Praise for *Mrs P's Journey*

'Crackingly presented'
Times Literary Supplement

'Sarah Hartley . . . romps through the story of this heroine
whose legacy is the essential tool of all London's citizens and
visitors . . . Hartley clearly relished digging out the dirt on her
subject's early childhood and it makes a good story'
The Times

'A sympathetic view of an extraordinary woman who deserves
more acknowledgement not only for her contribution to making
life easier, but because of her stoical drive in pursuit of a simple
but brilliant idea'
Observer

'The book brings Phyllis to life in a wonderfully vivid way and
gives a real flavour of her determination, shrewdness and
originality'
Lavender Patten

'Engaging, vivid rollercoaster of a ride through the life of an
extraordinary woman . . . Phyllis's extraordinary and colourful
life is done justice by writer Sarah Hartley, who fleshes out early
memories into snapshots of immigrant life in Britain'
Evening Leader

'Sarah Hartley . . . offers welcome professional illumination'
Design Week

'A fascinating account of an extraordinary woman'
Taxi Magazine

'This reads far more like a novel a
The Insigh

Mrs P's Journey

The Remarkable Story of the Woman
Who Created the A-Z Map

Sarah Hartley

POCKET
BOOKS

LONDON · SYDNEY · NEW YORK · TOKYO · SINGAPORE · TORONTO

First published in Great Britain by Simon & Schuster UK Ltd, 2001
This edition published by Pocket Books, 2002
An imprint of Simon & Schuster UK Ltd
A Viacom Company

1 3 5 7 9 10 8 6 4 2

Simon & Schuster UK Ltd
Africa House
64–78 Kingsway
London WC2B 6AH

www.simonsays.co.uk

Simon & Schuster Australia
Sydney

A CIP catalogue record for this book is available
from the British Library

ISBN 0-7434-0876-4

Typeset in Granjon by SX Composing DTP, Rayleigh, Essex
Printed and bound in Great Britain by
Omnia Books Limited, Glasgow

The publishers have used their best endeavours to contact all copyright holders. They
will be glad to hear from anyone who recognises their photographs. Many thanks to
Dr Esme Wren and Mary West who provided the majority of illustrative material
used in this book. Sincere thanks also go to the Geographers' A-Z Map Company Ltd
who provided the images of the A-Z and also the paintings of Claridges and Waterloo
Bridge. Additional permission has been given by the *Daily Express* for use of the
pictures of Phyllis in France and outside the company premises.

For Mark

Contents

Foreword

I never had the privilege of meeting Phyllis Pearsall, so I will always wonder whether we would have liked each other. I know she would have scolded me at times for my slow writing – although I doubt she would have co-operated with a book in the first place. 'Why write about *me*?' she would have said. For my part, I would have probably found her inimitable chatter quite exhausting.

One thing I do know we both had in common is a love of walking around London. Of getting up and going. Anywhere and everywhere, just as we please – the nuisance of public transport replaced by two good feet. Phyllis did not learn to drive until the age of fifty-nine – after two hundred and sixty lessons – while I have never even tried to learn. We are also linked by a wonderful gift – our ability to catnap, me on a bed, she on a bench or under a bridge. Indeed, on Sunday, 28 August 1996, I was half asleep in the afternoon when I heard about her death on the radio news. So, I remember thinking to myself, a woman put together the cabby's bible, the book that lies on every Londoner's bookshelf and in every desk drawer. Who says we can't read maps?

The trickiest aspect of writing about someone who, by her own admission, would elaborate on the truth and indeed, came from a family who would do so liberally, was to record the truth. Many rumours have encircled Phyllis's life, and inevitably in a few interviews she gave, she even contradicted herself. Her memoirs tripped themselves over with such extraordinary anecdotes that, without evidence to prove otherwise, I can only assume them to be true. My task, however, has not been one of detective. I did not set out to prove or disprove her legendary journey or her traumatic childhood. Where I have come across conflicting research, I have included both. I have written the truth according to Phyllis. For I am convinced that every story, every memory and every encounter that she described, she believed to be true. Of course, when starting with such a shaky foundation, I have not felt uncomfortable interweaving elements of fiction into fact. But if truth be known, my fiction turned out to be much more mundane than her 'fact'. If there is a scene, or a word, or a character, you believe to be too fantastical, it is likely they are real.

My admiration for her strength of character is enormous. Never mind that she lived through two world wars. Her triumph over so many personal tragedies and the tenacious willpower that pushed her to achieve so much are qualities that most of us are too lazy and half-hearted to aspire to today.

And so to the thanks owed to all those people who have helped me on my journey. To my agent, Jo Frank, at A. P. Watt, for seeing the potential in my original feature for *Frank* magazine and, of course, to Tina Gaudoin, the former editor of *Frank*, who let me write the piece. To Helen Gummer, my publisher at Simon & Schuster and Katharine Young, my editor, and Joan Deitch, the copy editor, for their care and attention. To my sister, Pippa, and to my parents, Steven and Maggie, for their love and encouragement, and to Suzanne Glass for her good ear.

Special thanks must go to those lucky enough to have been a part of Phyllis's extraordinary life and who happily gave up their time to share their recollections. To her best friend, Esme M. Wren, for her enthusiasm in keeping the memory of Phyllis alive;

to her niece, Mary West, for her beautiful photographic collection; to Jean-Pierre and Karen Gross for their anecdotes and hospitality; to Barbara Trollip, Derek and Ellen Jameson and Lavender Patten.

A big thank you also to Phyllis's original team – her boys, the only men who remained loyal throughout her life: Nigel Syrett, Fred Bond and David Churchill. Thank you also to Peter Barber, Deputy Librarian of Maps at the British Library.

CHAPTER ONE

Tracing the Source

Studying the map of a city is like reading the palm of a hand. Once you have spread it out and laid it flat it is impossible, for the first few seconds, to take everything in. But the longer you gaze at the riddles of lines, the more there is to see. Patterns start to form; then blink and you will be able to note the bold grooves, the high areas, the dips, the contours and prominent markings. With a map, a topographical imprint of human history lies before you on a single sheet of paper. Plagues, fires, wars, health, poverty, revolutions, inventions and constructions – all have left their imprint on the land. No amount of demolition and rebuilding and modernising can alter the core structure of a city.

So, too, will a hand portray and betray the past, whether it reveals soft skin and cosseted existence, or dark rivets chiselled by humility and sensitivity. And like hardened calluses, experiences cannot be sloughed away to reveal a clean, youthful appearance, they simply accumulate and patiently wait to reflect the future.

In the same way, the restless talents brought together in the personality of Phyllis Pearsall were not the result of creating a new soul, but of a fusion of fractious energy snatched from the generations before her. Destiny it seems, branded her with a complex blueprint, addled by peaks and dales already trodden by her parents.

Few will recognise her name, which gives no hint of the fact that she was one of the twentieth century's most intriguing

1

entrepreneurs and self-made millionaires. 'Phyllis Pearsall' sounds so simple and straightforward, it would not be out of place on a Sunday school register.

Yet who has not heard of, or bought or borrowed her greatest achievement – the world's bestselling map of London – the *A-Z*? More than sixty million copies have been sold since publication in 1936. Since then, the expansion of the company she founded, the Geographers' Map Company Limited, has seen the publication of over 250 titles, which include an *A-Z* map for all major cities in the UK.

Some people may see maps as purely scientific things, methodical and mathematical. With their rigid grids and co-ordinates, which are minutely and devotionally drawn up, they may seem the antithesis of anything 'creative'. The same people would expect the first female map publisher and founder of a cartographic empire to be as dull and dry as the tonnes of blank white paper shipped in for printing her maps.

But Phyllis Pearsall was nothing so conventional. How, you might think, could a stiflingly slow profession allow for a livewire, hyperactive genius to disrupt their monastic hush? Enter one half-Irish/Italian, half-Jewish/Hungarian thirty-year-old divorced artist whose naiveté endeared her to them and whose tenacity terrified them.

The life which will unfold before you never knew the comfort of gentle plateaux, nor did it ascend steadily into adulthood. Normality, for Phyllis, was always a series of extremes: mountains one week and canyons the next. Remarkably, throughout all her achievements and failures, richness and poverty, happiness and tragedy, she kept walking, her eyes fixed on the horizon. Who amongst us does not turn and look back, to take a peek at what they have left behind, whether it was loved or loathed? Phyllis Pearsall never allowed herself to do so.

Bolstered by huge resources of energy, she possessed strength and courage not only to start a super-human project such as single-handedly mapping the 23,000 streets and house numbers of London – but to actually complete it.

But the mind can lift and carry the body only so far. On her journey, Phyllis's health would fail her many times – as would her family – and both in the most devastating way. Yet over and over again, the mysterious streak of perseverance in her nature dragged her onwards.

A shadow over five foot tall, her personality was vast. As a grown woman, it was said that she had the presence of a prima ballerina. Sensitive, gentle and artistic she may have been, but Phyllis was able to create this external impression of lightness solely because she was underpinned by a shatterproof steel infrastructure, which pulled her nerves as taut as metal wire.

Phyllis knew whether the routes she was forced to take or the directions she chose freely had been the best ones for her. As it was, even if she had turned back, it is hard to believe she could have been confronted by a steeper path or a more rugged terrain than the one she took.

Those who cite her surreal story as a Chinese whisper of exaggeration and self-publicity should now step forwards, and take a glimpse inside the curious world where Phyllis Isobella Gross, the little girl known as 'PIG', was born.

It was his gypsy blood that led Alexander (or Sandor as his mother called him) Grosz to wander through Europe, staying a little time in each country, sniffing out any quick money business and stacking up influential friends like calling cards before disappearing overnight. A loner, Sandor refused to share the limelight with anyone other than himself. Beware, it is said, of men who do not have close friends. He was the sort of person who could not countenance taking orders or being beholden to any other; in truth he had all the prerequisites of a despot. 'Oleaginous' was how many described his behaviour, while others refused to be taken in by his shameless self-promotion. As any hostess who tentatively penned his name into the guest list for a dinner or ball would reveal, Sandor Grosz was high-maintenance, and the genuine amusement he promised to deliver only marginally outweighed his irritation factor.

Whether he was well educated, no one could truly be sure. 'I am,' he told dinner-party guests, 'the first boy from Csurog, a tiny village outside Budapest, to win a high-school scholarship. I have been,' he would add, unaware that his gloating was tainting the deliciousness of the soup, 'inseparable from my textbooks since I was six years old.'

If we are to believe his own account, just before the turn of the twentieth century, Sandor Grosz graduated from Budapest University, where he had found himself drawn to the acting profession. To the ladies and gentlemen present, he spun a colourful tale of the day when, as a thirteen-year-old boy, he had squandered his money on a ticket to see a travelling circus that had stopped in Csurog.

'I was mesmerised by the gleaming bodies of the gold-robed acrobats and sequinned tight-rope walker, and from that evening on, I lusted after the glamour of performing.'

Indeed, Sandor had convinced himself that the stage was a single bubble of fantasy in an otherwise tawdry world. How much better, he thought, to become an actor and resist a mundane municipal job, perhaps as a town clerk or civil servant. As for performing in front of an audience, Sandor never questioned his talent. He was a natural.

Yet in reality, life on tour harboured few prospects. Damp nights spent in tatty theatres scented by stale backstage costumes and beer, in exchange for a few tiny coins, left his belly sore and his young skin flexed across his cheekbones.

And then he snapped. Just like that. One day, in the provinces, stepping out onto the small dusty stage for a matinée performance of *The Merchant of Venice*, he was thrown by the sight of the portly Mayor in the front row, his pickled body trying to burst through his made-to-measure pinstriped suit, his fleshy hands trembling on the stockinged knees of his young mistress. Why this repelled Sandor so much, no one knows. Perhaps the gluttonous pleasures money and power could bring had taunted his own stirring physical desires. No matter – he had tasted that it was time for a change of scene and of character.

The walking away cannot have been easy. Was he a hard man? Yes. The secret thought to his own survival would be this unnerving habit of dropping his friends, family, and his business – everything, in fact, except for the clothes he was wearing – to disappear and reinvent himself elsewhere. With no past to acknowledge, how can a fresh start not be successful?

A few years before, his younger brother Gyula had died of consumption at the age of seventeen and so Sandor had found himself relied upon by his crippled, widowed mother. He knew that she prayed that one day, he would take over her general store. How could he tell her he was leaving, he fretted. The news would devastate her.

Even as a boy, Sandor had stashed away plans to run as far from his scrape-by rural hamlet of Csurog as he could, and head for a country where he would be granted the extravagant life he truly believed he deserved.

Sandor finally made up for his early privations twenty years later, when he became a father, first to a boy, Tony, and then to a daughter, Phyllis. The urgency with which he would snaffle up toys and gifts for them seemed obscene. It never entered his head that his greed for treats might spoil them. Teddy bears, golly-wogs, Parisian dolls with blinky eyes, dappled rocking horses, wooden hoops and paints and brushes were frittered out like sweets. 'How I used to envy the boy in my village who had toys,' Sandor would crow, 'but not any more!'

But back to that moment onstage, as Sandor bent for his final bow, his face slack with disappointment at the weak applause . . . He removed his make-up for the last time, deliberately and slowly, shed his actor's skin but cannily kept the round and rich tones he had acquired in the profession. Yes, it was time to leave Hungary. My journey must begin, he thought, where my life began.

As the last light crept out that night, his mother watched Sandor planting a row of tiny saplings beside the house and understood the trees were a parting gift. My boy, she thought to herself, will never live in his homeland again.

'These,' Sandor said, pulling his mother close and dabbing her rheumy eyes, 'these will grow strong and protect you from the August sun.'

And with that Sandor Grosz simply walked out on his mother, his job and his past.

Had Sandor stumbled across the Latin phrase *carpe diem*, he would have clasped it to his chest and repeated it over and over and flourished it in front of anyone who sneered at his reckless bravado. Neither he, nor later his daughter Phyllis, recognised the notion of hesitation. They always 'seized the day', whatever it may have cost them.

As he travelled across Europe, Sandor's slippery tongue would trick its way in and out and around every social class and their debutante daughters. Potential mothers-in-law would describe him to their husbands as a well-connected bachelor from

Hungary, a sophisticated gentleman with cornflower-blue eyes. With their daughters they would coo over his handsome profile and short but perfect physique. Somehow, Sandor's smooth chestnut skin was always plump and clean as if he had just paid a visit to the barber. Even in a crowded *salon du thé*, his face never shone, so he never had to fumble for his pocket handkerchief and dab at his brow. Flamboyant hand movements were interpreted as aristocratic, and his walking cane as the stamp of good breeding. With that well-oiled voice as his only tool, he would, a good few years later, talk his way into a wealthy lifestyle in Hampstead, North London. That same voice would also lose him a wife, two children, his fortune and his company.

English spoken with a Hungarian accent was a novelty – quite enchanting – and this doll-dressed little man knew how to silence a room as he acted out a true tale of adventure and heroism (the ladies liked that best) from his homeland. His short arms would flap the air as he came to the punch line, his body seemingly electrified by his own enthusiasm. 'Where did you say he came from?' women would ask one another. 'What did you say he did?' their husbands would enquire amongst themselves.

The year was 1900 when Sandor Grosz landed by ferry at Dover and made tracks to London, the largest city in the Western world, where one in three of its 5.5 million citizens lived below the poverty line and 250,000 existed in workhouses. Unaware of his own miniscule but significant role in Britain's future, Sandor was confident that here was the place to build his fortune. He was determined to become one of the 41.5 million citizens residing in Britain and a member of the British Empire, the biggest and the richest the world had ever known. An empire that covered 11.5 million square miles or one-fifth of the land mass of the globe; one in every four human beings lived within its boundaries and nearly one billion spoke the English language.

Why twenty-year-old Sandor chose to head for London at that point remains a mystery. Perhaps he had sucked dry his sources of hospitality overseas, for all he carried was one small pigskin valise and a few farthings in the pockets of his damson tweed suit. But it was more than likely that he was side-stepping enlistment for military service with the Austro-Hungarian Army by fleeing from his native Budapest. In exchange for freedom, and not for the first time in his life, he would succumb to the dragging ache of loneliness and the shame of being a penniless immigrant.

As with many men before him and many today, his priority was to secure himself a pretty young girl for a wife. Attaining respectability was, he decided, of paramount importance before setting himself up in business. What business? Well, that would come to him. He would think of something.

In those days, the Elephant and Castle area of South London was not dominated by a shocking pink shopping centre, and the pavements were not pock-marked by chewing gum or littered with McDonald's fast-food wrappings. Flanked by parkland, the creamery was a respectable meeting place for courting couples and it was here that fifteen-year-old Bella Crowley earned pocket-money as a part-time waitress, after school and at weekends. As Sandor Grosz plotted his next move, he decided to spend his last few coins on a glass of milk. He had not eaten for two days but that would not, he thought, stop him from smiling as he breezed into the creamery one Sunday afternoon.

As this gesture did little to prompt a reaction from the other customers, he flipped character and acted self-consciously alone, nursing his tall glass and toying with the white paper straws. And then Sandor allowed his eyes to feast on the young ladies present. His waitress, he concluded, was plain. If there was one thing that he would later drum into the heads of his children, it was that both members of a couple should be good-looking.

Scanning her body, he saw that her fitted white blouse and long charcoal skirt suited her very well, and her glossy waist-length dark braids revealed fine health. Her large eyes – a hazelnut brown – were unremarkable. But she would do.

'One more apple, one more ginger, one stewed pears and cream,' Bella was singing in her head as she scooped out ice cream into lily-shaped glasses for three gentlemen seated under the candy-striped awning outside. The girl had found that the combination of it being a Sunday and the first sunshine of the new century, helped her to forget a pile of Latin homework that lay in wait for her return. She sighed and asked Our Lady very politely if she might be spared this ominous task.

Looking up from behind the oak serving counter her eye swerved to a small, nutmeg-coloured man who seemed ill-at-ease in his gaudy, foreign suit. He beckoned Bella over, and as she inclined her inquisitive head, he whispered very charmingly into her ear.

A proposal.

My first, she thought.

'To marry you, I want,' he murmured seductively.

This was the first time that Bella Crowley encountered her future husband. Like the many other women who came to know and love and later revile him, Bella Crowley often regretted the day Sandor Grosz disrupted her quiet, unsophisticated life and turned it into a Victorian high melodrama.

CHAPTER TWO

Heading in a New Direction

If you believe in fate then perhaps Isabella Crowley, of Peckham Rye, South London, daughter of Arthur, a lapsed Irish-Catholic priest and Maria, an Italian, was always destined for a stormy ride through life. You might argue that all convent-educated girls turn out wilful, but at the dawn of the twentieth century, Bella would seize upon the radical causes of a new age as if she was possessed. 'How can women possibly move ahead,' she demanded, 'with a Queen at the helm who has practically buried herself alive?' 'How can women possibly think of deserting their families in the name of emancipation?' replied her father dryly.

On the ground floor of their shambling Victorian villa, a dwindling second-hand piano shop kept the Crowley house in a perpetual state of discord. They were a wild lot, according to Phyllis's niece, Mary West. Neighbours would strain to hear if the fast passionate arguments were being conducted in Italian or high-speed Dublinese. Rarely did Mrs Crowley leave the tiled confines of the kitchen, where she began kneading bread on the refectory table long before the Wyandotte hens started up in the back yard, and where she steamed and starched the men's shirts well into the following morning.

Bella had no need to question why her mother's strong slate-coloured hair had been invaded by white, nor why her swollen hands bore more scalds and scars than her father's. Devotion, the girl decided, was too akin to sacrifice.

Perhaps as the middle child, in a stifling and rowdy household, Bella felt her voice evaporate as she competed against her five brothers and three sisters. When I am grown, I will not go quietly into some marriage, she thought as she wrote in her diary, seated at her desk in the attic box room. I will make them all sit up and listen – with plays performed at the theatre perhaps. The psychologists among us may nod sagely as we learn that as an adult, Bella won the attention she sought by taking up the Suffragette cause. Even when she had streaked past her teenage years, Bella would be consumed by restless self-seeking behaviour that was for her as destructive as it was liberating.

If Victorian women repressed and constricted their sexuality behind overtight underpinnings, then Bella Crowley effectively ripped out all the intricate bindings of *her* clothes to allow herself to breathe in all that life had to offer, fully and deeply.

Long after the floral wallpaper in Bella's bare bedroom had crisped and faded, as had the sounds of her quick steps in the hallway, her parents would squabble over their Sunday roast as to which of their rogue relatives might have contributed to the girl's unreasonable behaviour. 'Why else would she be so disobedient?' her mother would repeat, fretful that out of a brood of nine, even one had turned out bad.

Without doubt Bella was a man's woman. Tall enough to retain her dignity if she swept into a rage but even so, small enough to tuck her arm deftly under that of a gentleman and then to rest her head with a sigh, lightly on their shoulder. She was, in short, the sort of woman *not* to leave alone with one's fiancé – if he was of a weakish disposition. Phyllis Pearsall, her only daughter, would portray Bella in much the same way that the popular novelist of her mother's day, Thomas Hardy, depicted his flibbertigibbet character, Sue Bridehead, in his novel *Jude the Obscure*. Ironically, Bella Crowley was the female mirror image of

Sandor Grosz. *With one crucial difference.* Whereas for Bella, Sandor was the only recipient of her love and devotion, Sandor was incapable of returning the honour. To be spoilt, fussed over and respected was, he believed, what a man should expect from his wife. How foolish, he believed, for any woman to truly expect a man to be faithful. After all, if she was given trinkets and trappings and children – what more could she want?

And how exactly did Bella see herself? Her giggling was not reserved for special occasions and she never rationed flashing her eyes in the direction of anyone who might be looking. In fact, whether she was swathed in sable as Mrs Gross of Claygate or posing naked as Delilah for her American artist lover, by the time the soil was sprinkled over Bella's pauper's coffin she had run up a long list of eyebrow-raising achievements. Slated by critics for her outrageous feminist play *Break the Walls Down*, performed at the Savoy Theatre, she abandoned her two children for her lover, wrote children's books, was a victim of domestic violence, a drug addict who battled with alcoholism and spent her final years in Bedlam mental hospital. And all this before the age of fifty.

But back to the easy days of the creamery, where the young Isabella had felt her ears burn at the flood of words that slipped out from the foreign gentleman. Was this love at first sight? No. Rather it was the dangerous introduction of two unchannelled energies, whose combined personalities were toxic. Like a malevolent thunderstorm, they would surround and singe any unfortunates who became caught up in their lives.

They both understood that the following months were a mere formality. A handwritten note from Mr Crowley invited Mr Sandor Grosz to Saturday-afternoon tea. All members of the family had been alerted by Mrs Crowley as to the importance of this occasion. 'And would all of you please,' she begged, 'see to it that your hair is brushed and your nails scrubbed.'

'Why, Mater?' whined Charlie, Bella's seven-year-old brother. 'Why must I wear my Sunday best on a Saturday?'

The sweet mix of shaving soap and fruitcake smells slipped through the house.

'Now tell me, what exactly is your young man like then?' asked Frank, sidling up to his favourite younger sister who was rubbing lavender wax into the banister rails.

'Let him speak for himself,' Bella replied smartly, pursing her lips tightly as she shrugged her shoulders.

From a boarding house in Islington, Sandor Grosz meandered a good six miles through the West End and over the Embankment to Peckham on a stomach that had lain empty for five days. It is surprising how pride can keep you alive. Starving, Sandor convinced himself, is a matter of will.

To ward off his hunger, Sandor's mind teased him with images of Csurog. And of his mother, wiping her eyes as she relived her favourite tragedy. Of her beloved Zoltan – her husband and Sandor's father.

I begged him not to leave the house. He wanted to play cards with his friends. A blizzard sang outside the door. 'You'll catch your death of cold,' I said. I was six months pregnant with my second baby, but still I laid down in front of the door. He put on his sheepskins. He said not a word to me. I screamed, 'Don't go, Zoltan!' He stepped over me and went into the darkness. They found him a week later. Upright in his cart. Frozen with his horse.

The moral of the tale sidled into Sandor's consciousness. The stubbornness that keeps us alive may well kill us in the end . . .

In his urgency, Sandor arrived an hour early for tea. It is true that a gentleman would have kept himself away until the appointed time, but Sandor's preoccupation with his own well-being meant this was not even a consideration. 'At last an English family, at last an entry into the heart of England,' he sighed, taking a run up the brick steps to lunge at the front door bell-rope.

It was Bella who coyly greeted him, swamped by a cleaning overall, a duster bandaging her hair and a broom in her hand.

The following scene might, indeed ought, to have put an end to their romance. Instead, Sandor's words instilled in Bella an insecurity about her appearance that never left her. A flash also appears of Sandor's lifelong battle to enforce his own will, and subjugate that of his wife. In later life, Phyllis would say that, not only was her mother shamed from that moment on about her provincial choice of apparel, but that her religious beliefs and duties would also be 'sledge-hammered out of her'.

'Glamour mattered to him immensely,' Phyllis once said of her father, in a newspaper interview, 'but women didn't. They were just people to get into bed with.'

Disappointingly for Sandor, his future wife would turn out to be neither weak nor submissive – and what animal, however big or small, does not fight its captor?

'Never will you dress so terrible again! My wife must always be attractive,' said Sandor in disgust at Bella's charlady disguise.

Tears and whimpers followed as she charged up the stairs to return buoyantly in a navy blue dress. 'This is what you were supposed to see me wearing,' she smiled coquettishly.

'That I like,' nodded Sandor, who was duly let over the threshold.

So desperate with hunger was he, that Sandor struggled to pace himself with the plump white bread and strawberry jam tea. Rendered mute by the presence of her suitor, Bella examined and re-examined and then counted the eye-hooks on her black patent boots. In turn, Sandor was overwhelmed by her parents' hospitality and he gauged, quite inaccurately (for they were not a wealthy family) from the mint-thin porcelain, that he had bagged a fine future. Without a moment's consideration, Sandor suddenly sank down on one knee and then, with an embarrassing flourish of his hand, kissed that of his sweetheart, and proposed. Sandor performed before the ten members of the family – clustered in the front parlour, with only the sound of the grandfather clock as accompanying music.

'But tell me, Mr Gross, that you are a Catholic Hungarian and not a Jewish Hungarian?' Mr Crowley enquired, taken aback by this gratuitous display of sentiment.

'The inquisition,' Arthur Crowley explained later that night to his wife, 'was because I did not want to see our daughter fall into eternal damnation – at least not before the age of sixteen.'

But as easily as a fish slips through a fisherman's hands, Sandor replied in the affirmative. 'I am Catholic,' he declared, 'and I would be honoured to marry your daughter.'

'Your prospects?'

'Excellent.' He lied as easily as the first time, brushing the crumbs from either side of his mouth.

A heat haze simmered on the brow of Lavender Hill. The late summer afternoon had paralysed the women and children who slouched down to the river; even the occasional dull clacking of horses' hooves was leaden. Viewed from above the rows of terraced villas, a lone figure busied himself up and down the garden paths, carrying a clanking assortment of oil lamps that swung from his shoulders. 'Kerosene?' Sandor would say years later. 'Why, the smell still makes me sick to my stomach!'

The housewives who cautiously opened their back doors to Sandor were suspicious of his dove-white shirt, with the cuffs turned up only once, and his squeaky shoes that tat-tatted as he sped on to the next house, whistling. His prices were not dear, but goodness – why would a respectable man be flogging gas lamps in August? Gambling, assumed many of the women as they returned to their chores, tut-tutting, or perhaps a bad investment overseas.

As with any family tale repeated from one sibling to another, from grandmother to grandchild, the emphasis fluctuates into its own reality. A favourite anecdote is stretched a little further, the dull character is written out and an extra line or two welded in for a funnier ending.

Phyllis could recite her family history without blinking, but so too could her elder brother Tony. Whose memory or interpretation of their past is more accurate will never be discovered, but Sandor's modest start as an Englishman had a more heroic feel in Tony's unfinished memoirs.

'Within a few days of my father arriving in London, he had been robbed of the little money he had brought with him and was penniless. But soon he made himself a fortune.

'One day he overheard two men talking Hungarian in a tea shop. This was a strange enough coincidence in London in those days, but he heard one of them telling the other how he had just made money by selling gas mantels, a new invention from Germany. My father begged and borrowed money with which he bought gas mantels and in a short time had enough capital to strike out.'

But selling oil lamps from door to door does not sound profitable. Your average London working man would have sniffed at it, but 'pitiful' and 'demeaning' were words that Sandor did not understand. Then again, your average London working man did not dream night after night of gorging on gold sovereigns.

My dream is a peculiar one, reflected Sandor as he shaved in chill water early one morning. He thrust out his greedy chin, surveyed his Roman profile and settled for it being a sign of future affluence.

'This is not the sort of business a gentleman wants to pursue,' Mr Crowley remarked to Sandor, exasperated that his future son-in-law was unable to grasp the basics of the British class system.

'Too late,' muttered Sandor who, armed with the natural patois of a salesman, had already saved six sovereigns in a Rowntrees toffee tin.

Elopement with Bella was his next move. The following morning, Sandor settled the bill at his boarding house, leaving no trace of his stay. Which was just as well, for the Crowley clan had finally challenged him about his true faith. 'You have nudged,' began Mrs Crowley, 'roast pork around your plate one time too many. I ask you, sir, why you refuse that meat, as if to take one mouthful would be against your religion!'

A mortifying silence fell on the gathering, until Sandor stood up, bowed and backed out of the room. Brothers Frank and Charlie would have given chase. It is a certainty that Bella fled to her bedroom, in the firm belief that she was about to die of grief.

I forbid you, Arthur Crowley wrote to the bogus Catholic, *to see my daughter and I forbid you to enter my home.*

Bella was inconsolable until one night, after midnight, when Sandor hurled pebbles at the window of her bedroom.

'Knot your sheets!' he called up. 'Two or three if you can. Hurry now!'

Bella dangled and swung and squirmed down on to the lawn below.

'We are going to Dublin,' Sandor informed his fiancée.

'But lovers get married at Gretna Green,' she replied, tugging at his cloak.

Sandor found his heart plummeting to his feet. Then, as those in the first flush of passion are wont to do, he acquiesced to his fiancée's alternative plan. My little one is wild, he thought, never suspecting for a minute that he would ever have trouble in training her.

The fugitives headed north on the early train from King's Cross railway station.

'This is such a splendid idea . . .' shouted Bella as they scurried aboard, but the word *adventure* evaporated as the simmering train let out a deep sigh. Four hours passed. 'Nothing is so dreary as an empty train,' Sandor said out loud to himself. His only relief from boredom was running his eye over the dimly-lit ghost-carriages. Mouldy swathes of hills and mountains bulged as daylight loomed. He could not shake off the small pressure on his shoulder, caused by the dead weight of Bella's sleeping head.

Being with someone can feel lonely, thought Sandor, until a red-haired trolley waitress asked if Sir would perhaps like to take a brandy. Whatever their flirtatious exchange, after Sandor had drained his glass, his foot tapped in eagerness to disembark and to marry the woman lying beside him, if only to quench his physical desires.

To say that Sandor Grosz was incapable of fidelity would be no exaggeration. Today, his family do not conceal the fact that Sandor's voracious and unpredictable philandering proved the undoing of his marriage. Like many powerful and influential men, as Sandor's success increased, so too did the need for the relief that came from brief sexual encounters.

Once over the border, the unlikely pair were united in Gretna Green's small register office. 'The last ceremony of the day,' an official said with a wink, as if the timing of their marriage was more than a little significant. To banish his feelings of being an immigrant, Sandor swirled his signature in the marriage register with his anglicised name – Gross. Bella, intoxicated by her own boldness and swallowed up by her new husband, ordered the memory of her childhood to disappear.

'Bel-la Gro-ss,' she spelt aloud, neatly leaving her mark.

As they celebrated over a hearthside dinner of smokies and whisky in the Keeper's Inn, neither could have predicted that their newly joined lives would remain that way for less than twenty years.

When asked about her childhood, Phyllis Pearsall – like the sorcerer's apprentice – could summon up decades of dialogue even half a century later. Conversations – some intimate, some frightening, many contradictory – were repeated by her in a uniformly sing-song voice. A slightly thin voice, it was powerful nevertheless. Rattling at the pace of a Gilbert and Sullivan operetta, the sentences in her privately published memoirs *Fleet Street, Tite Street, Queer Street* and *A-Z The Personal Story from Bedsitter to Household Name* tripped from one slapstick vignette to another, without malice or regret.

Phyllis saw to it that there were no intervals in the vaudeville performance that became the Gross family history. Backstage misery as she records it, never happened. Restraint was trampled upon as the pair acted out their own high dramas in front of each other. Tears, undying love, impassioned pleas for mercy, hysterical laughter – moderation had never set foot inside the front door of the Gross house.

Something in all of this does not ring true – in Phyllis's version of the truth, that is. One listens for her shrill voice. As it begins to seep to the surface of the brain, Phyllis Pearsall takes on the persona of two other female writers, Jean Rhys and Anaïs Nin. All three were contemporaries of sorts: stubborn, mischievous, lonely souls who doused themselves in men but never found peace with them or with their own company. Each penned copious amounts according to the truth – as they perceived it, as they found it and as they wanted it to be. Their formula? Take one fact, conversation or incident. Add one heaped spoonful of elaboration and one of wit. Leave to soak overnight to plump up for a delicious interpretation of the truth. Serve neat. But here was a mind that understood and spoke eight languages. Here was a woman whose eyes, despite sixty years of detailed work, never shrank from brilliance to require glasses. Reading fast was a sport, speaking just as quickly was a game, too. Ask any one of her friends and they would say that Phyllis could repeat, verbatim, an entire afternoon's conversation without hesitation. So what is real and not far from real are perhaps just blinks apart.

CHAPTER THREE

A Heavy Burden to Carry

1901

A restlessness nipped at the ankles of the newly married Mr and Mrs Gross. They slept fitfully, ate sporadically and, as with any couple thrown together, each feared upsetting the other. Perhaps it is a condition common among immigrants who imagine the ground shifting under their feet before any roots have taken. Maybe the pair were colluding in their own healthy appetites for everything unattainable, or maybe they had touched on their incompatibility.

Fuelled by an almost inhuman energy, they worked eighteen-hour days without a honeymoon and without holidays in a rat-infested oil-lamp shop, that Sandor had spent his savings on, in Brixton, South London. Never missing a trick, Sandor even sold pornographic postcards from his back door – until he was cautioned by the police.

Within a year, the rush amongst the middle classes for electricity was on. This, Sandor sensed, was his future, and the oil-lamp business began to flicker and fade as he stretched their profits to purchase stores in Birmingham, Manchester and Glasgow.

The couple's reward was their first home – a new, redbrick terraced house in Court Lane Gardens, Dulwich, which Sandor named 'Budapest'. I am King of all I survey, he must have thought, as he viewed the fine Wilton carpets, the pretty maidservant and rose trees in the front garden. In later years, though, constantly moving house would become another outward symptom of their unhappiness.

When seventeen-year-old Bella fell pregnant with their first child, the very next year, it was Sandor's triumph. 'I did it, I did it!' Phyllis records as her father's words after the baby, a boy, was born.

For Bella, the birth wrenched and wrung out most of the life from her. Weakened to the point of death, the chances of recovery were believed by the physician in attendance to be slim. A priest was summoned and her limp body was made comfortable. Sandor wailed as he caressed and plaited her hair to make her ready for the casket, as if, thought the physician, he was a mourner from one of those foreign countries.

It was partly Sandor's sobbing and fussing which finally coaxed back Bella's spirit which, if truth be known, was wallowing in his uncompromised attention. The physician advised Sandor to treat Bella to a boat trip, 'to revive,' he whispered, 'the little soul'.

The frailty of women, Sandor mused, as he finally managed to bundle his ailing wife aboard a boat at Tower Bridge, which took them on a ten-day trip along the eastern coastline up to Berwick-on-Tweed. Whether Bella reluctantly left her baby under Sandor's instructions, or whether she happily gave him over to a wet-nurse is unclear. But the couple were not to see their firstborn again.

The seas were rough and the spray revitalising. Storms delayed their return by one day. It was dead of night when the boat docked and there, on the quay, an elderly couple huddled under an umbrella, their forms swinging in and out of vision as a storm lamp flashed across them.

An ominous presence, sensed Bella, who instinctively recognised her estranged parents. Without ceremony, Maria Crowley greeted them with the news that their baby son had died that morning of an infection.

A single wail from Bella, stranger than any noise they had ever heard, rose out from the depths of her crumpled body.

'I did not even name him. What punishment is this? I did not even name him. My baby will go to hell.'

With some difficulty her parents propped up their daughter and together they embraced her grief. Somehow no one noticed that Sandor remained outside the huddle, apparently unmoved.

Bella was to take to her bed until she could no longer fight the lingering, invasive depression that hinted at the mental illness she would fall prey to until her death.

I cannot abide this weakness. How am I to cope? thought her husband. Observing his wife convulsing with tears repulsed him. He marched out of whichever room she happened to be in – their bedroom, the empty nursery, or the front parlour – perhaps to take a turn in the garden, perhaps to retire to his study. But what about compassion? Did that ever stir in the pit of his belly? Guilt occasionally, but compassion – no.

Despite his impoverished upbringing, Sandor's invincible health only served to emphasise Bella's frailty; her valiant efforts to plump up her own milky-skinned fragility with sheer will-power were futile.

'Anything that interrupts business is a nuisance,' Sandor once told his daughter. 'Illness, weddings, death. I may seem selfish but that is how it is. When I see somebody crippled or hear someone has died, I'm glad it isn't me.'

The frustration of his wife, according to Phyllis, culminated in the first of many angry outbursts.

'Pull yourself together!' he yelled again at the little figure, bandaged in shawls, motionless on their bed. *'Pull yourself together!'*

The Crowley family rallied round at afternoon tea, their favourite gathering, giving free rein to disgusted whispers of how their son-in-law was treating their poor, dear Bella. 'And perhaps his only child too,' tutted Mrs Crowley.

Whenever he could manage it, Sandor sneaked out of their company. In the hall he pulled out a handkerchief from his top pocket and rubbed his eyes until onion raw. He stepped back into the parlour as Maria Crowley was pouring tea, his head bowed.

'Perhaps I was too harsh. I misjudged poor Sandor,' she remarked to her husband on their way home.

Sick is how Sandor felt when the couple were left alone again. All this business is making me sick, he thought. Homesick, he diagnosed. I long to see my poor dear mother.

'Come, we shall take a trip,' he whispered to Bella. 'To Csurog. A belated honeymoon, my love.'

Another chance, Bella believed. She would try to be strong again for Sandor. But it was too late; the damage was done. Perhaps it was his desire to find in Bella the peasant strength with which his mother bore her troubles, but Sandor did nothing to encourage or reassure his wife.

For now, the fresh breeze of being on the move again, criss-crossing Europe on a two-month trip, and the absence of daily domesticity preserved their relationship, although the young woman's body would take two years to recover from the loss.

On 19 March 1905, Imre, a gentle soul who would later be known as Anthony or Tony, was born in Dulwich. As if by genetic rebellion, his talents when an adult would be artistic and could not have been less important to his father.

The following year, on 25 September 1906, Phyllis Isobella Gross was born. A small baby, she grew into a tiny child, with her father's cornflower-coloured eyes set in a heart-shaped face framed by masses of dark, wavy ringlets. Shortly before his death

in 1957, her father revealed to Phyllis that neither he nor her
mother had ever considered her a beauty. 'A spiritless suet
pudding she called you.'

Self-absorbed she might have shown herself to be, but as a
mother Bella truly believed her children were her priority. It is
unlikely, therefore, that she would ever have remarked that her
daughter resembled a pudding or lacked spirit. Yet the phrase,
which would have been instantly dismissed by anyone who had
met Phyllis, carried all the provocative characteristics typically
used by Sandor to stir, to insult and to goad into action. If he
thought his authority or supremacy as head of his family and of
his business, were at risk (which he obviously assumed in this case
– despite nearing death), he would try to reassert his position. One
of his favourite aggressive tactics was to undermine Phyllis, just
as he could not resist undermining the confidence and capabilities
of his wife.

Admittedly, when standing side by side with her convention
ally beautiful mother, Phyllis was happy to be eclipsed, so she
never felt the need to compete with her. Phyllis's colourful artistic
dress sense and short chaotic hair haloed a sensitive rather than a
pretty face. But if there was one thing that struck every one of her
friends and colleagues, it was her spirit – always present in her
inquisitive blue eyes and keen energy.

Unlike her formally trained sibling, Phyllis preferred spontaneous painting, and sketching and writing. From the moment
she first picked up a whiskery sable brush, she trained her eye to
be accurate, and when she prepared her palette, she felt like a true
artist.

'Where, oh my goodness where,' Sandor shouted in exasperation to Bella, years later, at their home in Claygate, 'do these
children get this feminine art obsession from?' His eyes punched
those of his wife in search of the answer, and their dinner of duck

and port wine sauce congealed on the plate. Bella looked up at the chandelier to stop her tears from brimming over. '*Who will make the money?*' Sandor shouted over and over again.

CHAPTER FOUR

Geographia: Marking Out the Future

How amazing it would be, if in the infancy of the twenty-first century we were to unfold the most up-to-date Ordnance Survey map of London and then compare it to another from the turn of the *last* century, only to discover that the modern, parasitic conurbations mounting one another, and the thin, multiple boundaries encroaching and gnawing down every last defensive line of green, were slowly *receding* rather than advancing with time.

And instead of the march of progress demanding ever more sophisticated cities and suburbia, what if we were to rebel and take up the more worthy challenge of keeping the lines on a map and so too, in our lives, as simple and as straight as we could? Yet we are too greedy to adjust the speed at which we move – too greedy for more. For more what? Well, that we don't know until we see it.

For Sandor Gross the greed began in 1908, when he had begun to lose his quivering fear of writing cheques. 'I am surrounded,' he said to himself, 'by an infectious breed, whose single most important desire is to explore and to expand. Social climbers. I'll show them.'

And he did.

Queen Victoria had been dead for seven years. Her stringent

personality, which had soured the nation for forty years and frowned on the happy-go-lucky British psyche, evaporated and, as if waking from a slumber, the Heart of the Empire stirred. The pace of life quickened. The pulse of cities strengthened. Birmingham, Leeds, Nottingham, Liverpool and Manchester stretched their boundaries.

Fifteen years earlier, England, Scotland and Wales had been mapped by the Ordnance Survey at twenty-five inches to the mile. The Victorian obsession with drawing thick rules around the Empire had then turned its attention to internal labelling and defining. The lines were pushed back as nearly half a million Britons a year sought new lives and resettled in other parts of the Empire.

Within this country, over a million migrants were on the move from the East and West of England to London, seeking positions as skilled artisans or domestic servants. Whitechapel and Southwark became home to the Irish who filled jobs as labourers, shoemakers and tailors. They were joined in the East End sweatshops by a swelling number of over 100,000 Jews, fleeing persecution in Eastern Europe. The working classes spawned a new class – the lower middle class – made up of clerks, book-keepers and schoolteachers, who jostled for space alongside the middle classes. A small but militant band of women, led by Christabel and Emmeline Pankhurst, demanded votes for women. The Suffragettes built up their numbers and carried out radical, sometimes violent protests.

Huge social divisions across the East and West End of London sparked disgruntlement and competitiveness. Money, in this new century, was to be earned, not inherited. More so than ever, for London was a working city with eleven docks clearing over 10,000 ships a year for export. Marmalade, gas light, India rubber, leather and sugar consumed the days of the East End workers. Factories

replaced workshops and business offices invaded the City. Fleet
Street, Holborn, the Strand, Oxford Street and Regent Street
pulled the smart and richer inhabitants from the North, South and
East of the River Thames towards the West End. Knightsbridge,
Kensington and Bayswater saw a rash of department stores such as
Whiteley's, which boasted, 'We sell everything from a pin to an
elephant.' Humble drapers' shops were soon deemed too old-
fashioned. Marks and Spencer opened a Penny Bazaar on the
Edgware Road, and W.H. Smith established railway station
bookstalls. It would be the following year before Harry G.
Selfridge presented his grand store on Oxford Street – 'dedicated
to the service of women' – which employed over 3,000 members of
staff in 160 departments. H.C. Harrod was already the talk of the
town after his grocer's shop on the Brompton Road had continued
to expand since its opening in 1850. Now set on a 20-acre site,
Harrod's drew the crowds by installing the first moving staircase
in 1898. Indeed, more than 15,000 multiple stores vied for
attention on Britain's high streets, from Boots the chemist, to
Lipton's the grocers, and shoe shop Freeman, Hardy & Willis.

In the first six years of the century, the first electric trams, the
first double-decker buses, the first telephone boxes, the first
taxicabs and the first fire brigade had all sprung up in London.
The suburb of Ealing saw the creation of the British film
industry, while Shepherd's Bush hosted the 1908 Olympic
Games. The financial capital of the world looked indefatigable as
the population topped seven million.

A world in sepia was soon to breathe in colour. Science, com-
munication, transport and travel were exercised by their great
champions Guglielmo Marconi, Henry Ford, Thomas Edison
and Alexander Graham Bell, and pushed to their limits. Rushing
and racing and running became twentieth-century diseases as
everyone tried to make their mark on the new century.

Automobiles, telephones, telegrams, photographs – *can we get there sooner, can we speak this minute, can we warn them now, can I see what they look like today* – became a reality.

Time was indeed of the essence. Little did anyone suspect that this seemingly unstoppable sprint in global development was about to be cruelly nipped in the bud by the Great War. On 4 August 1914, Prime Minister Herbert Asquith declared war on Germany. Over the next four years, millions of men would lose their lives in a conflict that cost millions of pounds.

It was on the morning of 13 June 1917 that fourteen German bombers launched the first aircraft attack on London. They dropped four tonnes of bombs, most falling within a mile of Liverpool Street Station. Over 837 people were killed and 1,437 injured. The city quickly transformed itself into an armed camp. An outer circle of airfields provided fighter protection; an inner circle of searchlights and anti-aircraft guns covered the capital itself. The annihilation and destruction as well as the anger and resentment that resulted from the Great War were the very antithesis of progress and birth. But it would be the making of Alexander Gross.

'What is it,' enquired Sandor of his wife over a breakfast plate of steaming kippers one morning, 'that brother of yours does, when he is not out bicycling, to make all that money?'

'It's not just any bicycling. He is World Amateur Bicycle Champion. And I think you will find that Frank sells geographical maps. Freelance. Door to door – what a chore,' replied Bella.

Sandor did not hear Bella's giggles. Money, he thought to himself, is not far away. Not far away at all. And so, in the brazen manner that characterised Sandor Gross's business style, he pushed away his kippers and left his wife without a word, to arrange a meeting within the hour with his brother-in-law.

Maps. It could have been selling potatoes. It could have been importing tea. Whether Sandor had ever unfolded a map in his life is doubtful. You see, the actual means of accruing a fortune were, to Sandor, quite irrelevant.

To many, Alexander Gross will be remembered as a significant figure in map publishing, but the altruism found in many great pioneers was sorely lacking in him. Although desperate to be one *of* the people, he had no feelings *for* the people; he was hardly brimming with enthusiasm to inform the masses and it is doubtful that he cared one jot about revolutionising how Great Britain was depicted. His imagination never toyed with the picture of an Edwardian family setting off in their brand new automobile guided by one of his maps. Sandor Gross considered the profit and the product – and that was all.

And so fate beckoned Sandor down a path marked *mapping*.

'I won't keep you, Frank,' Sandor said briskly. 'Now, I've always thought I would one day become a publisher. How about I produce the maps for you to sell? I like the idea of the British Isles, the World, London and Birmingham.'

A handshake. A deal done. 'Quick business,' Sandor would later tell his daughter, 'means quick profit.' In less than a week, he had sold his Brixton shop for a thousand pounds to make way for the development of Brixton Railway Station. He advertised on a Monday for a map draughtsman to work from home and hired one James Duncan, who had just completed his apprenticeship the previous day. Mr Duncan's task? To draw up a map of the British Isles in one week.

'With respect, sir,' he told his new employer, 'you cannot know the trade. It will take me years.'

'I will give you more money and hire more people. Then you can give me my map.'

Several more draughtsmen were hired and an office in John

31

Street was leased. One by one, the provincial lamp shops were sold off to pay their salaries.

'Time,' the draughtsmen must have muttered amongst themselves, 'no amount of investment can conquer time.'

Over ten months ticked away. Not one map was ready.

'It is the detail, sir,' explained Mr Duncan to Sandor. 'That's what takes the time.'

According to Phyllis, in exasperation her father then bellowed through the office. 'Am I working, Mr Duncan – for my unborn grandchildren?'

Sandor had no need, no interest or inclination to turn his attention to any facts about the profession. Why would he? What size and weight paper to be used. How many sheets to a ream. How many reams for a print run. What type of nibs for the pens. What colour inks. How many square inches to the mile. How best to devise the key.

'What did I love about oil lamps? Nothing. Maps? I long to see my name printed over and over again at the bottom of each copy. *Produced under the direction of Alexander Gross.*'

The careful hours devoted to gathering information, checking Ordnance Survey facts, trawling through spelling, changes in borders, countries, routes and names, of places and roads . . . the knowledge that his staff moved with exacting thoroughness did not pacify Sandor one bit.

'I don't care what it takes or how you do it – just get the job done.'

Now the product itself provoked a more positive response. Sandor's ears had twitched as he interrogated Frank. 'How much can we sell them for? How many can we sell? How fast can more copies be printed, once the first batch is sold?'

Sandor's least concern was always his staff. To gain an understanding, an empathy, with the quiet men whose contentment lay in the laborious charting of coastlines and mountains, streets and churches with as much care as if they were engraving the gravestones of their loved ones was, for their employer, an indulgent misuse of his working day. They, in turn, may have held 'the Guvnor' as he was known, in high regard, but they reserved still greater reverence for their art. Untouched by his agitating presence, their pens did not falter as they pressed on at a professional pace.

However, their dedicated eyes and measured, methodical hands only served to unnerve Sandor. If ever a man's character might be custom-made to suit his business, the meticulous nature of mapping and the boisterous Sandor Gross could not have been a more ludicrous mismatch.

As any cartographic old-timers will tell you, the reason that draughtsmen remain silent is because if they chatter there is a chance that droplets of saliva may rehydrate the ink on their boards, ruining hundreds of hours of work. And so to silence. For just as the offices were calming by their very noiselessness (save the rips of paper turning and ink brushes swilling in water jars), so Sandor could not stop himself from acting as bellows to a feeble fire.

Slamming doors.

Shouting.

Walking with heavy footsteps.

The financial research, the production planning, the structures, the discussions, the signings and any number of prudent details crucial to founding a prosperous business, Sandor glided over with a sniff.

It is unlikely that father – or in later years, daughter, too – even when hanging on the edge of bankruptcy, ever had a true grasp of the enormity of their commitments. In his favour though, Sandor may have chased fast money and success as if it were his salvation, but he never abandoned his staff while they slaved through the hours. Unlike his brother-in-law Frank Crowley, whose idea of sound business practices included long liquid lunches and an afternoon nap, Sandor was rarely out of earshot of his office. For despite the grand image of himself as the proprietor, the director, the chairman and the English City gentleman standing triumphant in his dreams, Sandor dismissed the notion of entrusting his future to anyone other than himself.

If I fail, he thought, the humiliation will settle only on my shoulders. If I achieve some status in society and I am recognised as a luminary in Britain's upper classes, then the applause and adulation can swell only in my belly.

To have delegated or shared the business would have gnawed away at his pride. For no matter how much Sandor succeeded in being the English businessman, he was also driven to display the traits of an immigrant: insufferable self-reliance and self-motivation. At whatever cost.

How much better it would be to think of Sandor's motives as testing the stamina of his daughter every time he challenged her inefficient thinking, rather than believe him to have been a belligerent tyrant. But in all honesty, Sandor failed to grasp why he should have held the women in his life in high regard, and his reasoning deteriorated even further when they showed the slightest bit of intelligence, wit or independence. It is clear from Phyllis's memoirs that Sandor was a sour and arrogant man who never so much as tipped a nod at either his wife or daughter's achievements.

Yet be careful not to dilute any picture of Phyllis by seeing her as a sweet innocent, dipping her toes in the choppy waters of the business world. She knew perfectly well that, albeit diminutive in stature, she cut a formidable figure. Were we to fault her style, it would be that she failed to perfect her father's art of bluffing or elaborating on subjects about which she knew nothing. Most of her map publishing skills (and she would be the first to admit this) were gleaned from the wisdom of those in her circle – from the youngest apprentice to her father's old-timers. Risk was, for Phyllis and her father before her, attractive and compelling. Yet sometimes it paid off and sometimes it did not.

Within a day of Sandor being forced to lay off his entire staff, Mr Duncan put his final touches to the map of the British Isles. *Produced under the direction of Alexander Gross* were the words written in a fine hand in the bottom lefthand corner of the map.

Sandor summoned his wife to see the finished products. One hundred maps were varnished and mounted on cloth and rollers, to be used in boardrooms. The technical term, Frank informed Bella, was CRV or Cloth Rolled Version. Another one hundred were cut to fold in hard cases, for desks. And to avoid the additional cost of dispatching pink-checked salesboys, Sandor and Bella united in pitching their sales wits against Frank. Lazy by nature and not averse to mooching for several hours over a Cuban cigar and a decent brandy, Frank's mistake in the race was to have made discreet appointments with company chairmen, heads of banks and institutions.

'Tactics, Bella, learn from me about tactics,' Sandor nudged his wife, as they marched into every office from Trafalgar Square to Ludgate Circus. In each one they deposited a map and a price. Within two hours they returned – to collect the map, or the money.

'One, two, three left unsold out of one hundred is excellent,' announced Bella.

Frank shrugged at his own effort of selling ten. Sandor did not consider this a satisfactory outcome, and paced the floor. And this is where he then made a crucial mistake. Do not fire your brother-in-law. I repeat, do not fire your brother-in-law unless you want to make an enemy of your wife.

'Why would you not give Frank a second chance?' Bella wept later that evening. 'Do you know nothing of fair play?'

'It may be more mundane, my dear,' Sandor told his wife, 'but I'd rather use wholesalers and shops than rely on that ignorant bastard for my livelihood.'

The idea had most likely come to Sandor mere seconds before he met Lord Burnham. In the pit of his belly a tumbling, a falling. A half breath as Sandor teased out his inhibitions and seized upon a plan. A political animal he was not, but ambition reversed his thinking. His left eye, quivering around the crowded reception, landed on the tall, proud gentleman surrounded respectfully by three smaller men, all riveted by whatever little anecdote he was telling.

Never had Sandor felt such an outsider. I want to stand alongside them, he thought savagely. To nod, to challenge, to be a wit.

Other guests may have been honoured to be introduced to Mr Alexander Gross, the successful new map publisher, but this achievement had already lost its lustre for him. 'There is Lord Burnham!' exclaimed Aunt Rosa. 'My, look how they fawn over him.

'Introduce me now.'

'I beg your pardon? *Now?*'

'Yes, do it now, for mercy's sake.'

For as luck would have it, Sandor's aunt, Rosa Grosz, was a leading journalist on Budapest's newspaper *Petzer Lloyd* and had been selected for a foreign exchange with correspondents from the *Daily Telegraph* newspaper in London. And there, among the correspondents, mingling with his guests, was their host, the proprietor of the *Daily Telegraph*, Lord Burnham. And here came Sandor Gross, his Aunt Rosa steps behind.

'Do you know the exact meaning of the word 'Balkans', Lord Burnham?'

No sweeteners. No humour. No social graces, Lord Burnham must have thought. And yet by all accounts, he laughed when Sandor accosted him.

'Who doesn't? It means trouble,' he replied easily.

'Well, it is the trouble I have in mind. Have you ever thought of reproducing maps to pinpoint news?'

'No newspaper has ever tried it.'

'Then why not the *Daily Telegraph*? The Ottoman Empire is crumbling. The Balkan States are on the verge of revolt. I could supply you with the detailed maps you'll need – at a moment's notice.'

Perhaps it was his audacity that won the peer round. But it is more likely that Lord Burnham caught a whiff of a new gimmick, one that would give him an edge over his rivals. Sales would soon pick up with the start of war in Europe, and what paper would the public want to buy? The *Daily Telegraph*.

CHAPTER FIVE

Charting the Changing Face of Europe

Turn it upside down, twist it to the west and then to the east, try to flatten it and ease out the creases. Do what you can to make it any the clearer, but a map will not provide any answers, it will only provide choices – for rarely will it reveal a single road or lone path to any one destination. Perhaps four or five are marked, some spindly, criss-crossing rivers, or entangling small villages and some are bolder, running smooth and broad like a confident smile. Once your eye has flicked back and forth from one road to the other, exploring the options, measuring the quickest way, you reach a decision and set off. What you do not yet know is whether your choice was, in fact, the right one.

The paths that beckoned Phyllis Pearsall on her life's journey appeared to her as young as two years of age. It is true that the first of these might have guided her to a cosy role as a wife and mother, her days uncomplicated by business concerns. The second path beguiled Phyllis into the world of mapping. It was her parents' world – a grand world of oceans and mountains, that encompassed the slipperiest of details, from the smallest speck of a house number in a tiny street terrace, to sizes and scales as big as the universe, charting battles in foreign lands and wars over foreign seas.

It was an unexplored world, and as a little girl she would try to piece it together as it flashed past sun-filled rail carriages as Mr and Mrs Gross bundled their children on last-minute trips across Europe to Austria, Hungary, Italy and France.

Every snapshot of experience, be it the bloated body of a little drowned body bobbing among the debris in a Venice canal, or the Polish count who shot himself dead on the beach in front of his fiancée after losing his fortune in Monte Carlo, Phyllis would see or perhaps learn to see through her mother's compassionate eyes.

'There's always too much for my eyes to take in,' Phyllis would declare as an older woman, and it was spoken with a sense of panic which seemed to increase, rather than decrease with age. Even on her regular trips from her home in Sussex to the National Portrait Gallery in London, she would concentrate on looking at only one or two portraits. 'That is quite enough,' she would say after an hour, as if her insight into those people she had focused on was as much a burden as a delight.

Her father's eye had a harshness to it, a meanness which, despite an instinct for adventure, could not help but dissect a hotel or a dining cart or a theatre for opportunities, whether it be of the business or female kind.

Whether Phyllis ever regretted the influence her parents had on her life can only be guessed. She certainly never criticised them in that respect. As for role models, Phyllis could not have wished for stronger ones when it came to Sandor and Bella's enlightened approach to work. Imagine that your father, pressed and polished from his black shoes to his winged collar and morning coat, stepped into the office with his umbrella neatly rolled and flipped open his gold pocket watch to check his punctuality – 8 a.m. – every morning without fail.

One hour later, your mother, having overseen your breakfast and instructed the nurse, swept into those same offices at 55 Fleet Street, Geographia, named after a shop your father had once passed in Berlin – Photographia. Your father's desk was set square in the middle of his large office; in that same office, in an alcove, your mother was seated at a smaller desk. When they returned together from the City, they greeted you at 6 p.m. They were business partners. They were the new breed of middle class; aspirational and ambitious. But for a young woman and a mother at that, to have been in professional employment of her own volition and with the blessing of her husband was almost unheard of then.

Together Bella and Sandor oversaw their new map publishing firm which, until its expansion after five years, worked exclusively for the *Daily Telegraph*. The pair were, according to Lord Burnham, 'making milestones in newspaper history'.

Sandor greedily anticipated that the rumblings in Eastern Europe would flare into bloodier conflicts and thus secure his fortune, according to his son Tony, who wrote in his diary:

In the end wars did him a world of good. Everybody wanted maps into which to stick little pin flags to mark the battle lines, defeats and victories. So you can see I was brought up more or less as a rich man's son.

After three mapping scoops, Sandor signed a five-year contract with the *Daily Telegraph*. The first was his 1908 map of Bulgaria after Prince Ferdinand proclaimed himself Tsar and his country independent of Turkey; this was chased by his map of Bosnia-Herzogovina after Franz-Josef annexed it to his Austro-Hungarian Empire in celebration of his Diamond Jubilee; and finally Geographia produced a map of Crete when its Assembly voted for union with Greece.

The flurry of commissions brought in by Sandor ruffled Mr Duncan's cartography department. The speed and demands of a newspaper had been a revelation to their time-sensitive work. They wilted under 'the Guvnor's' new Stop Press mania and were pushed to cut, to mask, to join, to fudge, their professional training compromised, their reputations at risk.

'Do not dare tell me you will not finish on time,' Sandor railed.

'Better get it out inaccurate than not get it out at all,' Sandor was warned in turn by Sir John Le Sage, editor of the *Daily Telegraph*.

Sandor returned later to the office on most nights, having stopped off at an Embankment stall so that he might ply his men with ham rolls and tea and his own supply of cherry brandy.

The last touches and crucial final checks on the maps came sometimes as late as 5.30 a.m. Then the transfers were rolled and run through the early morning streets to the printer's in Shepherdess Walk, off the City Road. Bribing the printer in order to gazump another print run was not uncommon. 'Just the once,' rang out as regularly as the damp-collar panic felt by Mr Duncan. Time and time again Geographia crashed into their deadlines with only luck as a back-up. With the first dawn chorus, elation and triumph rippled through the staff. But their contentment only lasted until the next map order – and often that was the same day.

In her memoirs, Phyllis recalled the first time that she, aged two, and Tony, aged three, were permitted into the Geographia offices. Not, of course, during the sweaty confusion of a deadline crisis – for that spectacle might have left a less pleasant impression on the little girl. It was on the occasion of the Lord Mayor's show – and the floats and procession then, as they do today, headed west from St Paul's Cathedral and up Fleet Street. Dressed smartly in a flowery frock, with black patent shoes and her hair neatly brushed, Phyllis stood on the balcony, flicking a Union Jack flag back and forth against the crowds below. In her mouth she sucked hard on a sugar cube covered in camphor oil, administered by her mother to stop the November air causing the sniffles. She, Phyllis and Tony were joined by Sandor to cheer on the parade. For Sandor, the happy picture they made sealed his great satisfaction.

To be flanked by my own handsome family, in my own office, with my own staff, above the throngs, I feel, he told himself, as patriotic as a true Londoner.

'Why doesn't little Phyllis have a go at a wee drawing of a map?' suggested Mr Duncan afterwards, as a reward for her impeccable behaviour. Lifting her on to his high pine stool, he balanced a pen in her hand and guided it to the ink saucer on his bench. He dipped it once into the oily black liquid and then drifted it over to the tracing paper, where he gently steadied her awkward fingers. Phyllis held her breath as she began to mark an outline of a map. Bella watched her daughter's tiny fist wobble and swerve. Several minutes passed. The lines on the paper were heavy with splotches as the pen dribbled, but her hand kept moving until her imaginary country was born. They applauded her fierce concentration.

'That's a fine map you've drawn, Phyllis,' said Mr Duncan. 'How I hope, Mrs Gross,' he said to Bella, 'that your daughter follows in your footsteps.'

CHAPTER SIX

Detours and Dead Ends

In the swirls of her subconscious and memory, it is highly likely that Phyllis interpreted her family's erratic dashes around Europe when she was between the ages of four and ten, and their perpetual moving house, as a soothing, lulling momentum. For on such a trip the happy package of mother, father, sister and brother were tied tightly together, and the attention of both parents was bound to their children.

As an adult, the yearning to roam was, for Phyllis, in part an urge to rekindle the closeness and contentment they had shared back then and sadly, would never manage to share again. At fourteen years old, Phyllis would be a witness to her own parents cutting themselves free of their familial bindings and then standing by, as if helpless, while their son and daughter had their childhood wrenched away from them.

Abandonment, like a bereavement, manifests itself in various guises and for Phyllis, although she pushed on regardless, her search for that lost time, lost love and lost future, never allowed her to feel entirely free of her past. Perhaps if those early years had been miserable, her education sketchy and her prospects few, then her sense of loss might not have been so profound. Even so, the wise woman that Phyllis became, did refrain from treading a path back to old haunts in a sad attempt to resuscitate those days. To try and retrace, say, a Sunday walk across the Downs taken years ago, or to revisit a pretty market town you once stopped off in when you were younger, Phyllis understood was truly a mistake. Not feeling regret, or not allowing herself to feel regret would prove to be one of Phyllis's most enduring character traits. A great strength? Perhaps not. Her refusal to succumb to the temptations of nostalgia meant that she never, even in her final years, sat down alone to take tea with her past. *On we go* – was her own personal motto.

At home, Phyllis and her brother, Tony, were not nearly so happy. For without the illusion of space and freedom given by exotic foreign vistas like the Riviera, or Lake Lugano, the conflict between Sandor and Bella swelled in the confines of the house and their marriage started to tear at the seams. While at home, who can imagine what strains the children were party to, long before school age? Phyllis once said: 'Dinner parties were our chief dread; and the new cold tone in our parents' raised voices after the guests had gone. Barefoot, in our pyjamas, our arms about each other, we would crouch, shivering on the landing at the top of the stairs, fearful that the ranting – with Papa shouting Mama down – would end in violence.'

As with the unpredictable nature of world events that erupt overnight without a breath of rumour beforehand, so too did Geographia burst into full-speed action, giving no advance warning, lurching from one map to another, chasing and plotting the course of invasions, attacks, retreats, explosions and coups that occurred in the years immediately preceding the Great War. And it was just this spontaneous steaming towards a deadline that kept Sandor alive. It force-fed his megalomaniac tendencies, for he was now praised for being indispensable to the *Daily Telegraph*, and permitted him to neglect what he undoubtedly felt was the mundane routine of family life. Bella and the children were left to trail behind in his affections, a poor second to his job.

No one is so craved, so missed, and so loved as the absent father, the aloof patriarch whose brilliance is heightened by his very remoteness. The long after-tea hours, spent idly scuffing her shoes in the front garden, plucking rose petals, and waiting, waiting, waiting, for the clickety-click of her father's steps to herald his arrival home, would lodge forever in Phyllis's mind. Indeed, she would spend the rest of her life hoping to attract the attention and admiration of her father, her persistence undiminished whatever his behaviour or however adverse his reaction to her.

It started with her first ever letter to her parents from Roedean, her boarding school in Brighton, Sussex. Aged ten, she simply wrote:

Dear Mama and Papa,
With Love, Phyllis.

Her reluctance to divulge to them the misery they insisted on putting her through was not reciprocated. Within a few years, weekly letters would become for Sandor and Bella sharpened tools for propaganda as their marriage soured, each bargaining, pleading and condemning the other to their daughter.

I have divorced your mother. She admits adultery. How your mother has persistently deceived me, wronged me, and how she has wronged you and Tony. Never have I been unfaithful to your mother. Alas, though it hurts me to say so, to your unnatural, unfeeling mother.

As adults the destructive closeness between father and daughter would grow as their professional paths crossed into mapping; their differences would be thrashed out in a spontaneous flurry of correspondence, often by letter and even more often by telegram after Sandor moved to America. Why they did not simply pick up the telephone to sort out the following problems hints that both Sandor and Phyllis thrived on exasperating the other – Sandor with his innate bossiness and Phyllis with her innate naiveté:

MAP IT

MAP WHAT

MAP CORONATION ROUTE

Yet the impatient tone of Sandor's voice was never challenged by his daughter. Even when she was in her forties, her letters often began:

My Darling Friend and Father,
I know how wise you are . . .

and were signed:

Lovingly and gratefully, Phyllis

Sandor was not touched by his daughter's longing for approval – as a girl, or as a grown woman. Far away, he reeled in the daily challenge of a newspaper, where the brief might change direction at any moment. There were no anxieties or low points, only highs of various peaks. The professional recognition that he received was partly due to his intuition, for he never failed to elaborate on any country or war he half knew about, and also for motivating, albeit not always by fair means, his team of draughtsmen at Geographia, to pick up speed and produce excellent maps to newspaper deadlines that might otherwise have taken months.

So too might print journalism have ensnared Phyllis, if maps had still been in such demand from newspapers twenty years later, for father and daughter shared the speeding brain of a quick wit and the natural resource craved by every professional – unlimited energy.

Even in the final months of her life, aged eighty-nine, when Phyllis was dying from melanoma cancer, and liquids were all her stomach could tolerate, her energy was inspiring. Over an April weekend, she and her best friend, Dr Esme Wren, travelled early in the mornings to London by taxi, so that Phyllis could paint the beautiful exterior of Claridges – her last work. As she was wheelchair-bound, the porters brought out a table for her paints. Over many hours, she delved into her final reserves of concentration to get the façade just so, while Esme walked around Mayfair. Then it was back home in the taxi, and up again early the next day, to start all over again.

Yet where did Bella rank in Sandor's life – his once proudly displayed business partner and adoring wife and mother to his children? There is a saying that goes something like this: when a husband influences his wife, he will always tell her he has done so, but when a wife influences her husband, she would be wise to never let him know. And aye, there's the rub.

Bella harboured a different, more creative strain of intelligence than Sandor's, which frustrated him, and despite his sharp rebuttals of her brilliant ideas, Bella refused to stay mute. 'How on earth will that work, Bella? What a ridiculous suggestion! Leave important business matters to *me*.' Those same brilliant ideas would then be polished by Sandor and flagged up as his own.

In later years, Bella turned to writing, to fill in the time after the children had gone to bed and before her husband requested her company at dinner. She submitted a series of children's stories to the publisher, Cassells. Her pink excitement, when they offered her a three-year contract, with £500 a year plus royalties, could hardly be contained.

'Look, Sandor,' said Bella after opening the letter at breakfast. 'I am to be a children's author. My nom de plume, I've decided, will be Vernon Bell. You can call me Vernie.'

Her husband's mouth turned itself downwards.

Scanning the details, he snorted and then skimmed the letter back to her across the table and continued to eat his kippers. 'Why give them the profit?' he grunted between mouthfuls. 'We'll publish them ourselves.'

The stories were printed, but Bella never saw a penny.

Outside the office, Sandor's competitive streak ruined their time together. Once, having employed a lady dance teacher to give private lessons, he sulked after only half an hour, as he watched his wife prove lighter on her feet and spin merrily with the teacher along to the tune of, 'If you were the only girl in the world and I was the only boy . . .'

Sandor grew to resent his wife's English breeding. Her English accent. Her giggle. Women, in his homeland, never questioned the authority of a man. *Never*. A husband was obeyed, respected and left free to do just as he pleased. Of course, one desired a wife who was something more than a street girl, but not one who wished to be the centre of attention. Bella, he decided, had too much to say. She sent smiles and whistles rippling among his staff, entranced and flirted with his friends and, most despicable of all, thought Sandor, she did not allow him to correct her faults.

Sandor even came to resent his daughter, partly for her resilience, which reminded him so much of himself, and partly for what he believed to be her undeserved mapping success. HOW CAN YOU, he wrote in one telegram, after she had asked his advice about printers for the *A-Z*, TAKE WEEKS ON A JOB I COULD ACCOMPLISH IN A TRICE?

Despite his disparagement, Bella's dedication to her job with Sandor at Geographia did not ebb. Slipping thousands of maps into envelopes, addressing and mailing them ran into many wearisome hours. 'For him the glory, for me the donkey-work,' Bella quipped to her children, seemingly without qualms that her grumbles would be squirrelled away in their tiny, yet analytical minds. And soon her watery eyes and little sighs stacked up higher and higher until their judgement was swayed, forcing Phyllis and Tony to take their mother's side in what some would argue ought to have been their parents' private dispute.

*

It was early on 8 May 1910 in Venice, where the Gross family were taking a spring break during the Easter holidays. Sandor had left the hotel in search of an English newspaper. Within minutes, he returned waving one as he ran up the Hotel Daniele's marble steps. Into their bedroom he charged.

'Get up now. Get up all of you, and pack. King Edward the Seventh is dead. I must get to London so I can map the funeral route!'

Clothes. Suitcases. Chaos. Phyllis yanked on her trousers over her pyjamas and put both feet into one leg. She tripped.

'Where did these clumsy children come from?' muttered her father.

No moments were spared for sadness or reflection. Two days earlier the King had succumbed, the paper reported, to bronchitis. His funeral, Sandor believed, would be within ten days. When Sandor had wired instructions to Mr Duncan in London, he, Bella, Tony and Phyllis scrambled to board the first train home.

'It's a new project, children – now let's all concentrate.' Fixated by his plan, Sandor elaborated out loud as they whizzed past grey stone suburbs and then on board the ferry back to England. 'I shall get them to widen the streets on the funeral route, thicken their outlines . . .'

'Why not run a black border around the edges, like a mourning card?' Bella suggested to her husband.

'Don't you think I haven't already thought of that?' he snapped.

Within five days the map was a reality. Spread across a sheet of stiff white paper, it became a sombre memento, bought by thousands to mark the closing of a chapter in British history.

*

The culmination of Bella's marital humiliation would come in 1913, in the form of what was, in retrospect, a ground-breaking play. The plot and characters of *Break the Walls Down* were extraordinarily emancipated, despite the fact that the Votes for Women Campaign was still some years away.

In the play, the female protagonist sets up her own dress-making business behind her husband's back and employs a French couturier. When her husband discovers the arrangement, he jealously dismisses her efforts. However, while her company flourishes, his declines and in the final scene – at a creditor's meeting – she steps in to save him from bankruptcy.

In her own mind, Bella must have fantasised that *she* was the sole director of Geographia. Indeed, she displayed all the necessary skills for the job, and without over-stretching the finances, as her husband was prone to do. In the wobbly first few months of their company, Bella must surely have bitten her tongue many times when she saw just how close Sandor was prepared to take them to financial ruin. To save him, to do something that would make him indebted to her, grateful to her and to love her absolutely was Bella's motivation in writing the play.

But her fantasy remained just that.

'I've written a play, Sandor.'

'Fetch it, then. So that is what you have been up to. Read it to me.' By all accounts, Sandor was transfixed as Bella read the three-act play. Midnight passed.

'Well? Please do not laugh, Sandor. What do you think?'

'The fruit of my educational influence. Brilliant.'

Sandor then telephoned his friend, the actor Willy Pogany. 'I know it's late, Willy, but come to the house and listen to a new play – Bella's masterpiece and mine.'

'This is very fine, Sandor. I'd be proud to be in such a play,' said Willy, after he had read it aloud with Bella.

'Then I shall finance a production,' the little man announced. 'Find the best cast you can, my friend.'

Today, the sum Sandor lavished on the project would run into thousands of pounds. *Break the Walls Down* was performed at the Savoy Theatre, in London's West End, after a run of *A Midsummer Night's Dream*. Sadly, no amount of chocolates and orchids and champagne, served in the finest red velvet box, could make up for the critics' words. They shredded every line of Bella's work and dismissed it as Suffragette nonsense. *A woman in business? Oh dear no.*

Quite simply, the critics believed that the British public were not ready for strong women – especially not those who were also financially astute. The play ran for one week.

Always poised to accept the blame, Bella lacked the courage to realise that her ideas were way ahead of the times. 'I am so sorry to have cost you all that money Sandor,' she said shamefacedly. 'How kind you are to me.'

'Then let it be a lesson to you. My wife will not be a martyr to women's rights.'

This ritual of Sandor encouraging his wife to achieve something, in the sure knowledge that she would fail so he could then gloat of his superiority, was nothing new for Phyllis. From the age of seven or eight she had observed the rise of her father, in wealth, in importance and in the domination of his family. His assured ascent did not come without its pains. She and Tony watched as he practised the slow, calculating demoralisation of their mother.

The incident that would stand out most clearly in Phyllis's memory occurred one late summer afternoon in 1914, when a garden party was held at their beautiful home, The Firs, in Claygate, Surrey. All the wounded soldiers and their families who lived in the town had been invited and 'no expense', Sandor had declared, 'was to be spared, for these fine men.' For days the farm and garden had been ransacked for flowers, vegetables, strawberries and peaches. The sight of these pale young men in uniform, many on crutches, all smiling as they hobbled or were wheeled past the rhododendrons onto the lawns, pinched Bella's stomach, although she would have never allowed it to show. Although Sandor keenly led the mothers, the girlfriends and wives by the arm to tour the rose garden or admire the fine lilies on the pond, his eyes slid uneasily over the wounded servicemen. Perhaps he was reminded of the uniform he might have worn to protect his own country, and perhaps he was embarrassed by the scars he knew he could never have borne so courageously.

Bella, however, was not afraid to shake the stubs, where there should have been hands, or to smile into the dark hollows that should have held an eye, or to wink at a quiet boy with no legs at all. Her sadness channelled itself into delight, into kindness and cheerfulness, so that for however short a time it might be, Bella would make these maimed young men feel happy.

'Mama, spot-lighted by an inner glow, exquisite in white georgette, her trim waist belted, her hat at a becoming angle, seemed everywhere,' Phyllis tells us. 'She joined in games, jokes, laughed, let nobody feel left out. Slowly as the guests departed, they congratulated Papa – much to his vexation . . . "Your wife was wonderful," they told him. "Your wife was the life and the soul of the party."'

Apparently Sandor waited until the maids had left for the evening, and then he exploded. 'So you fancy yourself as Prima Donna, do you? Do you? *Do you?*' he bawled.

As he smashed his fist on the kitchen table, crockery spun itself and shattered, while the remnants of a strawberry pavlova jumped into the air and landed under the nose of the family retriever, Blackie.

'Children, go to your rooms and get into bed,' Bella said in a calm voice. 'Please hurry now.'

The noise of shouting drowned all the laughter that had, for once, filled the house and lawns of The Firs, before the children had even reached the top of the staircase.

'All this luxury – is it progress, Sandor?'

They were the last words Phyllis heard before she buried her head in her linen sheets. It was not bedtime. It was barely after six o'clock. No matter. Neither Tony nor Phyllis made a fuss. And somewhere, albeit small, a part of Phyllis began to daydream about what she might someday achieve, to validate her own existence and that of her mother.

CHAPTER SEVEN

Parallel Lines

When Phyllis Pearsall was around eight years old, an incident occurred in her family that nearly ended in tragedy. What a lucky escape, you might think, but it could, instead, be seen as a vicious warning – from God, from fate, from whatever power you believe in. Yet only their mother would prophesise beyond the event. Coming from an Irish/Italian family, Bella's strict Catholic observation was topped up by a healthy respect for superstitions that had been drummed into her since a child.

'Look, children, there's a piebald horse. Make a wish.' Or, 'Don't put those new shoes on the table – it will bring bad luck.'

Sandor had been expanding his geographical business by devising and drawing up maps for pioneer aviators based at Hendon, North London. The accuracy of their flight paths so far had been limited, due to distorted readings given by the compass because of the magnetic pull on their planes' engines; this meant they could only navigate via landmarks. To advance their flying, Sandor devised extra-large-scale plans of England, after countless hours spent in the cockpit of a bi-plane, taking aerial photographs.

Such was his success at improving the quality of maps that he became internationally known in aviation circles and was even commissioned to draw up a route map for Jules Védrines, the French competitor in the 1911 *Daily Mail Thousand-Mile Air Race Round England and Scotland*, which was reportedly watched by over two million people across the country.

'Bring your family to meet us. Let your little girl and boy sit in the cockpit.' The pilots warmed to the man who was devoting the majority of his spare time to improving their flying conditions. 'Would you like to learn to fly, Sandor?' they asked him every time he strapped himself into the cockpit and crossed himself.

'Not if I was asked by the King himself,' he would chuckle.

Then, as a treat one Saturday morning, Sandor took the pilots up on their kind offer and drove the children and Bella to the Hendon aerodrome. Skinny landing strips were fringed with little planes. A few groaned and dipped and soared in the sky above. The wind was light.

Phyllis and Tony were then introduced to one Mr Gates, a widower, who according to Sandor spent hours in the clouds searching for his late wife.

'Come and feel her lovely smooth body,' said Mr Gates, encouraging the giddy children to pat the red metal shell. Shrieks. Tony crawled underneath the body of the plane and sprawled on his back.

'Look at me under here,' he crowed.

Phyllis tapped the propeller.

'Up we go, little ones,' Mr Gates said, lending an arm as they clambered up into the cockpit.

Flash.

'Smile for the birdies,' said Bella, her camera poised.

They smiled.

Flash, flash.

'Let me take them for a spin, Sandor,' said Mr Gates.

'Yes! Yes!' came the shrill replies of Bella, Phyllis and Tony.

'I forbid it.'

'Oh, please!' begged Bella and the children.

'*No.*'

Forlorn, their heads bowed, the children slunk down from the cockpit and sought the enfolding arms of their mother. She kissed their heads before turning her attention to the pilot.

'Smile, Mr Gates,' said Bella. 'One for the family album, my dear.'

They all stood back to watch the sprightly Mr Gates leap into the cockpit, the propeller now fuzzing and whirring. The wheel-chocks were removed and the plane staggered into the soft clouds.

Another flash.

Not from Bella's camera.

Silence as black smoke and red flames engulfed the giant fly and then a sickening drone as it flipped, twisted, and was pulled hard towards the earth before crunching into the field below with a cracking explosion.

Unless you are a parent it is hard to comprehend the emotions that must have overwhelmed the couple. Not only had they witnessed the horrific incineration of a dear man, but also the fragility and insignificance in the universe of their own family.

'Sandor, you saved their lives,' sobbed Bella. 'Thank you and bless you. Promise me you'll never fly. And children – promise me that you won't either.'

CHAPTER EIGHT

Pack Up Your Troubles in Your Old Kitbag (and Smile, Smile, Smile)

It was a European crisis, but for a few men it came as a godsend. The man who made the flags, the man who made black armbands and the man who owned the ammunition factory watched their profits sprint out of sight. And so did Sandor Gross.

Their generous benefactor was one King Nicholas of Montenegro. On 8 October 1912, he had fired the first shot from his revolver and declared war on Turkey. Ten days later, Turkey declared war on Bulgaria and Serbia. Two weeks earlier, the splash in the *Daily Telegraph* had proclaimed a Serbo-Bulgarian treaty. Even so, the editors seemed to dismiss the potential threat to the rest of Europe but Sandor, insisting on the seriousness of the situation, made an appointment to see the editor.

'Do you know what this means?' he demanded, and rumour has it that he thumped his fist upon the desk of Sir John Le Sage. 'This means war. Full-scale war.'

According to Phyllis, Sir John then skipped around his desk, kissing the air. For if there is one thing to make a newspaper editor drool with delight, it is a good old-fashioned war.

'What do you have up your sleeve, Gross?' he asked.

'A 30 × 40 inches coloured *Daily Telegraph Map of the Balkans* folded into self cover.'

'When can I have it?'

'Two weeks today.'

The scale of panic at Geographia was predictable, unavoidable and unbearable. The pressure on Sandor to show Sir John the completed work on time was flimsy compared to the pressure he put on his staff. 'Not one of you can afford to let me down,' he told them.

The map was delivered. By the deadline. Sales of the *Daily Telegraph* soared. And so Mr and Mrs Gross, formerly of Dulwich, could afford to move to the prosperous North-West of London. They purchased a newly built, squarely spacious corner house on North End Road, nestled in the heart of the literary quarter, between Hampstead Pond and Golders Green.

'How happy can a man be, Bella?' he rejoiced. 'Anna Pavlova blows kisses to my children from her garden – imagine that!'

One Lily Seidel, a Swiss governess, was employed to instruct the young Phyllis and Tony in German and French.

My governess, Phyllis noted in her memoirs, *had rather thick ankles*. Which was just as well, for had Lily's fragile beauty extended to her legs, Bella would almost certainly have dismissed her, for her husband's restlessness had stirred. His wife was the tormented witness to his lazily disguised infidelities. At night, the countless other women she knew had slept with Sandor stalked her dreams, as did the shadowy, laughing forms of those she would never discover.

Perhaps their openness was a European trait, but neither parent considered discretion an essential part of their marriage, and Tony and Phyllis were forced to watch helplessly as their mother's unhappiness settled around them and their father's eyes widened lustfully in the company of women.

Unlike most mothers of her day, Bella threw scorn on the perfect family. Why try to pretend that this game was a happy one? To conceal her humiliation and her anger at their father would serve no purpose, and so her gentle face darkened and her tiny waist shrank further.

Yet what Sandor had never bargained for was that Bella would fight off the opposition. Take the woman whose body twinkled with emeralds and rubies at the Royalty Theatre. No matter the play – Arnold Bennett's *Milestones*. When the lights came up at the interval, Sandor's arm was caressing the stranger's chair, his head cocked towards hers. Swiftly, he redirected his attention back towards his wife, but like every adulterous man, his reactions were seconds behind the female observing him.

The next morning, her composure swinging between hysterical and an unnerving calm, Bella rifled through her husband's dinner jacket and found, as she knew she would, the woman's name and address scribbled on a programme.

Hatless, coatless, she stormed into the offices of Geographia, slapped the programme on her husband's desk and flung a pot of black ink over his face and shirt.

Like black blood, the liquid ran down his cheeks. Sandor snorted as he reached for his breast-pocket handkerchief. 'Can I help it if the woman liked me?' he complained, putting her in the wrong immediately. 'Don't you trust me, Bella?'

'You use me,' she replied passionately. 'You use me for your business. I'm not coming in this week!'

'What about the Birmingham index proofs?'

His speedy acceptance into British society meant that Sandor had to dissociate himself from his past. It cannot have been easy for him to let go of the thoughts of how he might have been called up to fight for his country and for his family. But his mother – well, she was never far from his mind.

In the winter of 1913, Sandor caught the scent of war again. Without a second opinion he instructed Mr Duncan to hire more men.

'We need another map of Europe,' he decided. 'This time, we shift the focus. Let's take a good look at potential battle areas in Austria, then France, Germany and Western Russia. Give me a hundred thousand copies as soon as possible.'

This time, his initiative did not receive the hoped for endorsement. Shouted down in an editorial meeting at the *Daily Telegraph*, and accused of scaremongering, Sandor did not even get as far as explaining the mock-up he had unrolled for them to examine.

'You English do not anticipate trouble until it hits you between the eyes,' he fumed.

Two days later, the threat of war with Germany became apparent after the heir to the Austrian and Hungarian thrones, Archduke Franz Ferdinand, was assassinated in Sarajevo.

'About that map, Gross,' said his editor. 'How soon could you get it to me?'

'I have a hundred thousand copies all ready to go. With the *Daily Telegraph* title, of course.'

The death of Sir Joseph Chamberlain and the rise of Lloyd George as Chancellor of the Exchequer fuelled Sandor's deepest fears, especially for the safety of his mother in Csurog, which stretched across the vulnerable Slav-Magyar border in south-west Hungary.

MOTHER COMING TO GET YOU.

NO. NO. NO. I WILL NOT LEAVE MY HOME. WHATEVER.

Somehow the safety of his own wife and children neither

entered his head nor his heart, as he informed them over dinner that night that it was their duty to go and save his mother.

'Will it be dangerous?' Phyllis asked.

'As dangerous as you want to make it.'

Like little foreign correspondents, Phyllis and Tony packed their tiny suitcases for what Sandor always called the journey of a lifetime, which turned out to be a trip lasting from June until August. It would be the first time the children saw their paternal grandmother – and the last.

As they crossed the Channel and drove across France, through Switzerland and Austria into Hungary, Phyllis drew a map in her mind of the shapes of faces, houses, and fields in each country. But there could be no stranger contrast, she believed, than in Hungary, between the smell of the buttercup-soft leather upholstery inside their chauffeur-driven car and the dusty barren landscape outside, scattered with peasants who stopped to stare, their bundles of wood balanced on their heads. Phyllis stared just as hard at trundling carts carrying barefoot urchins swaying home after a day at school, or so she presumed; Sandor told her they had been out goatherding.

Her father, she realised, felt no shame at having been born in a village where the children ran to touch her skirts, where the beetroot soup was considered lunch and dinner, and teeth were optional. Then there was her beautiful, walnut-faced grandmama, stout, in her one black and white polka-dot dress, sighing, 'Oh, well,' after everything and not quite understanding exactly what Phyllis was saying. Yet her smile ran broadly across her worn-out cheeks at the sight of family gathered around her.

I want that, thought Phyllis. I want that happiness, when I grow up.

It was not an overnight transformation, but gradually, the tiny things that Phyllis noted during her stay – the singing boy next door with a stump for a leg, the blind woman who walked four miles to fetch her ox each day, and the roaming skinny dogs – made her realise that all the jewellery boxes, all the dolls, all the prize cups that every girl at school dreamed of weren't half as important as freedom.

Grandmama would not leave her home. As Sandor and Bella began their farewells, Phyllis wanted to say goodbye, she told them, to the village geese. Off she went, with every intention of setting the birds free. She hated watching them twist around in their tiny pens and see them force fed until they were nearly sick.

Within minutes, Phyllis was running back to her parents, followed by a honking, squawking flock of geese.

Bella yelled out: 'I'm proud of you, darling, fighting cruelty to animals in foreign countries. Up the Union Jack!' before diving into their waiting car.

Sandor shooed his mother inside. 'Do not look at what that naughty girl has done,' he instructed her. 'Remember Phyllis as good.'

During the war, many of the families in Csurog were decimated; sons, brothers and fathers were taken and shot on their knees in muddy ditches. Sandor's mother went on to live another two years, before she died a slow, painful death from gangrene that spread from her leg to the rest of her body.

On their return journey, according to Phyllis, her brother had tried, and failed, to take a photograph from the Hotel Adlon in Berlin of Kaiser Wilhelm on horseback riding ahead of his foot guards.

'This is not good,' said Bella. 'Sandor, we must leave immediately.'

On 4 August 1914, German troops entered Belgium at Gemmerich and that same morning, the Gross family set foot back in England.

CHAPTER NINE

Growing Without Direction

A maze. That is how Phyllis thought of Roedean. A whitewashed maze haunted by echoes of distant footsteps, distressed violins, death knells and Latin chanting. Upstairs and down, and into the warren of passages, Phyllis, a little changeling in navy-blue serge and black woollen stockings, fled, flushed with panic. 'Over hill, over dale, I do wander everywhere, swifter than the moon's sphere,' she huffed Puck's lines as she scurried, her hands deliberately fluttering like fairy wings.

Just remember, Phyllis would remind herself, that the front of the building slopes downward towards the sea and the back of school is always warmer. Picking up the pace to a near run, she would unfurl her fingers to detect any change in temperature. Cooler. A draught near her ears. And she was late, late, late again, for lessons.

'What *exactly* is it that you are doing, Phyllis Gross? What in goodness name are you doing out of the classroom?' The teachers never caught her, but that did not stop Phyllis from constantly hearing their voices during her wanderings. Yet the fear of being found, of being lost, or of falling down a hole like Alice, did little to persuade Phyllis that the company of her peers, and hours locked in a classroom were a more sage use of the day. And anyway, if it hadn't been for the discovery of the linen cupboard, she might well have found herself summoned to greet her parents who would arrive, time after time, unannounced and arguing. As Phyllis reached twelve or thirteen, her shame was expelled in deep breaths as she descended into the main hall to intervene.

But for now, she curled in safety and silence, dozing for hours in the starchy heat. Make no mistake, Phyllis was not a lazy pupil. When pinned behind her wooden desk in the front row of the classroom, her pencils sharpened and sitting soldier straight, the girl's eyes would never leave the mistress. As a grown woman, her management style was much the same: her attention to events was absolute, her practicality extreme – she boasted that she used every pencil in the Geographers' Map Company until it was worn down to a stub. But like her father, if Phyllis's imagination was not coaxed out immediately and patted on the head then her spirit, closely followed by her body, was apt to drift off.

The lavender-polished corridors at Roedean leading to back stairs or smaller classrooms or to the dorms disorientated Phyllis – but rarely enough to deter her from tweaking the handles on the door to this or that cupboard, or wondering why the doors to the east wing next to Miss Waldron and Matron were bolted, or slipping along the top passage until she quivered on account of the sea storm sizzling under the window panes. As any Brighton resident will tell you, the sea on the Sussex coast is a placid stretch of dull oyster capable of twisting into a mood worthy of any adolescent.

For some the sea acts as a metronome by tempering their restlessness and lulling their subconscious, but even the dragging lure of the waves could not harness the troublesome teenaged girls cooped up at Roedean. Despite the hypnotic call of the sea, somewhere out in the blackness, Phyllis herself was the sort of child whose body twitched while the night passed, sometimes sleep-walking, her eyelashes rippling as her eyes stammered from left to right under the lids. Her legs would flicker too, as in her dreams she ran up and down the sodden streets of London shouting out for her parents.

Phyllis's first day at Roedean was, coincidentally, the date of her tenth birthday. Wrought-iron gates were an ominous sign, she thought as her car sped up the drive edging the playing-fields. Even the seagulls were trying to warn her. Flee, flee, *fleeeeeee*. 'How funny it would be to see a *Keep In* sign instead of *Keep Out*,' Phyllis had joked nervously. 'I am off to prison!'

Set back from the cliff edges, the magnificent buildings gave shelter to a ragbag assortment of girls who, in return for a large fee, had been deposited into the capable hands of one Miss Penelope Lawrence in the hope that they would turn out well.

'We have a new pupil joining us today, and I hope everyone will make an effort to welcome her, please.' That is what one would hope to hear. Phyllis did not. Instead, the woman told her briskly: 'I am Miss Waldron, your house-mistress. Look, learn and listen and we shall both be doing very well. The unofficial motto here is "Girls should be seen and not heard." Adhere to it and you will make no enemy of me.'

She smelt. Of disinfectant, of mothballs and of silky stale talcum powder. Of spinster. Mama would be so sad for you, reflected Phyllis, trying to peer at Miss Waldron's turkey chins wobbling, while balancing a pile of pink exercise books, an atlas and a Bible in her arms. So sad, that you live in a grey suit and a grey blouse that have leaked upwards into your face, turning even that into a concrete hue.

'Well, child?'

Phyllis gave her the fake smile reserved for Mama's relatives. Fortunately, the house-mistress considered it an adequate response.

Everyone can recall their first six hours at a new school, and whether their future there turned out to be happy or not, that day is photographed and filed away in a mental folder marked *Traumatic*.

Years afterwards, at a dinner party, someone will relate how, on their first day at school, they went without lunch because they couldn't find the refectory and were too scared to ask. Then someone else will confess how they stole another pupil's pencil case because it was pine with a slide-off top and they preferred it to their fluffy orange pouch with a dodgy zip. And everyone joins in with their own story.

As an adult, Phyllis did not need any cajoling into releasing *her* past. She would spread before her with pride the dusty Roedean memories which she polished like precious stones before bequeathing them to the listener to be equally admired and revered. The relish and warmth with which they were handled allowed them a certain romance, a certain value. Smiling broadly, as she always did when describing any subject with any degree of pain attached, Phyllis never wavered from branding her school-days as cruel misery. The truth was perhaps rather more mundane: Phyllis Gross was just another pupil who failed to erase the marks of institutionalism from her life's report.

Although she rose to captain of Lacrosse ('Fearless' was the nickname given to the cannon-ball of terror who once smashed another girl's teeth out as she criss-crossed the pitch, all in the name of Junior House), Phyllis was the antithesis of the team player. But in a photograph taken at Roedean that has now faded from monochrome to sepia brown, Phyllis is caught for an instant on a terrace, looking happy and relaxed. Her head is inclined to one side, her hair misbehaving, a smile keenly wide and her skinny legs turned inwards in their black tights. Her arm pulls tight around the shoulders of another pupil, also grinning. It is stuck into Tony Gross's album, now kept by his daughter, Mary, and beneath the picture in his careful childhood hand the caption reads *Phyllis and A. Batten*.

Her teachers considered Phyllis to be an indulged, muddle-dressed girl (*her people are refugees turned millionaires, you know*), a natural loner and a natural target. Bored bullies picked her over with the ferocity of a wild pack of wolves. Victim. If Phyllis ever screamed, punched, kicked, bit or retaliated against her aggressors is not known. It had been a different story when she and Tony had attended the same school, Phyllis aged four and her brother five. Although he was the elder, according to her memoirs, and no doubt she was a tiny scrap of a thing, she would fight with all her might to try and pull the bullies off her brother.

A bell tolled and Miss Waldron plucked Phyllis from the classroom after her second lesson – History. Phyllis was deciding whether she would have rather been a Tudor or a Stuart when she was interrupted. 'Ordinarily you would now make your way to the dining room for cocoa break. Then we have French, Tennis and Mathematics, followed by luncheon. This afternoon we have Poetry, Needlework and Physics. You haven't lost your timetable, have you, Phyllis?'

'No, Miss Waldron.'

In fact, the school secretary, Miss Young, had failed to give one to the new girl, but even aged ten she had sense enough to recognise the futility of such an admission. In her memoirs, Phyllis Pearsall records her next encounter so vividly that it is best seen through her eyes. *Tear-blinded, I trotted behind Miss Waldron up the carpeted stairs of her private quarters and along dingy corridors, towards frightening shrill voices emanating from a room, which we entered. All talk ceased abruptly. The big girls cramming it alarmed me even more. In the menacing silence, Miss Waldron introduced me: 'This is Phyllis. She is ten years old today,' and left me to their mercy. They closed in on me. Cicely, the largest – daughter, I learnt later, of*

*renowned Polar explorer Ernest Shackleton – poked her face within
an inch of mine, grimacing: 'So you're the birthday girl! Show us your
presents then.'*

The other slouching girls must have edged forward with
Cicely. Buried deep in her coffin-sized silver trunk, wrapped
beneath the soft piles of cotton vests and slips, Phyllis fumbled for
three china dolls. Precious, thought Phyllis, as she uncovered
their porcelain cheeks, their blue eyes rattling. It does not matter
which of the girls sprang at Phyllis first. The others soon muscled
in and snatched at the blonde, ash and russet horse-hair tresses of
Belinda, Elizabeth and Hatty. Sniggering, they ripped at the
velvet and the linen and the frills, tearing at the white cotton
undergarments. With a strength that the games mistress could
only dream of witnessing in the gymnasium they jumped and
stamped on the dolls' heads. Shards of china sprayed their ankles.
When broken arms and severed heads lay dismembered at
Phyllis's feet, the girls, shocked at their own spent aggression,
slunk out.

A lifelong suspicion of strangers might have arisen from this
hateful incident, but years later, one of her original members of
staff at the Geographers' Map Company, Nigel Syrett, would
explain one of Phyllis's greatest attributes – which had also been
her greatest weakness:

'She was a rotten judge of character, we all knew that. She
trusted everyone until they proved themselves otherwise. "Hello,
darling, how are you?" she would say to someone she was
introduced to and embrace them in her warmth, whether she had
met them before or not. And of course they would respond
likewise, until sometimes their true character revealed itself.'

From then on Phyllis knew that her time at Roedean would be
a troubled one. Letting oneself be overcome by grief, she had
learnt from observing her mother, was a sign of weakness to be

reserved for extreme occasions. Once, from under the velvet drapes of the dining-room table cloth, Phyllis had spied her mother hurl down her silk-trussed body prostrate at the feet of her father (who was lighting a cigar) when her request for, 'A little – oh, just a little!' increase in her clothing allowance was categorically rejected.

'And that, my good lady Bella, is my first and final answer.'

'But . . . but . . .' cut in the distraught woman, 'how can I ever be seen in Town in the same—'

Here Phyllis remembered a particularly spectacular combination of her mother spluttering, clutching a wrung-out handkerchief to her pulsating bosom and stealing gulps of air.

'– the same, the-the s-s-same tired, shabby, d-d-dresses . . .'

And with that, Bella Gross unleashed her sobs, beating red fists on to Sandor's patent shoes, her torrents of wailing rising higher and higher until she battered her husband into submission.

I am not sure, thought Phyllis with all the practicality of a girl who never cared a fig about clothes, that it was worth all *that* bother.

Crying now, she decided as she scooped up the doll parts and hurled them out of the open window, would make me look a baby. At least they have noticed me.

That morning at home, which would, as it turned out, be her last ever living at home, had not been so triumphant.

'There'll be no molly-coddling where you're going, my girl,' Sandor had offered as his parting advice, probably as a fatherly-take-it-on-the-chin sort of thing. Unfortunately, Phyllis's usual strength had abandoned her that day and Miss Seidel had to be summoned to assist Mr Gross in unclasping his daughter's hands from around the waist of Mrs Gross. Frizzy plaits, a velour hat and angry screams were blotted out by soft, perfumed furs.

'My darling, you are fairly squeezing the very life from me,' were Bella's last words to Phyllis, and once set free by the governess, she remarked tritely to her husband that she so preferred to dress her baby in Viennese frocks.

It was a forlorn and crumpled Phyllis who clambered into the automobile. Did she entreat her parents not to make her go as they waved her smaller and smaller out of the drive? No.

'Big school will be good for you,' Nanny had promised, nodding at the driver who then made little agreement noises and nods too.

'Please do not send me away.' She tried to say the words but her lips wobbled and let her down.

Nanny yanked out a handkerchief from her sleeve and crunched Phyllis's nose. 'Now blow.'

That had seemed centuries ago. Whatever was she doing here? 'Birthdays do not get much sorrier than this. This is a really sorry day,' sighed Phyllis as she perched on the window seat to survey the doll bone pattern on the lawn below. A sea gust flicked at her cheeks and Phyllis sank down on to the seat to think back to her ninth birthday.

'That was in nineteen hundred and fifteen,' she declared. 'At home,' she huffed. 'At home in Claygate. That's Surrey, you know,' she told the blank rose petal walls and stern iron beds.

'Wakey, wakey, rise and shine, Birthday Girl!' Sandor Gross had boomed as he ascended the nursery stairs.

'Am I here? Have I made it? Number Nine at laaaaaaaaast!' Phyllis had screamed, and presumed that jumping up and down on her bed would be excused today.

Tony hooted. 'Wait for me. Wait for me!' He wheeled into the nursery clutching a red balloon and a fat parcel.

'Where is Mama? Where is she?' Phyllis cried.

'Darling girl, she is waiting outside for you.'

'Mama? Why outside?'

'Well, some surprises are too big to be left alone by themselves.'
Shrieks.
More shrieks.
Sandor covered his ears. '*Children!*'
Silence.

'Phyllis, we must ask you please to do us the great honour of following us on to the lawn. But I must insist that you first . . .' And with that Sandor had whipped out from his breast-pocket a yellow blindfold.

'Miss Seidel, Erik and Else!' bellowed Sandor. 'Come and see, come and see. A treat for all our eyes.'

Now, huddled in the window-seat corner, Phyllis let herself feel again the light cotton of her nightgown turn stiff in the cold as she stumbled out into the smoky autumn air. Bare feet, wet feet and iced grass.

'Mama, Mama, they are bringing me. Are you there?'

'Here I am, darling. With the one gift for our birthday girl we could not wrap.'

A gasp.

'Have you ever wanted a present from Africa?'

Once again Phyllis heard her mother's stifled giggles and recalled her knees growing weaker beneath her.

Tony had then let loose a strange snorting noise that boys of his age do when they are embarrassed or over-excited. 'Come ooooon,' he had managed before becoming engulfed by snorts.

Sandor had enfolded his daughter's head. Softly, he kissed her hair and yanked off the blindfold.

And there, shivering on the grass, was a baby elephant. Elijah.

'When he gets too big,' her father had declared, 'we shall give him to the zoo.'

Extreme moments of elation such as this might have turned Phyllis into a spoilt brat, but the similarities between Bella and her daughter only went so far. Within a year of Elijah the elephant, reality had shoved Mr and Mrs Gross and their fantastical lives off to one side.

Four years at boarding school proved the academic making of Phyllis. She became the geography whizz and the winner of the essay competition. For any good teacher, curiosity, charm and intelligence in a pupil are fine attributes that bring with them the additional benefit of popularity, with both staff and peers. However, like her father before her, Phyllis was a step out of syncopation with everyone she encountered. Her speech ran a little too fast, her wit was just a little too clever, her innocence a little too unbelievable.

Loneliness drove Phyllis to hoard and to read books obsessively as if, like her dolls, they too might be wrenched from her at any minute. She wrote fanatically but her hours of thought would be pushed firmly to the bottom of the waste-paper basket, such was her fear of Miss Waldron reading her letters home aloud.

Dear Mama and Papa, With love, Phyllis read the tightly looped words enclosed in little manilla envelopes every week.

Her memory tuned into a high frequency, she photographed great chunks of text that would be regurgitated effortlessly in class. By the end of her life, Phyllis had learnt much of the Scriptures by heart and never forgot a name. Indeed, she may not have realised as much at the time, but she possessed the same restless ambition, the precocious confidence and unassailable charm of Sandor Gross, entrepreneur and millionaire.

CHAPTER TEN

Overtaking the Past

November, 1919

After a night of snowfall, a freezing morning had cast a blue hush over The Firs. As the story goes, Bella had taken her horse out alone, before dawn, one Friday morning, 'for quietude and solitude' into the bristling green of Oxshott Woods. She would have been breathing in the pine air, her eyes closed and listening to find out if the brook's babble had been muffled by ice. Nobody knows why, but for the first time in many years she rode side-saddle, so when her horse slipped, stumbled and then fell, she found herself unable to dismount and was crushed beneath the animal. Nobody knows either, why Sandor did not raise the alarm when his wife did not return several hours before he left for London. The children, who were at their respective schools, would only hear about their mother's accident in a letter from Sandor, three days later:

Could it be Nemesis? Your mother has been seriously injured. In a riding accident. Crushed under her horse. Fractured skull and spine, the doctors say. You know her courage. She dragged herself to the road. How, nobody knows. There she was found hours later, unconscious.

The Nemesis that Sandor referred to concerned a trick he had played on 'the ghastly Miss Waldron' as he called her, only the week before. Miss Waldron, now accustomed to breaking tragic news of fathers and brothers killed in action to her girls, had summoned Phyllis to her study after breakfast. Her rarely seen tenderness as she sat beside Phyllis on her sofa alarmed her pupil a great deal.

'I'm so very sorry, Phyllis. I'm afraid it's your mother. She is seriously ill and has asked to see you. We have arranged for you to be put on the next train to Victoria and your father will meet you there.' She squeezed her pupil's hand, which unfortunately only served to prompt a stream of tears.

Wretched, is how Phyllis recalled that train journey. Her blazer pockets bulging with handkerchiefs, she climbed into an empty carriage and let her tears flow freely as she pictured her darling mother call out her name as she writhed in pain. To her surprise, her father appeared uncrumpled by worry as he paced the platform, and even less so when he caught sight of his daughter, running towards him, snivelling.

'Is Mama dead? What has happened? Tell me, Papa!'

'Dry your tears. I cannot stand that nonsense. Your mother is waiting for us at King's Cross Station, with a new dance frock for you and, she informs me, buttercup-yellow patent shoes. We are off to Derby, for Tony's Speech Day celebrations.'

'But Miss Waldron . . .'

'I say damn that Miss Waldron, *and* her rules.'

The relief of being reunited with her family and able to catch her own dear mother around the waist, transformed Phyllis's grief into pure happiness during what turned out to be three memorable days. Unfortunately, the grand deception, as she thought of it, would turn out to be not so grand after all. When Phyllis returned to Roedean, no one asked after her mother or even spoke to her. Silence fell in the common room when Phyllis walked in.

Cicely shoved a letter under her nose. 'Listen, everyone. What do you have to say about this, Phyllis? Thought you wouldn't get found out? Your people must have no morals whatsoever. "Dear

Cicely, Why couldn't you get up here for Speech Day? The sister of my stinking fag did – I trust you take it out on her." So you cried wolf, eh? No one will ever believe anything you ever say again. Get out.'

Just as the meanness of Cicely was beginning to pall (being pinched in the corridor, mud smeared on her pillow and the family photograph pinned above her bed scribbled over), Sandor's letter arrived.

The next day, as his car pulled up at Roedean, Phyllis could see that nights of lost sleep had dragged on his face.

'Your mother has asked to see you.'

He shook hands with Miss Waldron before bundling his mute daughter into the car. They drove for two hours in silence to Guildford Cottage Hospital. Inside, the raw smells and noises of death and illness stuck themselves in her memory. Whispers. Uniforms. The white of the nurses. The black of the nuns. The distinctive chloroform odour, that made her nose run, would release memories of that day, over twelve years later, as she visited her mother in quite a different place – Bedlam. Tears, uninvited, began to trickle as Phyllis and her father were led up the stairs by a matron.

'Please be aware that your mother's pain will be aggravated by every movement and sound,' the woman warned them.

But no one had thought to warn the thirteen-year-old girl of what she might expect to find.

In her mother's darkened room, the body that lay in front of her was huge. As Phyllis drew nearer, she gave a little gasp. A slow rattle of breath shook in and out of her mother's mouth. Her face, unrecognisable, was a purple landscape of pulped hills, her eye-sockets blackened, her eyes bulged shut. Distorted by shaving, her engorged head was tightly bandaged.

Phyllis's tears stopped, as did her feet, unable to move closer towards the body. 'Don't worry, Mama,' she blurted, 'I can still see it is you.'

A cracked voice: 'My wings are clipped.'

'Time for your morphine, Mrs Gross.'

The head and spinal injuries that Bella sustained were almost identical to those that her daughter would receive in a plane crash over twenty-five years later. Both women would find their recovery impeded by returning to work too soon, and be witness to their lives changing beyond all recognition. In Bella's case, she would literally never be the same person again.

Today, brain scans would have probably shown up a degree of brain damage that at most might have triggered what seems to have been a severe personality disorder and at least, left her with severe headaches for the rest of her life.

After two months in hospital, they moved Bella to a nursing home not far from Claygate. Her mother, Maria Crowley, who took the train daily from Peckham Rye, said bedside prayers for her daughter and for her son-in-law, whose temper, she believed, was the work of the devil.

In her memoirs, Phyllis described the excruciating cruelty that her father unleashed, without restraint, on her mother during his short visits, irrespective of whether it disturbed his daughter, other patients, or Bella herself:

Papa, provoked beyond endurance by her slow progress, her inability to talk rationally, shouted at her, 'I can't bear illness. Why should this happen to me? Pull yourself together, Bella. There's nothing wrong with you!'

'I'm sorry, Sandor, for the mess,' Bella slurred. 'Everything spoilt for you and the children. My own fault.'

Sandor walked towards the door. The next words he spoke, which clawed their way into Bella's disorientated mind, would be his most destructive.

'It is terrible for a man like me to be tied to one woman for the rest of his life.'

The physical strength that Bella must have summoned up in the darkness, after her husband, mother and daughter had left, to pack, to tremble into her clothes, to steady her way down the corridor and then take a taxi to a hotel, was phenomenal. Yet it was her anger that so galvanised her damaged spine and fractured skull into working, long before they were ready to do so.

When the doctors informed Sandor of the disappearance of Mrs Gross, they enquired whether there was anything he might have said to upset his wife.

'None of your business,' he snapped. 'I pay you, don't I?'

The house felt like an empty butterfly cocoon without her mother. Despite her pleas to stay until Bella was found, Phyllis was packed off back to school. Her miserable window vigils had irritated Sandor beyond endurance. There, ludicrous nightmares tore up her sleep, so much so that the teachers instructed her to sleep a little extra at the weekends. Her imagination, that had come in so handy for creative essays, had turned against her; as she looked out across the sea, she wondered if she caught sight of a hand, a leg, a body, her mother, drowning before her eyes.

Two weeks later, a letter arrived at The Firs addressed to Alexander Gross.

Dear Sandor,

I know how often I have disappointed you. Now I have given you your freedom. The freedom you asked for.

Yours, Bella.

The following day, a Sunday, Else the housekeeper found Bella collapsed on the doorstep of The Firs and tucked her into bed, before the master came home from a pheasant shoot with his neighbour, General Livingstone.

By Tuesday, Sandor had coaxed his pale wife back into the

office, where he believed she would be most useful to him, rather than allowing her to stay at home. When she shuddered at his orders and no longer gave clever retorts to questions as she used to, by all accounts he shouted. In a three-storey office filled with the quietest of workers – draughtsmen – he shouted.

Even as the stairs wobbled beneath her and the typewriter keys rattled her ears, she took slow steady breaths as she entered the drawing office. 'I am so sorry. My husband is not himself today.' Her eyes lowered, she smiled at the silence and made her way out on to the street.

Just after the death of her unnamed firstborn, it became clear that in order to continue as Mrs Gross, Bella had two options. To subjugate her desires and opinions and shape a life in subservient shadows, or to fight, and sustain many bruises along the way for what she believed was meet and right.

The only option, she believed then, was the one that would keep her imagination alive. She still believed it. As it was, this fight would beat her beyond recognition. Was she a battered wife? Sandor never so much as raised a hand to her, but physically, she would turn on herself. Mentally, her self-worth was knocked repeatedly until she could no longer judge her own merit. The only difference between Bella and her daughter was that Phyllis had the advantage of seeing her mother's sorry example of a disastrous marriage, and Phyllis would not, unlike Bella, be in love with her husband.

'She must go for six months to Dinard, a few miles west of St Malo,' the family physician advised Bella when he called on her at The Firs. 'For its restorative coastal air, and,' he whispered, patting her damp hand, 'to get away from your husband.'

'Your dear wife is very highly strung,' he told Sandor.

'Highly strung! So am I highly strung,' he quipped.

Perhaps it would have been for the best if, when the schools shut for summer, Phyllis and Tony had been palmed off on their grandparents for a modest British holiday. But to give him his due, unlike most fathers of that time, and some nowadays, Sandor was not in the slightest bit daunted at travelling with his two lively children.

For Phyllis, those weeks flashed by in her memory as a precarious, unpredictable adventure in Europe. Her father's attention was constantly diverted and distracted by women as they caught trains from one country to another. On the Orient Express to Vienna, he became acquainted with what Phyllis recalled as 'a compliant countess', complete with a gold front tooth.

Most anxious that his children should not impinge on his sexual indulgences, their good behaviour (not running away, not fighting over the biggest bed and turning up dressed for dinner at 8 p.m. every night) was rewarded with gold crowns, which Sandor would press into their palms and tell them to spend freely each morning, so that he might entertain his new friend.

The giddy fun of running around fairgrounds, riding on big wheels, eating roasted hazelnuts and jam crêpes and trying their luck on hoopla stalls (where Phyllis and Tony once won a bottle of champagne, drank the lot and fell asleep under a fortune-teller's table), freed their minds from the deep anxiety surrounding their mother.

In those days, such scrapes and near-misses were deemed character-building for children. Run away to sea at fourteen? Travel alone by ship to Australia at ten? A wife and three children by twenty? The liberating childhood afforded to our grandparents could not be further from the twenty-first-century teenagers who are driven to and from school and where the average age for a man to leave home is twenty-five years old.

THE WRECK WILL BE WAITING FOR YOU AT LUCERNE.

So read the telegram from Bella that Sandor opened one morning, a month into their trip. He sent word back that they would indeed take the train the next afternoon to Lucerne. The sense that his wife was close at hand did not cut short his antics, however. In fact, he dusted down his thespian skills and became more daring in his act to attract women. To the treacle-hearted dowagers, he was a widower. To the young heiresses, he had been deserted. And to the extremely beautiful, the children were not his own but those of his poor dead sister. He reeled them in, the Viennese, the Swiss, the French, the Germans, and spat them out too, fleeing with Phyllis and Tony before any of them could attach themselves to his coat-tails.

The next encounter with Bella, whatever good intentions either may have had, would run away with itself, drawing them both on over two months to the end of their marriage.

Phyllis, who claimed never to have been shielded from any aspect of her parents' relationship, devoted a good section of her memories to these events that would divide her family for ever.

The long French windows in the hotel dining room were open on to Lake Lucerne. Out in the dark night, mountain tops glowed as lightning flashed across them. As the orchestra played Hoffmann's *Barcarolle* Sandor insisted that he, Phyllis and Tony were shown to a table for four.

'Your mother is late. To humiliate me.' He ordered juicy watermelon, but Phyllis felt sick and could not touch it and Tony said he would wait for Mama.

'Eat, both of you!'

All three ate in silence, the noise of their cutlery grating on their ears. Then Phyllis heard a lull in the conversation, and remembered looking up:

There she stood; her face was chalk-white, framed in a black crepe-

de-chine hut, black Pacquin frock – fringed and concertina-pleated.
She remained immobile, except for haunted, darting, shadowed eyes,
scanning the guests.

Sandor did not make a move. Nor, as she approached the table,
did he stand up or kiss her. 'Please kiss her. Please, Papa,' Phyllis
cried, as she left her chair to hold the thin, unresponsive body of
her mother.

The fixed gazes of Sandor and Bella hardened. 'Now we are all
here,' said Phyllis, braving the silence, 'let's agree on going up the
Rigi tomorrow.' Like statues coming alive, the husband and wife
suddenly began to talk, to eat and, to their own surprise, all four
survived until pudding.

What turned out to be not so surprising was that as the family
took a turn about the lake the following morning, Bella fainted,
and Sandor's reaction, as passers-by started to stare, was less than
kind.

'Good God,' he muttered. 'Do I have to endure this?'

The little hands that lay beneath Bella's head, while Tony
flicked drops of lake-water on his mother's face, belonged to
Phyllis.

'Don't worry, Mama,' she whispered, cradling her mother's
grey face. 'Tony and I are here.' As Bella came round, they led her
to a bench, where all three squinted at the tiny figure of Sandor
making his way back to the hotel.

'Children, it's impossible,' she said, taking their hands in hers.
'I'm leaving for Dinard.'

The next time Bella would see her husband was as he burst in
on her as she lay on top of a bed, clad in nothing but a peach silk
slip, in the house of Monsieur le Docteur Tillier.

The confusion surrounding Bella's departure from the hotel
gave Phyllis, a curious child, the opportunity to play detective.
First, she had asked reception for a forwarding address for

Madame Gross's mail. 'Chez Monsieur le Docteur Tillier,' they said, as did the bellboys. Her work, she felt, was bound to be rewarded by her father, but unfortunately, the address was not that of the Dinard Convalescent Home.

Like a dog let loose amongst sheep, Sandor stormed into the dining room and out again, he tried to go for a walk to kill his anger, but ended up ordering his luggage to be brought down from his room. At once.

'Children, we are off to catch your mother. She has gone to meet her lover. All three of us will catch her *in flagrante delicto*!'

As the train to Dinard pulled out of the station, both Phyllis and Tony cried, much to their father's disgust. 'The shame of it – you, Phyllis, thirteen and Tony, fourteen years old.' But they continued to sob, afraid of what they might find and afraid of what they might hear.

It was well past midnight when the taxi driver stopped outside a well-lit Victorian corner house. Incensed by the beauty of the house, Sandor rang the bell, and kept his finger on the button.

'You will wake the dead,' grumbled the maid, as she unlocked the bolts and then flung open the door. 'Sir, whatever is the matter?'

Sandor grabbed his children's hands and ran up the stairs. 'Where is she? Where is my wife?'

He burst in on Bella, who was apparently alone. From a side door, a calm Frenchwoman in her sixties breezed through in black taffeta, her white hair held in a black Alice band. 'Explain yourself, Monsieur,' she said sternly.

The woman, Sandor discovered, was the mother of Dinard's most eminent doctor. It was she who, for companionship, had invited Bella to stay in her house. 'There is no lover,' she explained: 'Your wife is here alone.'

Phyllis fainted.

'*Ma cherie, ma cherie*,' was the whisper Phyllis heard as she stirred in the arms of the doctor's mother, who could not disguise the tail end of a vicious argument.

'Sandor, you have murdered my love. You thrive on scenes like this.'

'Apologise, or don't come home.'

'I'll leave. I'll go to Lisbon.'

True to Bella's unpredictable nature, the bill Sandor received the following week was for a return passage to Rio de Janeiro.

The relative sanity of Roedean was quite a relief, Phyllis decided after she had returned for the Michaelmas term, although she found herself unable to relate to tales of lawn tennis, picnics, rowing up the River Cam, tea parties at the Ritz and samphire-gathering on the beaches of Norfolk.

Pinned above her head, postcards of the Corvocado Mountain would be joined by ones from Botafogo Bay and Urba. On 6 September, a birthday card was missing from her mother, but made up for by a telegram from her father: MOTHER SENT YOU & TONY HORSE EACH. WHITE.

Enclosed was a note she had sent with the horse box to The Firs, which read: *For my darlings, Phyllis and Tony, with love from their Mama. I am now riding on a mule into the heartland of greenest Brazil, with a group of prospectors who I had many a dinner with on board ship. We are in search of radioactive minerals. Do not expect to hear from me until Christmas.*

Of all the bizarre things to happen, Bella's consortium would discover samarskite in the mines at Divinópolis. According to Phyllis, when they presented their find to Marie Curie for testing at her Institute of Radium in Paris, such was the richness of the mineral, they were each paid thousands of pounds.

The financial security brought about by Bella's journey had also freed her proud spirit. On her return to London, she sent three telegrams, one to Sandor, one to Phyllis and one to Tony.

All three read: FILING FOR DIVORCE. NEW LIFE.

CHAPTER ELEVEN

The Kishlany Trailing Behind

The cruelty of children must never be underestimated. As well as the physical brutality they feast upon, unhindered by any sense of morality – whether it be concocting stews from pulped worms or deserting a younger sibling stuck in the branches of a tree until the day's shadows have slunk away – their verbal taunts can splice confidence with the accuracy of a rapier sword.

Fortunately, the young 'ladies' at Roedean were also attracted to the superficial. Their hands would snatch at pink iced buns, satin dancing shoes and the shiniest of pennies while their curly heads fibbed about the father with the fastest car or the mother with the fattest string of pearls and the rubiest of lips.

Phyllis had no need to fib on *that* score, but she took no pride in her family's wealth, dreading their impromptu visits. Even now, on hearing the sound of hooves and seeing a couple riding towards the lacrosse pitch, she was chanting under her breath: '*Please do not. Please do not let. Please do not let it be. Please do not let it be them . . .*'

But it was.

Phyllis was now aged fourteen, and as she staggered against the March gales tearing over the lacrosse pitch at the end of Saturday practice, another girl overheard her mumbled mantra. 'Whatever is the matter with Pig?' she asked disdainfully.

But no one replied, since no one actually cared.

Only a month before, Miss Waldron had monitored her pupil

for signs of distress as she handed Phyllis a telegram to read before Prayers.

DARLING. MARRIED ALFRED LAST WEEK. GONE ON A PAINTING TOUR OF ARGENTINA. WISH US FINE WEATHER. MRS ALFRED E. ORR.

Scanning the words only once, Phyllis folded the white paper over and over again into a tiny square, tucked it up the sleeve of her sweater and, tilting her head sweetly, requested to be excused.

We will not, Miss Waldron reconsidered, need to worry about any tears from Phyllis.

What Miss Waldron does not understand, Phyllis had thought as she marched away, is that it doesn't matter to me, because it is all happening so far away. Anyway, Alfred may be Mother's chance for happiness.

Back to the lacrosse game amidst the March winds. Phyllis's mantra had proved useless – and here were the happy couple, two bright figures tacking their way down the moleskin curves of the South Downs.

'Why must she ride a horse?' Phyllis muttered, yet she already knew the answer.

This defiant symbol of her mother's rehabilitation was intended to be relayed to her former husband. What other reason could there be, when the pain crunching her back would ordinarily have been enough for Bella to take to her bed? Yet the injection of happiness that Alfred had given her enabled Bella to grind her teeth through the crippling seizures and pray that Sandor would hear of her well-being and be plagued by jealous thoughts.

The pair were still too far away for Phyllis to have been able to catch an American voice stabbing the air with curses. Curses on her mother.

'God dammit, Vernie, wait up, I said. Pull up your damn horse now, ma'am. I can't keep up!'

Gone was Phyllis's surge of light-headedness after the three goals for which she had fought so hard; in its stead, a hot rush of pain swelled her bruised thumb and twisted ankle as the other girls stopped playing to stare across the field. A flotilla of navy-blue games skirts and lacrosse sticks bobbed together. Like banshees, Cicely Shackleton and the other prefects wailed, 'Just look at that lady – she's riding astride. Oh, and look at what she is *wearing*!'

'Pig? I thought your people were in Argentina . . .' Cicely screeched back to Phyllis, then she, too, fell silent as the spectacle drew near. The girls gave a collective gasp, half in admiration and half in relief that no matter how provoking their own parents were, they would never subject them to humiliation on a grand scale such as this. For there, on a Western-style saddle astride an apocalyptic black horse rode Bella, in white Brazilian riding breeches and an exotically fringed white flamenco jacket, her feet encased in an exquisitely embroidered pair of black and scarlet patent leather boots.

'I say, look at that white sombrero,' the girls whispered.

This was the first time that Phyllis had set eyes on her mother's new husband and, she supposed, her stepfather. Here was one Alfred Everett Orr, a New Yorker, who could have had no idea at that time that his new wife would guide him up the English social ladder from commercial artist into a highly respected portrait painter, whose sitters would include the Prince of Wales and members of European royalty.

His connections may have sounded grand, but Phyllis was about to be exposed to yet another emotionally deprived adult whose artistic temperament was as fickle as his finances. The trouble with Alfred, Phyllis said as a grown woman, was that if sitters paid in advance he saw no reason to paint them, and if they didn't he was so upset he could not bring himself to do so.

She noted the slightly flaccid body, kitted out in a Savile Row suit of royal blue corduroy and a yellow silk cravat that underlined his angry red beard. 'Although this is the man Mama has married,' Phyllis later declared to the girls in the dorm, 'he is *not* to be mistaken for my father.' Phyllis said this even though at a young age, she sensed she would never actually like the man who was her father. Yet her love, loyalty and unconditional adoration for Sandor could not be swayed.

Whether Sandor conducted his relationship with his daughter with such brusque formality because snobbery deceived him into believing that is how an English patriarch ought to conduct himself, or whether it was simply how he treated everyone, apart from himself, is hard to discern. As it was, Phyllis would not hear of confronting or questioning her father's cruelty, nor in later years his lack of trust in her business skills. She never sought to fight against the injustice meted out by him. She took great pains to shine, to smile and to appeal to his gentle side that she prayed was dormant and not dead. Unlike her mother, Phyllis never resorted to ultimatums, to tears or to shouting. Even so, perhaps Phyllis was cleverer than that. Phyllis got her revenge in a subtler way. After all, who will question a man's true character when it is his own dear daughter who is writing about his life long after he is dead and buried?

'We had no principles in our family,' Phyllis once said in an interview. 'I was never told about right or wrong. Morals were never mentioned. I was told "meet your problems head on". But the main thing was to make money.'

Would Alfred fare any better as a strong, paternal figure? For one thing, Orr liked to drink – an unfortunate vice that within a couple of years had destroyed any order that Roedean had painstakingly instilled in Phyllis's life. So foul were the words that oozed from his drunken lips then, and so capricious were his needs that he, too, goaded Bella to the precipice of insanity many times.

In time, Phyllis recognised that Alfred's flame-coloured hair served as an indication of his irrational temper. Even then his skin, thickened by eczema and brandy, gave him the appearance of a stuffed pig, while his nose, thought Phyllis, resembled a large crimson plum. Anyone decent, she decided, would take one glance at Alfred's shoes – flimsy, black patent ones – and mark him down as a fake, a trickster, as gaudy and cheap as his brightly painted cufflinks.

Just when I was doing so well, Phyllis thought, her tiny feet squelching to a halt in the mud in front of Bella's horse. The wind scurried around her knees and her head dropped to examine her boots, as if in search of the adoration she kept especially for her dearest Mama but which had suddenly gone into hiding.

'We do not want any more Ghastly Scenes,' Miss Waldron had scolded Phyllis the last time Roedean had hosted a Gross gathering.

'What an unexpected pleasure,' the headmistress Miss Lawrence had announced, when first Bella and then Sandor had burst into the front hall within minutes of each other, one Tuesday evening after dinner.

'Do not let that philanderer speak to my daughter!' Bella had wept. 'I want to see Phyllis, I want to see my daughter . . .'

'Under no circumstances will you allow that whore to see Phyllis. It cannot be permitted. Look – just look at her behaviour!' Sandor had shouted.

'May I make it perfectly clear that such displays of hysteria will alarm the girls. Kindly refrain from this deplorable behaviour.'

Miss Lawrence's words had hung over the scene as Phyllis ran first to embrace her mother and then her father. An observer would have felt disquieted by the fact that the child's distressed reaction to her parents and her tears meant nothing to the man and woman whose play for power had driven them all the way from Surrey without any of their hateful energy dissipating.

You are so lucky Tony, stressed Phyllis, her nib pressed hard on the paper in a letter sent to her brother the following morning, *to be so far away at Repton. Mama and Papa are here all the time and you can imagine* . . .

And maybe to imagine was as much as Tony could do. For although Phyllis witnessed first-hand the disintegration of their parents' marriage, her brother's diary, typed in later life, recorded a more dispassionate view:

My father and mother were quarrelling and finally parted. This meant them both coming down separately to our schools to tell Phyllis, my sister, who was at Roedean, what a terrible person the other was. (This was particularly odious for Phyllis, as Brighton was so near Surrey.) They went there practically every week but luckily only came once to Repton, one after the other. These skirmishes went on, they sold our lovely house and garden at Claygate and set themselves up in a dark and dingy service flat in Westminster. They were dance mad like the rest of the world at that time. My father after the final separation went completely berserk on dancing with complete disregard for his business.

'Hold our horses, little girl,' Bella commanded Cicely, and with that she whoa-ed her horse and in a flourishing dismount, flung her reins at the mute prefect. A waft of familiar perfume caught up with saddle oil and steaming blankets drifted over the gathered crowd. Not one fleck of dirt sullied Bella's virgin outfit but no matter, she avoided the chance of spoiling her appearance by merely inclining forward to cup her daughter's face in her hands.

As her pearl earrings wriggled in the light, Phyllis gauged her mother's state. No pin-sized morphine pupils, no pinched cheekbones, no tremulous nerves. Glorious, is the word Phyllis decided on. Mama is gloriously happy. And she was right, for despite the agony of her back, Bella's cheeks were infused with fresh-air pink and her eyes were charcoaled not with shadowed lines of grief but from careful artistry.

'Phyllis, darling, are you permitted to offer us a little tea?' Bella cooed, her eyes expanding in the gaze of all these girls. This was precisely the sort of entrance Bella excelled in – for a fine performance. 'It seems as if only yesterday we were in Argentina,' Bella let out to no one in particular, 'and now we are resting in Brighton. How lucky you are, my darling, to see us.'

Selfless as she always was when it came to appeasing her parents, Phyllis probably did not give the future of her sub-prefect badge a second thought. Of course, forfeited it was later as she flouted the rules to lead the sauntering pair into the deserted refectory where afternoon tea was set out.

Wasting no time, Alfred flickered his fingers as his hands first plunged into a plateful of the regulation thick wads of white bread and then smeared them generously with gloopy red jam.

'Not quite like Nanny would have made it,' giggled Bella, who shooed away the unrefined platters proffered by Phyllis and swivelled her eyes around the room. Phyllis wobbled the weedy tea from the chipped pot and into a china beaker. 'Our first family tea,' smiled Bella as she pulled out one of the small splintery chairs at the end of the refectory table and sat down.

I can tell, thought Phyllis, there is a stranger among us. Sure enough, she detected Cicely sidling up to the table. Look how she smiles at Mama. Fancy trying to endear herself to my Mama!

Indeed, Cicely was entranced by Bella, whose every fairy gesture caused the tassels on her jacket to shiver. And Bella, who never missed a trick, sensed the opportunity for another commission for her new husband. She rapped Cicely on the arm with her dainty white kid gloves and said sweetly, 'Why, my dear, you must pay a little visit to our studio soon.'

Cicely flushed. And Phyllis was never tormented by her again.

CHAPTER TWELVE

Homing Instinct

'Who do you love better – your mother or me?'

It was a wicked question – the sort of question that only a parent desperately torn apart by a custody battle might ask of their child. Yet Sandor began asking that question long before he and Bella did divorce. It wasn't that there was a custody battle, as both parents were loath to give up their newfound freedom since Phyllis and Tony had been sent to boarding school. The children, it was decided, could please themselves.

What answer did Sandor expect his daughter to give when he tried to catch her out, time after time, with this same question, ever since she was eight years old?

Did he have some conscience or doubts, perhaps, about the quality of the affection (but never the presents) he gave to his children on the rare occasions he actually managed to see them before their bedtime? Had his daughter sweetly replied, 'Mama,' would that have weakened what love Sandor had for Phyllis, or simply fed his jealousy of Bella?

Phyllis always refused to answer him. Even then she matched her father's cunning and had acquired the cutely coy manner of her mother as a girl. She would not be drawn. Her eyes would flit and twirl but her lips remained clamped shut.

When Phyllis first realised just what fierce rivals her parents were, she never let on. But in later life she noted that her father's insecurity always seemed to raise its ugly head and lead to screaming rows after social occasions such as a dinner party hosted at The Firs. On a night sparkling with guests and silver, Bella had perhaps led the conversation and concocted the wittiest stories and the prettiest of summer puddings. Sandor still trailed behind the Home Counties aristocracy, since his accent even after twenty years in England still impeded the flow of his speech, like a crippled child trying to walk in callipers. His wife's success left him fuming with jealousy.

He also hated to be left at home while Bella went off to spend a day or two with her parents. Then, perhaps she might leave him in charge of his young offspring – with the assistance of a governess – and after a quickly blown kiss and a monstrous slam of the front door, it seemed that all at once there was no one there to adore him, to tell him how wonderful he truly was. It is the most useful thing a wife can do for her husband, Sandor believed.

'Sandor, how I worship and adore you,' Bella would tell him every morning, and each time she said it with as much sincerity as the first time. His mother had sighed, as she too told her son how much he was loved. And so, Sandor hoped, so too will my daughter.

But exclusivity was essential to Sandor.

And then the question would arise as Phyllis fetched his copy of the *Daily Telegraph* to put at his place for breakfast. He would stop eating his egg soldier, wipe his moustache of any yellow spots and then ask the question as if he was indeed enquiring about the prospects of a fine day without rain. 'Phyllis, who do you love better – your mother or me?'

The reaction Phyllis allowed herself to give was one of vague disinterest. Quite how she managed to feign such an emotion, so young, was in itself an achievement. Scoff as much as you like at my runaway hair, she had thought to herself. Ridicule my knees that are bruised and scabbed from climbing the apple trees. Don't even trouble yourself to glance at my sketches of the garden that have taken days to draw as carefully as I can. But, no matter your faults, Papa, my love for both you and Mama is equal, no matter how you hurt me or how much you try to barter with me.

What if she had said these words aloud? It is doubtful that she would have, not through cowardice but because Phyllis knew intuitively that if she had only one role in the family, it was to act as a pacifier to the other members.

'The impudence of my wife. My wife who dares to question my facts!' Sandor had screamed at Bella after one garden party. The sun had not yet gone down on the fluttering white tablecloths, and glasses stood cloudy with unfinished champagne. Tony had moved in on the strawberries huddled in a silver bowl and had sought solitude down by the pond.

The raised voices rattled the house as Sandor continued pacing to and fro in his study. Bella reclined on the chaise longue in the conservatory, fanning away the flies, her neck mottled red with angry blotches. Then she suddenly got to her feet and screamed up to no one in particular, a hoarse, wild sound that brought Sandor flying out of his room: 'I AM LEAVING THIS MARRIAGE!'

Phyllis, who had been stroking the cat and teasing it with leftover anchovy toasts, had at once sensed the seriousness of this statement. Quietly she crept into the conservatory where her mother was leaning against a wall, her mouth covered by a handkerchief; her father had crumpled weeping onto the chaise longue. She had taken the trembling hand of her mother and placed it gently into the trembling hand of her father. And she had left them there, consoling each other, but inconsolable in their marriage.

Cigar smoke seeping out from the study – that was one of Phyllis's early memories of her father at home. On long winter nights when the rest of the family were curled over books in the drawing room, he removed himself, with friends, to expound over elaborate and absurd business schemes. Games, reading, quizzes – to Sandor they were all a waste of his time. Only Bella understood how much her children would remember the hours of fun they had had, long after they had grown up. To listen to their laughter twisting around the house kept her head light and soothed her loneliness.

'Why not hop on the open-top bus to Clapham Common?' she'd say. Or she would insist they pull on their galoshes to go splashing about in the rain, or shoo them out of the nursery just before four o'clock and race them to the front door to meet the muffin man. It was Bella who saved Phyllis when the cook chased her around the kitchen table with a large carving knife, after she had politely enquired whether tea would be ever so much longer. By no means a petite lady, the cook made up for her lack of speed with her ferocious-sounding flat feet. Shrieks rang out and Bella ran to the kitchen to see her only daughter sprinting and crying and laughing with fear, unaware that she really might have been carved into little chunks for a casserole.

Calmly, Bella guided Phyllis out into the hallway and whispered down to her: 'I had no idea you could run so fast. We will have to do an egg and spoon race tomorrow.'

And promptly sent for the police.

But it might as well have been a different mother entirely who half-opened the front door of her house to a thirteen-year-old Phyllis, one July afternoon in 1920. The times when her daughter would have rushed into her mother's arms and let out a huge sigh of comfort had been locked away.

Dressed in trousers, Bella was whisking a bowl of eggs. The smell of spirits escaped from the hallway. She scowled, or maybe it was squinted, and then smiled at her daughter as if she didn't quite recognise her.

'Yes?' The door remained only half-opened.

'I don't suppose you might lend me a few pounds for the taxi fare from Victoria? I know it's a lot, I'm terribly sorry.'

'Is it the end of term?'

'No.'

'Why have you come to see me then?'

'I've been sent home. I thought Papa might have told you.'

But Sandor had not confided in his ex-wife, since he believed she would have sniggered at his current misfortune; instead, Bella had felt rather queasy at the news of her only real tie to money being as poor as she. The sly bankrupt, she discovered from Phyllis, had given strict instructions in a telegram to her at Roedean from his shabby Hotel Cecil on Tottenham Court Road, before he had left for America: I'VE BEEN ROBBED OF MY FORTUNE. YOU WILL HAVE TO LEAVE ROEDEAN FOR GOOD. TELL NO ONE. GET YOUR SHOES MENDED AND GET A WINTER COAT ON TICK.

For Phyllis, the trauma and humiliation of the past twenty-four hours had left her in a state of shock. The memory would smoulder on for the rest of her life.

At breakfast that morning, Miss Waldron had asked Phyllis twice, in front of all the other girls, if her father had sent her fare from Brighton to Victoria. There is a certain smugness that only teachers possess when they feel the need to exert extra special power over a pupil. Miss Waldron would have known that her pupil did not have a penny to her name, but she felt happier pricking her with the question just the same.

The arrogance of the *nouveau riche* families such as the Grosses had sent shivers through Miss Waldron and other members of staff at the school. Still, one rotten apple was about to be thrown out.

Her classmates no doubt hugged her goodbye. The teachers

pretended not to see – but Phyllis did not record any of those moments. In a breathless version that took less than five minutes to tell, she gave Bella an explanation for her sudden appearance. She'd been dropped off at Brighton railway station, and a porter had heaved her trunk in after her. 'Don't worry about the money, miss,' he'd said. 'All aboard now.'

A blank. No heartbeat. What of Tony?

Sitting bolt upright, her throat tight, she'd spent the hour-long journey to Victoria drawing an imaginary map of London, which she superimposed on the fields and towns running by. Papa, she knew, would be north of the river and west of Oxford Street, and Mama a little further to the north.

When her train pulled into Victoria she realised that no conductor would let her on a bus without a fare, so she waited for a taxi. The first stop was her father's hotel. She ran inside, but was informed by reception that he had checked out a week before.

'Straight on then,' she told the taxi driver. 'To my mother's in Ridgemount Gardens off Gower Street in Bloomsbury.'

Phyllis jumped out of the taxi and raced down the steps to the flat, but when she knocked on the door, a young man looked out quizzically. 'Mr and Mrs Orr? They moved last week to a studio in World's End, Chelsea.' He disappeared behind net curtains and reappeared with a scrap of paper with their address scribbled on. Shouting a thank you behind her, she ran back up the steps and passed the note through to the taxi driver.

'Please,' she puffed, 'can we go there?'

The man shook his head. 'Whatever happened to parents, eh? They're not the same these days. Fancy letting a little thing like you get herself home from school.'

As they headed down Shaftesbury Avenue, the heavens opened, as they always do when you are at your lowest ebb.

'Here's the street,' said the taxi driver, half an hour later. The numbers were unmarked or obscured by trees. 'You'll have to get out, love, and have a look.'

It was heavy rain, the sort that seeps through even a school blazer and shirt. Phyllis zig-zagged across the tiny street and hammered on the white door of the right number house, hoping desperately that it would open and reveal her mother.

'How clever of you to find me!' Bella turned her head and called back into the studio, 'Alfred! Do you have a couple of pounds on you?'

A huffing puffing noise approached and Alfred pushed past Bella to see who had arrived. The red-haired monster did not disappoint. With paint rubbed up his shirt-sleeves, his tummy bloated and his eyes blotched by drink, he scanned the little girl in uniform.

'Hey, Fearless Phyllis,' he grunted and turned on his heel.

Bella shrugged. Then the Maharajah of Patiala appeared, in full royal costume. He nodded at Phyllis and smiled at Bella. 'Allow me, Mrs Orr. Your husband is busy working on the background.' And with that he proffered the taxi driver a new ten-pound note.

'He is such a darling,' Bella whispered when he had retreated into the studio. 'You should see the ancient Egyptian scarab he gave me as a wedding gift. It had always brought him luck and he said, "May it do so even more abundantly for you". Imagine!' Bella started to laugh.

Then she took another look at her daughter who was now sitting on the trunk that the taxi-driver had just unloaded. 'Excuse me!' Bella shouted at the man, before he could drive away. 'Could you take my little girl to the nearest employment agency?'

Years later, Phyllis would write a vivid description of how her mother turned her away: *Jump in, Phyllis. It's been lovely seeing you, but you'll understand that you can't stay here. Poor Alfred could never put up with a child about the place. His artistic temperament has destroyed his stomach lining . . .'* Then, with a washing her hands of me farewell, advised, *'Take a live-in job, Phyllis, I know you'll enjoy it.'*

Never mind that later the same month, Alfred would agree to pay for Tony to go to the Slade. Without bitterness, Phyllis watched as her brother was encouraged to follow his passion and she was left to go her own way.

Phyllis repeated the dramatic story of her departure from Roedean in interviews, in her books and to her friends. Yet Tony's memoirs reveal quite another, more ordinary tale:

While I was at the Slade my sister Phyllis had been removed from Roedean and after a couple of terms in a local high school, my mother found a school in France for her. My mother took her to Fécamp, where she was enrolled at the local Collège de Jeunes Filles, in Normandy, where she remained a year or two.

During the Easter holidays, Phyllis found a room for me at a local locksmiths. Phyllis and I used to go sketching together. For lunch we used to buy bread and rabbit pâté. This was a delightful holiday. The locksmith's wife used to make me soup in the evening and we drank cider. I did a number of pen and wash drawings in Fécamp and when I returned to London I enrolled in the evening class at the Central School.

Whose tale is more accurate? It is hard to know which sibling to believe. But perhaps in Phyllis's mind this is what *truly* happened. In her reality, she truly was abandoned, she was sent away and she was without a family.

CHAPTER THIRTEEN

On Your Own Two Feet

As Phyllis turned around in the taxi, she moved her arm up, ready to wave goodbye. But as she rubbed her blazer sleeve to clear the patches of condensation on the back windscreen, she could see that no one was in the street. There was only a bread delivery boy on his bicycle, whistling in the rain.

Ten minutes later, the taxi pulled up outside the employment agency on Warwick Way. Phyllis sat tight. The rain was not going to stop for her.

'Come on, love. Out you get.' The driver hauled her trunk out of the car boot for the last time and opened her door. He put his arm around the mute body and coaxed her around the puddles and on to the pavement. 'On your own two feet now,' he said gently.

He put his hand out to shake hers. Phyllis automatically raised hers and as he shook it hard, a smile appeared on her face from nowhere.

'Good luck, love, wherever those feet take you.'

Inside the agency, a pair of pale reptilian eyes scrutinised the schoolgirl with the fuzzy plaits, whose bulging eyes, the woman believed, were the result of her throttlingly tight navy-blue tie.

'So what can you do?'

With the confidence of someone who knew she could do very little, Phyllis thrust out her answer. 'I'm fluent in three languages – French, Spanish and German.'

The woman turned to flick through a filing cabinet and pulled out a sheet of paper. 'This vacancy should suit you perfectly. They need an English pupil-teacher at the Collège de Jeunes Filles in Fécamp. Fare paid. Bed and board included.'

'Thank you, I'd like it very much.'

'Report to the headmistress tomorrow morning – her name is Madame Brettain. From Le Havre take the bus to Fécamp. Rue des Galeries.' The woman handed Phyllis a five-pound note.

Still dragging her trunk, Phyllis found a bus that would take her to Waterloo station, where she caught a train to Southampton and then boarded the night ferry to Le Havre. Somehow Phyllis managed to purchase her tickets and sail, unattended, on the little ferry overrun with French families returning home, without raising anyone's suspicions. Then at Le Havre, the French authorities simply waved her through.

Breakfast had been the usual hurried affair of tea and porridge in the school refectory over sixteen hours ago, but like her father before her, it was willpower and not her stomach that kept Phyllis going. No one ever saw Phyllis steam greedily through a plateful of food and still manage to gobble up a pudding too. A fussy eater, they had called her at Roedean, as they watched her fork prod listlessly at her plate. It was an easy mistake to imagine that the owner of such a tiny body, who expended such energy, would have the appetite of a man. Yet, even as an adult, Phyllis pecked at whatever was put in front of her, for she was not a lady of the kitchen. What a fuss people made about cooking and what a lot of bother, she believed. For her, food was not a life source, it was a social necessity, and even then, it often had the audacity to interrupt a lively conversation.

Water ran clear from the washstand taps in the ferry toilets, so Phyllis drank from those. To fritter the pennies she had left on a pie and a cup of tea, she considered would have been a ridiculous waste.

None of her family knew of her whereabouts, and little did she care. The agency may have kept her details, but who would go looking for those? It did not occur to Phyllis to contact Bella. The reason she had been sent away was, she deduced, some sort of test.

In reality, Bella could not spare an ounce of love or care for anyone else now but Alfred. For as a lover, he lavished on her the emotional sustenance Sandor had refused her for so many years. In return, the grateful recipient had, albeit unwittingly, near squeezed the emotional life out of him with her capricious demands. If only, Bella thought, Alfred could apply himself like Sandor. Yet when he *did* actually settle down to paint a portrait, he was lost for days in a haze of enthusiastic oil paints.

Since the moment when her mother, still whisking a bowl of eggs, had turned her back on her, after a casual flick of a wave, before closing the front door, Phyllis's confidence, which had never been all that buoyant even as a little girl, sank like a stone. What would have been the point of objecting? Ever since she had received her father's telegram, two days earlier, she had diligently followed any and all instructions with blank acceptance. It is too easy for us to say, 'That is just how things were back in the 1920s. One respected the wishes of one's parents.' Fortunately for Phyllis, her mind was in shock, while her body rummaged to find an extraordinary strength from somewhere to carry her through this crisis.

On we go.

At no point in her memoirs does Phyllis write of crying, feeling low, depressed or distressed or, even more surprisingly, hurt. Hurt by her beloved mother who could not even be bothered to mask the inconvenience her daughter had become. Did she not feel those emotions?

In truth, her mother's vulnerability was so painfully childlike to watch, that Phyllis did not trouble to explore, never mind wallow in, her own emotions. Five years later, at the age of nineteen, putting her mother's needs first again, Phyllis gave up her cabin on the *Flying Scotsman* sleeper to King's Cross for a seat in a second-class carriage, at Bella's request. The pair had just spent a few days together in Oban. The trip had allowed Bella to 'rest' from her husband. The money saved from the cabin, she explained, could be wonderfully spent on a kilt and sporran for her beloved Alfred. There was no question from Phyllis as to why her mother could not give up her *own* cabin; she simply curled up under a tartan rug and slept, her head resting against the damp glass of the window.

At 4 a.m., the night attendant shook her awake. Her mother was dying, he announced. The door to Bella's cabin had already been broken down, and they had discovered her unconscious body.

'A suicide – I can't feel a pulse,' the night attendant shouted.

Phyllis dashed water on her mother's face and prised the empty bottle of chloral from her grip. 'She will be all right,' Phyllis told the crowd that had gathered. 'I know it.' And so she did.

Money passed hands quickly, as two porters lifted the slumped, moaning body into a taxi. Phyllis refused to see the disapproving stares of the other passengers at the fallen woman, her feet trailing, her head rolling. And then, when she'd struggled to heave her mother through the front door of her home at 13 Mulberry Walk in Chelsea, she would not listen to the gunfire abuse dribbling down the beard of the American, who had worn nothing but his white silk pyjamas for a week.

'What you doin' here, snotty? What you gawpin' at me for? Think you know it all, huh? Go! Git! Scat! Scram!'

It was Phyllis who, with no home to go to, after undressing and tucking her mother into bed, ended up checking into a dreary room at the Royal Court Hotel. Too tired, too cold, she dozed fully dressed until her mother telephoned shortly after midnight, screaming that Alfred was trying to kill her. There was a smash, a crash and the line went dead.

After Phyllis had phoned the police to notify them of a murder, she ran up the King's Road and into the house, where Alfred was trying to strangle Bella. When Phyllis raised a bottle of whisky over the drunk's head, ready to bring it down and knock him out, Bella pleaded with her in a hoarse gasp, 'Don't hurt him, Phyllis. He doesn't mean it.'

It was Phyllis who let in the policemen and explained to them how dreadfully sorry they were to have called them out on such a trivial matter, as Alfred's hands were pulled from Bella's neck and he was led into the garden for questioning. And it was Phyllis to whom her mother clung, smoothing her hair and begging her daughter to take her away from this nightmare, anywhere – and why not back to Paris?

'Please don't cry, Mama,' Phyllis said. 'Yes, do come with me to Paris. I should love it. Please understand though that my bedsit is not at all what you are used to.' Her voice did not change in tone, nor sound anxious. Phyllis had seen too much to feel anything. What is more, her character was formed by a different age – one that would march through two world wars and the emancipation of women. Her generation would not understand the constant need for turning over, the unravelling and scraping away of past emotions that afflicts us these days and from which psycho-therapy grows rich and prospers.

Yet as a grown woman, Phyllis used to smile as she relayed the suffering she had stoically endured, delighting in the shock of the listener. Criticism of her mother or her father was not allowed, however, for that would have served only to underline the Gross family dysfunction and weaknesses, rather than to illuminate her own great strengths.

'But my mother was infatuated, dear. I've always accepted whatever happens,' she told Caroline Phillips in the *Evening Standard* a few years before her death.

Psychiatrists today might suggest that by showing no reaction to her sudden and unprovoked abandonment, Phyllis was storing up her anguish which would surely surface at some point as post-traumatic stress disorder. Her will was stronger than most, however, and if her serenity was a pretence then she kept it up until her death. Phyllis never allowed herself to pick through the misery of her circumstances, knowing that it might lead to the same dark mania from which her mother suffered. Instead, she stepped over the bad times and made herself walk in the opposite direction to depression.

On the ferry to Le Havre, the agency fee had not stretched to include a cabin so Phyllis circled the decks until she decided on a spot where she could spend the six-hour crossing. Fortunately, she never felt queasy on boats, but although she would go on to paint bobbing sailboats in so many of her canvases, to stand steadily on dry land was preferable. In the bow of the boat, she knelt up on the hard glossed wooden benches, staring out to sea. Through the briny rain she strained to make out the last of England, and was mesmerised by the waves undulating and beckoning her to lean further and further towards them.

Her stubborn resolve did not falter. Her mouth would have been numb from her teeth chattering. Any tears that did scurry down her cheeks were due solely to the cold south-easterly wind smarting her eyes. Like a hostage kept captive in solitary confinement, her view was monotone. Black sea, night sky. To pass the time, she dredged through her past and selected memories to play back in glorious colour.

1912. Nearly six years old. A Gross family holiday. 'Pig's ear pink', was how Bella had described their hotel on the seafront at Ventnor, on the southernmost tip of the Isle of Wight. They had taken a ferry from Portsmouth and out into the Solent. Running around on deck, Phyllis chased Tony, and Bella chased her. She heard the laughter. She counted her family. Everyone was there, including her grandparents and handsome Uncle Frank, her mother's favourite brother, whose relationship with his sister and her husband had not yet soured over 'differences in business practices' as Bella put it.

A quick jump to a few days later, to the promenade, where the warm day had teased everyone outside to take a stroll. Deck-chairs. Waves. Sea gulls. A laughing policeman. An accordion. And there was Uncle Frank waving from the sands where he paraded his champion cyclist's physique in a stripy bathing costume. She was holding someone's hand, she couldn't tell whose – probably Sandor's – and as she squeezed it lightly, she felt a squeeze back. The smell of sunshine in the breeze was edged with the sticky scent of the ha'penny barley-sugar canes that she had sucked on until her tongue was orange and sore.

Suddenly she was looking up at Uncle Frank. With one hand shielding his eyes and with one hand clasping his wriggling niece, he nodded into the haze. 'That's France out there,' he told her. 'Home to all things French.'

'I want to go there when I am grown up.' Grown-up to Phyllis meant when she was old enough to dress her hair down, order her own breakfast, or when she was tall enough to tug on a tram-bell cord.

Even then, on the boat to Le Havre, Phyllis could not tell at what age one became an adult. Roedean could have kept her a girl for at least another four years. As for after school, she had not even been given a week's warning of her departure and so had missed out on setting aside dreamtime to explore what might come next. Art, she supposed, would come into her future somewhere. While her schoolfriends would see their expensive education push on until they were eighteen, they would leave it behind at the school gates. University was considered a bizarre option, fit only for the brilliant, or for the clever, quirky girl, whose deficiency in beauty might just be rescued by her intellect. The blonde girls, the pearl girls, the debutantes, would chase light pastimes – tennis, riding, cookery, gardening and perhaps a little charity work, and more importantly, rich young men whose strong genes promised robust babies.

If Sandor's attitude towards women earning money appeared liberated, in fact it was only his peasant roots showing. Women were like horses and cattle; if they were young enough to stand and fit enough to walk, then they could work.

Wrenching off her navy school tie, Phyllis threw it out towards the trailing gulls. She then unknotted her knobbly plaits. Nothing could be done to disguise her English schoolgirl grey, knee-length socks and woollen tunic, however, and at that moment, she realised that her transformation into a woman wasn't going to be easy.

Geographically, England and France are not that far distant from each other. But later on, Phyllis would say that it was the peculiar smell of France that set the country apart from its Anglo-Saxon neighbour. When she first stepped down from the boat after it docked in Le Havre, the thin air was tainted with a stench of oysters, mussels and urine. If Tony had been with her, the pair would have screwed up their faces and shouted, '*Phwoar!!*' much to the consternation of their parents. But the pungent odour could not have unsettled her stomach more than the rank air below decks, which had reeked of sweat, damp and garlic.

As the other passengers noisily clambered down with their cases, some were embraced by relatives and others were swallowed up whole by the early autumn fog. Phyllis stood motionless on the drizzly quayside, with only the sound of foghorns as a welcome. Her hesitation was fleeting. Even at such a young age, she had an acute sense of reality; her mind did not try to disguise the truth. Bella would have only seen the dark-haired handsome captain, swaggering away from his ferry, and Sandor would have already been swept away in a car, having secured his onward journey by befriending the family with the most opulent luggage and furs on board. Yet for Phyllis, to take in these snapshots – of a trawler man in blue overalls peeing into the sea from beside a little sailboat, to the waddling woman with a basket strapped to her side, calling: '*Harengs, harengs, harengs frais!*' gave her a true sense that she might, without too much effort, disappear unnoticed into these foreign surroundings.

These smells and these sounds that were so alien to her then, would in years to come be an instant sign that she had arrived in France, the country where she always felt her artistic temperament could be truly unrestrained.

All the lost hours chanting French verbs in a sealed classroom were about to pay off. With a nervous voice, her accent a little weak, Phyllis approached a fisherman sitting on a lobster pot gutting cod, and enquired how far it was to Fécamp. He smeared the fish blood on to his apron and wiped his brow.

'*Ce n'est pas loin. Dix kilometres.*' He nodded towards the bus, its engine humming, parked next to a warehouse, and filling up with passengers. '*Dépêche-toi.*' And with that he put down his thick knife, stood up and effortlessly carried her trunk over to the bus.

'*Merci, Monsieur!*' With quick little steps she followed his own big strides. '*Merci, merci, Monsieur!*'

He carefully manoeuvred the trunk on to the bus. That small kindness brought tears to her eyes as the bus trundled over the cobbles and on to the coast road that led north to Fécamp. The love and generosity that had once spilled out so effortlessly from her own family, had appeared now, when she was most in need of it, from a stranger who owed her nothing. He may have been a spitting, rough wine drinking Normandy fisherman, but such kindness was second nature to him. Why was it not second nature to her own family any more?

How appropriate it would have been if the College had loomed into Phyllis's vision, its windows fastened with iron bars, its thick walls a heavy brown, its pupils mean and unruly. Instead, her new home awaited at the top of a steep narrow lane, in the wealthy seaport, where the breeze never lost its smell of salted cod. Phyllis was greeted by a pearly grey mansion – the sort that the English would mistake for a château – secluded from the rest of the town by wrought-iron gates enclosing the formal box-hedged grounds. Each sash window was framed by white shutters and a mist of lilac wisteria enveloped the west wall.

Shuffling on the gravel, an old concierge in tight ankle boots and a baggy white pinafore came muttering into sight, her shoulders stooped. Without a word to Phyllis, she unlocked the gates and pointed her way inside.

The chilled interior was checked with bright light, the walls white, the air still. The Michaelmas term would not start until the next day. Someone, somewhere, was baking cake. Her moment of calm was slashed by a dog, a Great Dane, that nearly knocked Phyllis off her feet. Slobbering on the black and white tiles, he let out a hollow bark at the funny-looking creature frozen in front of him.

'*Marcuuus! Marcuuus!*' From her shuttered office, a raspy voice wailed before the formidably short Madame la Directrice – Mme

Brettain – came running out to scold her hound. Her limp, sable-coloured hair was tweaked neatly into a chignon, her stomach and bosom were encased in heavy corsetry. The stiff collar of her white lace blouse supported her chins and her black crepe skirt dusted the floor as she walked.

'*Marcuus! Quelque fois . . .*' She stopped and did a double-take at what she almost mistook for a gypsy. Before her stood a shrimp of a girl, her sallow skin brightened by a pair of dark, curranty eyes, her unruly hair matted. The girl gave a little smile and a bob of a curtsey.

'*Bonjour, Madame. Je m'appelle Phyllis Gross.*'

Her heart, if headmistresses possess such a thing, softened. 'Where is your mother?' she asked. Those were the first and only words Madame ever spoke in English to Phyllis. Her disgust at seeing this young girl arrive unescorted was easily translated from the loud snort she let out.

Phyllis shrugged. '*Je ne sais pas.*'

However, despite being won over by an English miss, Mme Brettain was not, under any circumstances, going to let on that she had in any way found her amicable. With brusque efficiency Madame assigned Phyllis to her quarters with the servants. The room allocated to her – a tiny, white-walled cell with a bright skylight – had probably once been part of the pantry. The nearest lavatory was a long walk away and daddy-long-legs lurked with the moths in the corners, but it was to be her own, dear space.

Madame did not stop once to pause or ask her if she understood the instructions she was reeling off with a flip of the hand. Léonie, her adopted daughter, would be given lessons in conversational English during the school holidays. During termtime Phyllis would be teaching English conversation to all the pupils. With her spare time, she could continue her own education.

Spare time did not make its presence known.

Léonie, Phyllis noted, was an olive-skinned girl about her own age, whose right eye drooped slightly. Perhaps understandably, camaraderie with a contemporary, who had been brought in as a servant and a teacher, was not advisable. As it was, Léonie was already burdened with the stigma of her mother being head-mistress and was reluctant to look out for anyone else.

And with that as her lot, Léonie must have decided there and then to be difficult. She handed over to Phyllis her first task, a heaped basket of soiled linen. 'I will show you the laundry room,' she said under her breath. '*Voici. À bientôt.* There it is. See you later.'

Maybe then would have been a good moment to break down and cry, but now Phyllis – light-headed with hunger – was finding the challenges that were being slapped upon her, one after the other, quite amusing. She had not so much as lifted a lid on a laundry basket before, let alone seen the chore in action. Without any previous experience, she began to draw vats of boiling water and with wooden forks dropped each item into the steam. After an hour, sweating over lavender-swirled water and foaming bleach, Léonie returned.

'Leave that now, and come with me, please. It's time for you to eat.'

At the back of the building and down some green slate steps, Léonie led her into the factory-sized kitchen where Simone, the cook, put a large platter of rabbit meat and wine-fried potatoes in front of her. Phyllis had already felt her insides collapse in on themselves with hunger, yet not long after she had finished eating, Simone would relay to Madame that the English girl did not display the manners her country was renowned for, as she struggled for over an hour to force down and swallow her food, her elbows pointing heavenwards.

Settling in took less than a day. What soon became clear to

Phyllis was that, ever since she had left The Firs, she had been yearning for somewhere, a place where she did not have to practise so hard not to upset anyone, a place where she might wake up in the morning and not fret about what mean tricks the day held in store for her. Here at the private college were one hundred young ladies; tradesmen's daughters mixed with those of merchant seamen and shipping magnates. Some of the long-sleeved black pinafores worn as uniform were patched and sun-bleached, while others were newly pinned and trimmed. It did not matter. Nor, for the first time, did it matter that Phyllis stood inches below others her own age, that her shrunken arms belied her boy's strength nor that her buckled shoes, once smart black patent, looked considerably past their best. Laughter was not restricted to exclusive huddles and the tactile friendship among the pupils was sincere without being overly possessive.

After her first week, Phyllis sent a letter to her father. *This is real life, Papa. I have found it at last. I know that you have lost your fortune but I am grateful to have been catapulted into this place. Even rats preen their whiskers while I take my showers. How different from banal Roedean.*

Her memoirs echoed her happiness: *How gloriously unlike Roedean it was. In termtime hubbub instead of Roedean's refined hush; eagerness, including me, to learn – without the derogatory 'she's a swot' and eagerness amongst us teachers to teach.*

The French – or rather this Normandy brand of education – threw its emphasis on the practical, which Phyllis would never have seen at Roedean. Her hands, previously clumsy additions to her arms which excelled in dropping pencils or knocking vases, began to learn their purpose, as she mended deep-sea fishing nets for the local fishermen, embroidered items for trousseaux, learned how to wash, iron and fold linen and clothes correctly, and how to polish shoes. Her mind, that used to wander at any

113

opportunity, grew to understand focus. The blessed hours of tight concentration on hemstitch or embroidering initials on a bedlinen set brought all of Phyllis's attention into one tiny spot.

Here, a windy afternoon did not mean a cruel hour of lacrosse on a darkening pitch, praying for rain to come. Instead, the girls and teachers would set off on rambles that might trail into the early evening, as they chatted through the bosky Val de Clercs and moved up to the sailors' chapel, high above the cliff, where little votive candles and a prayer would be offered to Our Lady.

It was during this time that other people, like fellow teachers Jacqueline Bannier or Mademoiselle Gondy, began to slip in and out of Phyllis's everyday thoughts with her permission. Before, other people had bullied their way into her dreams; they were the nuisances, the boisterous intruders in her own happy space. Now she loved her mornings spent with Jacqueline, skimming through the outdoor market up the street, pinching the fowls for freshness, giggling at the squirming piles of fish, bartering for the cheapest price of rich Normandy butter for Simone the cook, or mimicking the husky farmers' cries of: '*Peaux de lapins! Peaux de lapins!*'

All at once, these memories mattered. And other people mattered. Other people who were not from her precious family began to have a currency. They too became precious, for the time they wanted to spend with Phyllis and for the time they wanted her to spend with them. Her voice grew louder.

CHAPTER FOURTEEN

Reaching Back

The Bannier family were big in ships' biscuits. They were the second wealthiest family in Fécamp, the first being the Meryons who owned much of the fishing fleet. Jacqueline, who at nineteen was their youngest daughter, had invited her young English friend to spend a few weeks at their summer home in Bec de Mortagne.

Fortunately, Madame Brettain had graciously allowed the pair to slip off at the start of the holidays, it being accepted that Phyllis had already pushed Léonie well beyond an average standard of spoken English.

Days spent with her one dear friend, chattering while raspberry picking or gathering mushrooms, or splashing about in the river, could not have been more wonderful for Phyllis. As one further act of friendship, Jacqueline had already arranged for some spare country clothes to be laid out as she felt awful that Phyllis owned one cream blouse and one thin black skirt, that had survived a year of pounding in the laundry.

Only one thing could have ruined the whole holiday – and it happened the day before Phyllis and Jacqueline were due to set off for Mortagne.

ARRIVING SUNDAY FOR FORTNIGHT WITH ALFRED. BOOK ROOMS.

The smile that had covered Phyllis's face became strained. How could she feel so dismayed about seeing her dear Mama?

115

After a long year without any contact, overcome by sudden guilt, Phyllis had hastily scribbled off a postcard to her mother. Rather foolishly, she seemed to include an invitation to visit her in the postscript of the pretty postcard of the harbour: *I do so very much hope to see you and Alfred soon.*

Madame Bannier explained to her daughter that she had no alternative but to extend the invitation to Bella and Alfred. '*Ce n'est pas un problème,*' she told Phyllis kindly. '*C'est mon plaisir.*'

Sunday. The water meadows were still asleep. At five o'clock in the morning, Jacqueline and Phyllis had gone fishing for crayfish, then tipped them into a little pail and slowly cooked them in white wine back in the kitchen on the wood-burning stove. By twelve noon, the long table under the apple trees in the orchard was ready to receive the chateaubriands, the trout, and the *tarte aux fraises*. A good deal of white pressed Normandy linen had been spread out; the tablecloths, the napkins, the cushions and the arabesque awning stretched out on giant poles.

Madame Bannier clucked around the servant girls before taking her place alongside Monsieur Bannier on a long swing hammock that gently rocked them out over the edge of the brook and back again. Wine bottles, tied by string to a rock in the little stream, chinked in the gentle ripple of the cool water. Madame Bannier whispered something in her husband's ear.

Bella never arrived.

Alfred never arrived.

The dogs never ran out along the avenue of cypress trees to greet the visitors, the gravel on the driveway never crunched with the tyres of a taxi. Jacqueline plaited and replaited Phyllis's hair. The flies moved in on the food shrouded in lace doilies.

'*Enfin*. Let us eat. Phyllis, do not worry yourself. Some delay has probably occurred. Your poor Maman will be worried to the pit of her stomach.'

But Phyllis knew this not to be the case. And she was right.

Two days later, Bella turned up unannounced. She was alone. Her eyes were red. She did not apologise. She did not kiss Phyllis. The first thing she said was: 'Have any letters arrived for me?'

They had not.

Bella, it seems, had left Alfred painting a Texan millionaire in the Highlands. She had grown tired of waiting in a damp castle library for the rain to lift, so Alfred could depict the man outside in his Stewart kilt. Without saying goodbye, she had flounced off and caught the next train to London. A few days were lost to her before she realised that she had quite forgotten where she was supposed to be next. But after a telephone conversation with Madame Brettain, who had steered her in the direction of Mortagne, all had become clear again.

Despite her fluent French, Bella left apologies and polite conversation to her daughter. She was beyond leaving any sort of impression and had certainly tossed aside any notions of flirting with M. Bannier. This was sulking – and sulking in possession of a secret supply of whisky did not become Bella one little bit.

Monsieur and Madame Bannier were not, could not, be won over. But for the sake of the little girl, who never left her mother's side, they indulged the Englishwoman whose sobbing in the night frightened them all.

'A cheese will cheer Alfred up,' Bella told her daughter. 'Then he'll miss me and come straight away. Send him a Normandy Camembert, darling and don't dawdle.' Thus Phyllis was dispatched by her mother to purchase a big, fat cheese.

After a week of silence from Alfred, neither the lavish teatime picnics carried to the cliff-tops, nor the noisy outings to rock-pool beaches for shrimping and paddling, could trick Bella out of her room.

'You have told them about my dreadful headaches?' she reminded Phyllis every morning as she fluffed powder across her face.

Relief came to everyone the very next morning. A whistling boy on a bike from the village was the handsome messenger: BUTLER DUMPED YOUR LOVING PUTRID CHEESE IN TRASHCAN CANNOT LIVE WITHOUT MY DARLING COME.

Within minutes, a happy pink flushed over Bella as she threw her belongings into three suitcases. The sound of laughter from her room surprised Madame Bannier and such was the joy, even from Phyllis, at her departure that out of the greenhouse, the kitchen and the parlour, the entire staff and family gathered to wave her off.

In later years, when Phyllis always remembered those invisible but powerful lines like fishing lines, that drew her mother first to her father and then later to Alfred; back and forth and back and forth, they let her spin out, far on her own, and then a single word of flattery, reeled her back in.

That is why, fifteen years later in 1935, when Phyllis eventually stepped away from her life as a married woman, it felt so very satisfying to *not* turn back, nor to reconnect – to feel the pull of her spouse yearning for her return, but to have the courage to wait until the line between them fell slack. She had too many memories of Bella, hauling suitcases and hatboxes roughly down the stairs, her hair ever so slightly out of place, her red lipstick and rouge applied with the heavy hand of an angry woman. She would stand, with her hands on her hips, the heel of her shoe cocked at an angle into the carpet as she directed bellboys from her hotel room to a waiting car, or stuffed the entire contents of her wardrobe into a trunk the size of Wales. Her voice higher and louder than normal, Bella secretly longed for someone to stop her, to come and rescue her. But they never did.

And each time she returned it would get a little bit worse.

Sometimes though, when the skin around Bella's eyes was waterlogged from crying and she could not button her coat without her hands faltering, instead of stumbling back into Alfred's life, she sought shelter with Phyllis.

She did this after one stormy interlude with Alfred in 1925. Bella was grateful for her daughter's invitation to Paris. As she shut the front door on the house in Mulberry Walk, the sadness that tugged at her was left behind. It would linger and coil itself instead around Alfred, slowly pulling his spirits down, as Bella caught a ferry with Phyllis to France.

'A slum of a room,' was how Phyllis described the cramped quarters in La Glacière, as she unlocked the door. She knew her mother would recoil at its greyness, but at first Bella seemed grateful just to be beyond Alfred's clutches. Her gratitude would last only a few hours, however. That first night, when the overhead Metro screeched into the station and went on doing so through the early hours, Bella howled in her bed, according to Phyllis, and tore at her hair: 'This hellish din will drive me mad!'

A letter early the next morning from her doctor, Mr Denison, gave her just the excuse she needed to leave:

Twice I've had to pull your husband out of the gas oven ... He can't believe you've thrown him over. He says he'll never drink again if only you'll come back. He talks and thinks of nothing else but you. Without you I don't think he can stand on his own feet. But can you stand up to such a task? Or will he pull you down with him? Only you, Mrs Orr, can decide.

Within the hour, Bella was transformed into a nervous, giggling girl and Phyllis escorted her to the Gare du Nord.

'My darling husband wants me after all,' Bella gushed. 'Be pleased for me.'

Back at Bec de Mortagne, the exposure of her dear friend Jacqueline and her gentle family to the disturbing conduct of her mother, left Phyllis unsettled. For the rest of her stay in Mortagne, the nights would not pass with sleep. Her solitary progress had been set back, thanks to the one person who ought to have cherished her daughter's talents in the presence of other parents. Phyllis had imagined her mother telling witty anecdotes about English life, her eyes and hands fluttering to the amazement of M. Bannier. Phyllis wanted them to fall in love with her mother and in turn, perhaps, they would fall in love with her too.

Phyllis returned alone to her college. Even before the start of the new term, everyone there, she concluded, would be told by Jacqueline about how unsuitable she was as a friend. Yet the familiar smell of hot laundry and madeleines, as well as the long lessons spent instructing Léonie, led her mind away from the chaos that had dragged her mother back to England. Perhaps on hearing of Bella's visit, Tony would write to Phyllis and suggest a quiet week together of gentle pursuits, for although they were not as close as they might be, brother and sister supported each other's perseverance with their parents.

We roamed all over the countryside drawing and fishing, Tony wrote in his memoirs, *I drawing, Phyllis fishing. We first caught crayfish in the river and brought them back to our pension. Mother came out again for a little while, but to our relief was soon bored and went back to London. It was then that my mother suddenly announced that she could no longer afford to keep me at the Slade and that I should go to Paris to the Académie Julian where a friend of Alfred's was a student. So I went to Paris.*

Until then, Tony had somehow managed to evade the wrath

and confusion of his mother. Since school, he had encouraged a remoteness between himself and his parents partly because, like Phyllis, he dreaded the excruciating embarrassment of their dramatic entrances and bizarre clothes, which stirred whispers in public and annoyance in private.

However, it was in Paris in December 1921, that fifteen-year-old Phyllis became embroiled in such a mess (not of her own making) that she was finally asked to leave the College.

Snow had been falling for a week before the telegram arrived. It was the day before Christmas Eve and the end of term. The paths had been swept to the church and lanterns lit the way to the carol services which had gone ahead as usual. Duck, pickled cabbage and hot mulled wine kept the pupils from getting the chills. At night, the common room turned into a curious gift factory of girls and teachers knitting woollen socks for brothers and fathers, sticking pressed flowers into bookmarks, while some baked gingerbread men and bottled jars of honey in the kitchen with Simone.

FAMILY REUNION. CHRISTMAS IN PARIS. TAKE TRAIN.

The telegram that Phyllis waved at Madame came as some relief. Her smile was infectious. For the second year running, no one had invited the little English girl home for Christmas and Madame Brettain could hardly have left her alone again in the school as it remained unheated until Epiphany.

'Make sure you are back in time for the new term,' the headmistress warned her.

In retrospect, even the notion of a family reunion was laughable. Presents were for children, and who wants to eat turkey when you can have the best foie gras and caviar in the world? A carnival – that was how Phyllis described that particular Christmas. From the intimate innocence of the boarding school, she was submerged into the raucous, gaudy, adult world

121

of Paris, from which neither Bella nor Tony did anything to protect her.

Of all the trains that Phyllis might have caught on Christmas Eve, the one that carried her from Fécamp to Gare St Lazare crashed. In the deep white of the countryside, windows split and shattered as carriages twisted off the rails into waves of snow. The temperature inside dropped to minus ten and for five hours the passengers, all uninjured, slapped each others' backs, opened brandy bottles wrapped as presents and forced their mouths to chatter through carols. Phyllis remembered a woman slapping her face, with a flap of her leather gloves.

'Do not fall asleep, *ma petite*, or you may never wake up again.'

When the train finally limped into the station, Phyllis was greeted by Tony and his friend Dick, both muffled up in heavy coats, scarves and berets.

'You've buggered up the whole afternoon,' Tony stormed. 'Why the bloody hell have I got to bother with a stupid kid like you!'

Words related to her terrifying train ordeal began to spill out of Phyllis's mouth, but her brother refused to listen.

'Shut UP!' He had heard enough tall stories already.

They must be already here, Phyllis deduced from his furious demeanour, that had nothing to do with her late arrival.

The threesome headed to the Boulevard Raspail where they were supposed to have gathered at noon. There in a grand suite, propped up in a flounced green brocade double bed, were Bella and Alfred. Crowding round them on the carpet were Tony's artist friends, including Balthus, who later became famous and who Phyllis recalled as a dirty-looking man. Long, unkempt hair hung down on to the shoulders of his paint- and grime-stained clothes, and like a character out of *La Bohème*, a cigarette butt hung from his loose lower lip.

All including host and hostess were Pernod-tipsy and the guests, while greedily gobbling their free eats, discussed their fervent creeds on art, philistines and social injustice.

If Phyllis had anticipated what we would now call quality time with her mother, she was very much mistaken. Bella was enjoying the show. For the next five days, a merry band of freeloading artists and authors latched on to the money-mad couple, whose amazing fox-fur coats and loud voices allowed them entry into places as diverse as the Opéra and the Jockey Club on Montparnasse.

Despite her festive glow, Bella humiliated her daughter by noticing (aloud) just how much time Dick, the tall, dark Irish artist, had spent staring at Phyllis. At sixteen years her senior, Phyllis thought he looked old enough to marry her mother.

'How do you like being the centre of attention, dear?' Bella smirked through a squint of smoke, half out of jealousy and half in the glorious knowledge that her daughter would never have half as many men try to seduce her as she had done.

But Phyllis wasn't the centre of attention. As the youngest in such a disparate family, no matter how warmly she smiled up at whoever was talking and tried to chip in with conversation, she was always an afterthought. Tony, it seems, had forgotten to book his sister a hotel room, but neither he nor Bella seemed anxious about where Phyllis would spend Christmas Eve. Thankfully Dick, mortified at the treatment of the schoolgirl, who looked ludicrous sitting among the intoxicated artists, left their company to telephone a family friend.

Phyllis later believed he bribed them to put her up for a couple of days. His discretion, among all the showy characters, was yet another gentle kindness that Phyllis would not forget.

Then the arguments began. Christmas Eve was all about Midnight Mass at Notre Dame, Bella declared. No, it wasn't. It was all about having a good time at the Ritz Bar, Alfred retaliated.

'Why can't you do just this one thing – for me?' Bella threw herself out of bed and stomped into the bathroom, quite forgetting that out of the pair of pyjamas she was sharing with Alfred, she was wearing the top . . . No one seemed to notice but Dick.

Alfred relented.

At the spectacle of Midnight Mass, where the smell of incense mixed with the icy breath of the Pernod drinkers, Alfred's genuflecting was decidedly out of practice and he tripped.

'*Shhhhhhh.*' Bella, her eyes closed throughout much of the service, elbowed her husband in the ribs. She squeezed Phyllis's hand. *Hark*.

Phyllis listened to the choir voices reverberating like sharpened crystal around the giant candlelit tomb. Her temperature started to rise and as she pinpointed a favourite shade of red in the Virgin Mary in the West Rose window, her world went black.

Her slight body came round shaking and coughing in the arms of Dick, who had lifted the slumped girl from Bella's feet – the older woman was trying to listen to the end of the *Adeste Fidelis* – and carried her outside into the Place du Parvis. From her swooned position, her head lolled back to see the Galerie des Chimères (gargoyles) ready to pounce on her. She let out a weak scream.

'I won't let them eat you,' Dick said, and kissed her on the forehead.

When Bella and Alfred and Tony shuffled out with the congregation, their concern was limited. Bella pulled on her daughter's arm. 'Stop coughing! It irritates Alfred. Never let your ill-health be a nuisance to others.'

As a gesture designed more to boost his alcoholic quota before

Christmas Day than to comfort his stepdaughter, Alfred placed his hand on Phyllis's head and prescribed hot grogs. Immediately.

From café to café they swayed. From the Rotonde to the Dome and then down to Boulevard St Germain for a drink or three at the Deux Magots. The hot brandy set fire to Phyllis's head and her eyes burnt into the two models whom the artists had waved over. They perched on the knees of Tony and Dick. They dipped their fingers into tumblers of whisky and giggled. 'We are wearing no knickers.'

Phyllis did not want to hear any more of their pretend whispers, so she leant on the bulky arms of Alfred, who was discussing which was the most dangerous venereal disease with a beautiful sculptress.

'I should take Phyllis home.' The low voice of Dick was drowned out by Bella's drunken tone. 'Keep her here. All this is good for my daughter's education!'

Alfred cried for absinthe. When the walls began to shimmy, the happy gang staggered into the cold. Their slow, arm-in-arm progress took them over the Pont de la Concorde and up the Rue Royale.

'Find me absinthe and oysters to tickle our juices,' Alfred cried.

Was there a Christmas Day that year? If there was, Phyllis could not remember one detail. The next few days skipped into one haze of light. The parties that alcohol and Alfred required to make their magic appear left Phyllis on the brink of collapse. No one heard her cough now above the noise of laughter, and her red cheeks they took for a sign of pleasure, not a raging temperature.

It was Dick, whose calm Irish voice had soothed her outside the church, who delivered her to the train station.

'You will be better off at school,' he said. 'Go back and rest. I'll be thinking of you.'

It was in fact, the worst thing Phyllis could have done.

The moment she set eyes on her limp walk and fevered temples, Madame screamed at Phyllis: 'You dare to return to work ill! This is too much. You have a holiday and you return like this? How could any self-respecting mother . . .'

Phyllis remembers Madame shoving her into the scullery and demanding that she iron a stack of damp linen for the girls' beds. She remembers the steam and the swimming sound of water, but not much after that. The doctor was summoned. He diagnosed pneumonia. Madame was told to inform Mr and Mrs Orr that their child's life was in danger. Petrified that Phyllis might die in her school, in her sickbay, the headmistress sent a telegram to Bella straight away.

Nothing.

As Madame nursed the burning child, her anger at Phyllis subsided. '*Mon petit. Mon pauvre petit,*' she would whisper as she patted a flannel on her brow.

A week later a parcel arrived.

To help my recovery Mama sent me a pale blue diaphanous Worth evening gown: 'Worn by Lady Brecknock for her portrait; and then discarded. You'll be able to alter it to fit. I've written to your father to tell him your ill news but I have not heard from him. Have you?'

How stupid Madame had been, to believe she would receive some thanks, some recognition from the rich Englishwoman, for bringing her daughter back from death.

Tant pis.

Pity was too good for Phyllis now and Madame literally sent her packing, as soon as the girl was strong enough to stand.

CHAPTER FIFTEEN

Il n'y a que le provisoire qui dure
(Only the temporary lasts)

The fast jazz noise of Paris had fixed itself in Phyllis's overheated imagination and bombarded her with a cacophony of notes even as she boarded the ferry back to Southampton. This time, her feet could reach to tap the floor as she sat on the wooden bench seats in the bow, facing out into the English Channel. Farewells to her first real friends at Fécamp had been rushed, too brief for tears, and anyway, no one would have been able to say anything sentimental above the howls of Marcus, who on sensing a departure had taken it upon himself to cover the departee in as much dog hair and slobber as possible.

Any passenger who glanced upwards from Phyllis's boots to her black lamb's-wool coat (a hand-me-down from Jacqueline), and the long dark plait that snaked down from her felt cloche, would have thought her a poised young woman, older than her sixteen years.

In her memoirs, Phyllis did not take this journey. After Fécamp, she headed straight for the Sorbonne, to enrol as an undergraduate in Philosophy, courtesy of a *Get Well Soon* cheque from her father who, despite a solid Swiss bank account, had chosen to settle in a measly one-bedroom apartment in Chicago.

Two years on, Sandor still felt utterly humiliated by his bankruptcy and had, once again, tossed aside his fickle past which no longer served a purpose. Of course, he could have sucked dry his savings in a Zürich bank, but oddly enough he quite enjoyed the pain and self-sacrifice of fanning the ashes of his past success into a bigger, roaring flame.

Instead of seeking out the European aristocracy in New York, he moved west to mix with clusters of Hungarian exiles and Eastern European immigrants, who taunted what they believed was his English accent, who questioned why a man with such dainty manners and bespoke suits would not confide in them, wondered why he refused their offers of beer in this time of Prohibition (he brewed his own) and why he picked up prostitutes.

On his second attempt to haul himself up from a 'pauper' to a noted businessman, it was anger that fuelled his ambition. 'That I, Sandor Gross, should have come to this,' he muttered to himself as he picked his way through bums begging on the street or dined in backroom bars where gangsters flipped coins and played poker for a living. Happy memories did not dare intrude. The twice-weekly dinner and lunch at the Savoy, the soothing chauffeur-driven Bentley, champagne before *The Magic Flute* at Covent Garden, his handsome mahogany desk. Lost. He had lost them all – his wife, his family, his reputation and his home. Only pride, Sandor later told Phyllis, had stopped him accepting a knighthood. 'I could not bear to see your mother flaunt herself as Lady Gross.'

Only pride, too, stopped him from ever telling his ex-wife he loved her. In a strange, destructive way Sandor *had* loved Bella. The times when she obeyed and did not stray from her pretty role as wife and mother. When she clung to him (but not too hard) for warmth, when she travelled on business with him and promised not to speak up in company. That is when he loved her.

With time and distance, the cruelty which had spat from him

when they were married, the resentment and jealousy he felt at her popularity, swilled around and disappeared. He could not accept that Bella no longer adored him and even deceived himself that given enough encouragement, she would return to him.

As for his children, out of guilt he mailed the occasional cheque to them, but he could no longer be expected to remember their birthdays. He was pushing himself hard through every possible working hour. Up at dawn. Dead at midnight. Even during the Depression, Sandor considered the hundreds of men waiting around the block for the soup kitchen to open to be lazy good-for-nothings.

At Staten Island, where he had first queued among the filthy masses, shuffling forward into the Land of the Brave, he recognised himself, twenty years earlier, in those with the trembling lips as he watched face after desperate face stutter to officials with a few words of English.

Understand this; it was not out of generosity that he established an English language night-school. Too ashamed and too mean to rent buildings downtown, he set up in the shadowy wooden sheds that ran alongside the Chicago rail and stockyards. Vulnerability – that would be the key to his success this time. Sandor reckoned that new immigrants could easily be parted from what little savings they had to learn the native tongue.

His classes gained a fine reputation for being effective and fast. How he wanted to shout at his feeble students: their frightened eyes and weak voices only goaded his impatience. But the irritation of Bella's voice that would chant alongside in his head as he repeated out loud each letter of the alphabet to a class, only made him more determined to succeed. Yet it would be another five years before he would walk, whistling down Wall Street, in the knowledge that his stocks and shares were soaring. His bank had agreed that he was now rich enough to start up a small map publishing corporation. 'Welcome to Riggs Bank, Mr Gross.'

Since adding to the annual 5,000 English divorce statistics, Sandor had submerged himself into a black bitterness over the institution of marriage. A prescription of testosterone would cure it, his American doctor believed. 'Have a little fun,' he suggested. 'Meet a nice dame.'

After Bella, Sandor would never meet another woman with whom he would share the rest of his life. He missed picking out hats or dresses for Bella in Bond Street (for he knew best what clothes suited her), he missed her splendid cooking and watching her put a spoon into the pot and then taste the stew and carefully wash the spoon before tasting it again.

A restlessness itched at his heart. He could dine on money until he felt sick, but nothing could satisfy his sexual appetite. Why? Even Sandor could not work it out. Of course, there were ladyfriends who hung on his arm when he became rich, and young things who hung on even harder when he became a millionaire, but even they could not stop the girls who came and went in the night.

He twisted and wrung out his pride, for it had done him little good, and begged Bella to leave Alfred.

Dear Sandor,

How dare you suggest I leave my beloved husband. May I remind you that long before I met my darling Alfred, it was your original ridiculous notion to pay me to take a lover in Brighton so that you could divorce ME. When it was I who was grateful for the occasions when I did not bump into one of your girlfriends at the theatre or Claridges. If you care to remember, while I refused such idiocy you agreed to pay me an allowance for the rest of my life. I have not seen one penny.

Bella.

Yet each man kills the thing he loves. Those words were darkly printed on the back cover of Phyllis's book *Fleet Street, Tite Street, Queer Street.* Who knows whether it referred to her father, her mother or her husband – or all of them? To squash, to strangle, to beat a love to death was certainly applicable to her father, who spilt out his regrets in reams of notes for a play that would never make the stage. Phyllis came across them amongst his things, after his death.

Sexual morality, Sandor wrote, *was about rules made for the impotent, by the impotent. Marriage was a conventional lie, love was nothing more than a weakness which must be rooted out.* And of his children: *I was pleased to find I felt nothing – nothing at all, at leaving them.*

Phyllis would indeed return to Paris, to study for a degree in Philosophy and Byzantine Art, but not for another two years. After she had disgraced herself at Fécamp, as Bella neatly put it, she made her way to her grandparents' house in Worthing.

The bus that dawdled along the south coast from Southampton in those days ran for four hours as it took in the pier at Southsea, the cornfields outside Chichester and the promenade at Bognor Regis before trundling into the seaside town. Worthing is only a few miles from Brighton, and Phyllis felt too close to that terrible school. She began to worry. Was that lady running from the rain Miss Waldron? Could that be the dreaded outline of Cicely Shackleton cycling towards her?

Any fears tiptoed away when she spotted her grandparents, huddled together at the station. Someone had shrunk them. Someone has shrunk my darling grandparents, Phyllis thought, as Grandfather raised his trilby and Grandmother waved a lace handkerchief, for what seemed like for ever.

'Will you look at her, Father. What a lady she has grown up to be. How like her Mama. And will you look at those fancy French boots . . .'

No sooner had Phyllis stepped down from the bus than she found herself cocooned in the sing-song babble of her grand-parents.

'Phyllis, what news we have for you. The snowdrops are out,' said Arthur Crowley, as if the five years since they had last seen her had only been five minutes. Nudges from his wife Maria interrupted him.

'Do you fancy an egg for your tea? What about you, Father? And you, Phyllis, do you fancy an egg for your tea? Maybe some malt loaf for afters. What do you say, Father? We have a little room prepared especially, with a desk. She'll like that, won't she, Father? She likes to write – just like her Mama. And we have Wellington boots for you, in case the weather doesn't pick up.'

For several reasons, Phyllis omitted this time from her memoirs. Firstly, she never truly assuaged the guilt of her burden to these two elderly people, whose passage from South London for a gentle retirement by the sea had begun only six months before. Once awash with all the carryings-on that comes with a home bursting with nine children, finally, the precious few years left of their lives had been set free.

For her own mother to have dismissed her as a nuisance, surely meant that she was a terrible liability. Phyllis tortured herself with the thought that these good people might pass away at any moment, their deaths precipitated by her unpleasant self.

She could not help but notice their eyes, cloudy behind thick round wire spectacles, that struggled with the grocer's bill. The dead blue bottles upturned on the kitchen tiles went unseen and her grandfather, whose hands had once swept across piano keys, now used valiant efforts to hold a fork, such were the terrible effects of his arthritis.

Whether he closed his ears off to his wife, talking herself through each movement of the teapot and kettle, repeating the same question over and over to him, or whether one really did need to speak up for Grandfather, Phyllis could never decide.

Grandmother climbed the wooden stairs up to the box room, one at a time.

'Gently does it.' She opened a door into a tiny apricot room, tucked under the roof of the Victorian villa. Here were the warm petal colours that reminded Phyllis of her bedroom at The Firs, which had been so absent in the hospital-white boarding-school. A cream Persian rug. A rocking chair. Brocade curtains. The small bed with its satin eiderdown had been lovingly made and Phyllis could only imagine how many hours it had taken the squabbling pair to tussle under the eaves with the sheets. Yet for two years she never unpacked.

'Who should I thank for the lovely fire?' Phyllis asked.

'Grandfather. We let young Lillian go. There are only the two of us now. What use have we for a little maidservant?'

The few pounds that Phyllis hid in a yellow Chinese silk purse under her pillow had been saved up from her additional chore of cleaning the boarding-school lavatories. The odious task meant nothing to Phyllis. The pleasure from having dix centimes pressed in her palm every week, she knew would have brought a smile to her father. Even if she retched at the stench of urine while scrubbing the porcelain, she would bring out her memory of him peering up from the financial pages of the *Daily Telegraph* at the breakfast table and wagging his finger. 'It's making money that counts.'

Of course, hundreds of hours spent on her knees in cubicles did not add up to very much at all, but Phyllis would slip a few coins into her grandmother's Lipton's tea caddie where she hid the housekeeping money, whenever she realised they had dined on leek soup and fish pie leftovers for at least a week.

The other reason that Phyllis did not relish this episode in her life was because it dragged her story backwards. Instead of forging ahead, alone against the world (as she saw it), to try her luck and talent in Paris as an artist, with nothing but a warm coat to her name, with one snap of her mother's fingers she had been reduced to a child once more.

Without taking a genuine interest in her welfare or future, Bella had reined her daughter in, as if she now had the proof that her youngest child was neither old enough nor wise enough to be trusted to live independently. The nearby convent school, where Phyllis was enrolled by her grandparents, seemed so provincial, so unsophisticated compared to Fécamp, with its pervasive disinfectant odour, its maroon gym-slips and golden ties, the tiny lavatories built for infants, the primary hand paintings pinned around the assembly hall, the name tags stitched in every pair of maroon knickers, the sloppy nursery lunches, the spottiness of the pallid girls who swore by Cuticura soap, and the plainness of the nuns.

It is unlikely that Phyllis would have been teased there, when she could have tied any one of her classmates up with her string of languages. Who would bully a girl who dressed her hair in a French plait, who had danced the Charleston in Paris, who had tasted champagne and who knew how to prepare lobster? The other pupils still traipsed to church on a Sunday, hand-in-hand with their parents, and considered a day's walking on the South Downs a treat.

Although by now Phyllis would have peaked in height at five feet, on her return from France she developed an upright bearing that suggested she was every bit the lady. Phyllis was not in the least bit grand though. Quietly, she pieced together the smatterings of History, English and Religious Education that had scattered after Roedean. On Saturdays, she would stride down at dawn to the fisherman's huts to help them mend their nets for an extra shilling or two. On Sundays, when the weather shone kindly on the promenade, Phyllis would pitch up her easel and sell her miniature seafront water colours to passers-by. They stood around and stared at the girl who squinted from under her straw hat, back and forth from paper to sea. 'First paint what made you want to do the scene in the first place,' Phyllis would advise amateur painters when she was older.

In breathless waves the green light of the sea appeared without hesitation and her brushes dipped and swirled greens into the water in her jam jar. Twenty minutes. That was all it took for her to complete a miniature. A large oil painting would take up to seven days, but she would not be able to afford oils until she was in her late twenties. Seven or eight water colours would be wrapped and tied in greaseproof paper and sold at a shilling a go. In her heart, Phyllis felt she would have happily given them away, for the pure thrill she got from standing in the fresh air and salty breeze, painting as much as her eyes could manage to see.

From her father she had inherited the ability to slip in and out of layers of the social strata, a skill which in itself would make her a loner. Those who met both father and daughter remembered them as bright and witty, but where did they truly fit in? Attachments, to her dear Mama, to Jacqueline, to anyone at all, had ended in misery for Phyllis. Like fireflies, her happiness was in the tiny, everyday conversations with strangers that flickered into her day and disappeared without a trace. Even as an older woman, her colleagues can recall her fantastical encounters that for Phyllis, were an ordinary part of her life:

'I was invited to the Philharmonic in New York last night. I'd got into the elevator from my floor at The Westbury, and began talking to the lady and gentleman beside me. It turned out he was the lead violinist and she the lead cellist and by the time we reached the lobby, they had asked me to join them as their guest for that evening's concert.'

After two abstemious years in the care of her grandparents, Phyllis successfully passed her Oxford local exams in English, History and Religious Education, and was into her eighteenth year in 1924. Her love of the south coast would stay with her and, like her grandparents before her, Phyllis would eventually turn her back on London, to settle a few miles away in Shoreham-on-Sea.

Phyllis stayed in Worthing a month longer than she had really intended, so she might tackle the chores her grandparents could no longer manage; scrubbing the front doorstep, boiling rhubarb jam, pegging out the Monday wash. Each night, as she played the piano for them, she knew it might be her last. The stack of colourful postcards that had flapped on the doormat every week from Tony in Paris began to clutter her bedroom mantelpiece. *Too many art classes, too many models. My apartment is overflowing with people. James Joyce came for dinner. What news? When are you joining me?*

I want to be in Paris, she thought.

And to Paris she went.

Unlike the River Thames, where the water has a certain masculinity, a dull, predictable flatness, the Seine is a thunderous, attention-seeking stretch of water – a female river, inconstant in her flow and ebullient. They say there are sixteen ways to cross her, that she is the life force that splits Paris in two and that every building of note watches over her or is just a spit away. The energy she releases spawns new life, while dragging away the weak ones. In winter, her voice sucks in mothers whose heads are leaden with absinthe, but no one stops to point at a flaccid, lily-limb flailing in the undertow. In summer, her roar soothes to a tone that calls those who want to escape the loneliness of their cold-stone apartments.

Here, sacks of kittens are drowned, dogs are abandoned and water rats multiply on scraps discarded by the men of *les Bouquinistes*. Artists sketch hopeless writers sprawled on benches, drowning in scrolls of paper, passed by prostitutes who loiter arm-in-arm or slip off their sandals to paddle.

Today, the commercial barges and *bateaux mouches* use the river for their own pleasure. She does not work much now. The lone fishermen who prayed for her to yield them her treasure have all but vanished. Sometimes the whale hulk of Notre Dame for all its white candles cannot match the comfort and protection given by her. She hides lovers, thieves, fugitives and runaways under the lichen-flecked bridges that drip with her damp.

It was beneath one such bridge, Pont St Michel, that joins Boulevard du Palais on Île de la Cité to Boulevard St Michel in the Latin Quarter, that Phyllis slept for over three weeks. Teenagers hitting the backpacker trail today would have amused her. 'Thailand! But my dear! They take credit cards and phone cards with them – I took a school trunk with my paints and a clean change of underwear.'

Only the Unexpected Happens was an apt title for a book of short stories Phyllis published herself in 1985. Indeed, it was predictable that anything Phyllis set out to do or anywhere she went (always with the best intentions), the plan would be kicked to the kerb as suddenly she found herself diverted, distracted or detained. As a child, Phyllis had sensed the white fury, as she called it, that swelled inside her father as he had wrestled with every circumstance and every person under his control. The more Sandor fought with them, the weaker he became if they finally beat him to the ground.

Phyllis never understood the crippling effects of control or of the resentment that dominated her father. Instead she chose to be fearless, like her mother – to embrace a light-hearted acceptance of what Sandor would have called tragedies, disasters, and misfortune. As with the time when she and Tony (no more than eight years of age) danced on the window-ledge of their Vienna hotel room, much to the horror of passers-by below. Or as with the middle-aged cheese man in Fécamp market who invited the schoolgirl for trips on his lorry during the holidays, so she might get to know the French countryside. She could have ended up dead in a ditch, but she trusted the man who shared his lunch with her. Who knows if she might have come to any harm had her jaunts continued?

No prayers would pass her lips and God would not come into her life for another thirty years, so it was not faith that kept her buoyant. Phyllis simply had no fear. Of anything.

So it was to be expected that from the moment her grand-parents had blown their last kisses to the little pilgrim off to join the dirt-poor intellectuals on the Left Bank, her journey would not be without incident.

TONY ON MY WAY. SEE YOU TOMORROW.

The telegram to her brother did arrive, but Tony was already drawing and painting in Picardy, on an autumn tour with his artist friend, Dick Pearsall.

Rue des Cannettes. Phyllis had sketched a map of Paris in her head, with especial focus on St Germain des Près, which she drew and redrew on the train ride to Gare du Nord. She walked the narrow slant of Rue des Beaux Arts. There was Tony, opening the door, his deep voice drawing her in, a Gauloise in his hand. A sibling squeeze, a quick ruffle of his dark hair and then his arms flapping as he shoos her up to his room.

It did not happen. She pulled the rope bell to the navy-blue door. Again and again. Silence. The pigeons on the lattice balcony above were laughing at her. Phyllis perched on her trunk and took out from her satchel a chunk of Dundee cake that Grandmother had wrapped for her journey. Scattering crumbs for the pigeons she watched as a woman across the street closed tight her balcony doors to the autumn evening. Wisps of air started to smell smoky. Of bacon and crispy leaves. She clenched her hands which might well have turned blue, but then everything took on a death shade in that light. The deserted Sunday-night streets allowed Phyllis to hear the bells ringing from the church of St Germain des Près, through eight, nine, ten and eleven o'clock. A gramophone crackled out from the house next door. Laughter from a man and a woman. The clinking of glasses – a romantic dinner, she thought. Tony would be out carousing and would stagger around the corner in a haze of revolutionary conversation, jangling his keys.

'Here is my little sister.' She reran the harsh words of his greeting when he had met her at the train station. And that had been Christmas.

Suddenly Phyllis did not want Tony to discover her, the stupid sister. Or to put her up. As quick as she could, she scrambled to her feet and wheeled her squeaking trunk away and off into the darkness.

Deeds not words. Deeds not words. She whispered the Suffragette motto as she hauled the trunk over cobbles to retrace on foot the route the taxi had taken from Gare du Nord. Left luggage. Her deeds were automatic. Her grasshopper brain jumped ahead. It planned her movements meticulously. Not a second spared for hesitation. Her eyes were dry and alert.

She did not see the odd look from a little whippet of a man with a greasy moustache who peered at her from behind the left-luggage counter. The few notes she carried were tucked neatly into her boots. Confused by the fact that he could not label her as a student, or a prostitute, he watched her numb fingers grapple with the centimes and the trunk that she passed over to him with a bright smile. He winked. Whoever she was, the man knew that with an innocent face like that, she would not last long in Paris.

And then Phyllis walked. Following her memory map, she headed back to the Left Bank, and knew that once she crossed Le Petit Pont, the Sorbonne would be only minutes away.

Rue des Écoles. Her breath stopped as she stared up at the ancient tomb of learning; a grey classical stone building guarded by statues that seemed to lean towards her. As her hand stroked the cold wall, she saw the original poor students of 1253 who, like her, would pass humbly through the courtyard and into its hallowed chambers.

Half an hour later and well past one o'clock, no one noticed the slight figure of a girl wander down in the darkness to the rush of the Seine, her pace dazed. The three years ahead of her were skipping through all the possibilities of Free Will. Her mother's last letter played itself back to her:

My Darling Child,

How marvellous that your father has finally managed to finish your education. You will be charmed by Paris. Remember that whatever it is in the world you decide to do (and who you choose to do it with) you act in the knowledge of your own Free Will. Learn from my mistakes. I gave up my own Free Will long ago.

Mrs Alfred Orr.

Under the Pont St Michel whispered voices, a girl, a boy, a man, trailed into her consciousness. Three pairs of eyes watched as Phyllis felt the damp on the wooden bench and then sniffed a copy of *Le Monde*, fluffed up from reading that lay in the grass. She opened out the pages and spread them neatly across the bench. They stopped their fumblings to watch as she crept up to a laurel bush and then heard the splatter of liquid on leaves.

'Do you want to join us in here?' the girl yelled, her voice echoing round and out.

Like a rabbit Phyllis stopped her breathing dead.

'Altogether warmer,' the man growled and then let out a whisky cackle, as the girl and boy joined in.

'Let me feel your warmth, little girl,' the man called out before cackling again.

If Phyllis could have smelt the hot breath that slipped itself under the girl's coat then she might have sensed the danger that crept around her, but sleep was ready to protect her. 'What you cannot see,' her mother had tapped on her nose when she was tiny, 'cannot give you nightmares.'

After wrapping the pages of the newspaper around herself against the river wind, she curled on her left side, facing the water, her hands a bony pillow. As she slid into darkness, the numbness in her legs and in her arms, she imagined drowsily, was nothing compared to the agony Renoir's beautiful model Danielle must have suffered.

CHAPTER SIXTEEN

Nabokov's First Nymphet

'I really starved in Paris, but I enjoyed it. That bit of poverty put money into perspective for me. I have never really wanted more than enough to keep me going and firmly expected a bedsitter to be my end.'

Leisure Painter, Spring, 1970

Studying at the Sorbonne was a great privilege for Phyllis, yet the stiff diploma that she received with a curtsey after three years of studying Philosophy and Byzantine Art should have been accompanied by a second one, that acknowledged the freefall experiences she had notched up *outside* her classes.

Paris was a wonderfully exciting place in the 1920s, and Phyllis gradually took full advantage of it. Paris was the city where Josephine Baker danced in *La Revue Nègre* wearing nothing but black feathers; it was the city where girls had discovered the suntan, the *Vogue* plucked eyebrow, the bob, Man Ray, red bow lips and the corset which, with her boyish figure, Phyllis surely didn't need. Like all students she dabbled; in men and in art.

After twenty-one nights sheltered by the Pont St Michel, Phyllis had painful bruises on her shoulders. So far, no one had tried to rape her; grubby fingers had not grabbed at her English skin, but only because she was lucky. The other 'outcasts', as she called them, who hid in the bushes and slept on the benches, were a bizarre mixture of Russian immigrants, crippled war veterans

142

and runaways. Riverlife diseases – tuberculosis, muggings and molestation – went on to claim many of them.

Occasionally, kindly strangers would cover the shivering girl with their unwanted copy of the day's newspaper, which Phyllis remembered as 'the warmest thing you can imagine'. The dates printed at the top of the copies of *Le Monde* were additionally useful: they helped her count down the days to the start of term at the Sorbonne.

Within her first week, Phyllis had pinpointed the cleanest museum lavatories from the Champs-Elysées to Montparnasse and had worked out when to stand outside the kitchens to Brasserie Lipp for their discarded trays of sauerkraut and sausages.

In the years to follow Phyllis would inherit two watches from her Mama and be presented with one by her employees, but she never bothered to wear one – she always guessed the right time. In Paris, just by sniffing the dampness, she could tell what time of day it was:

Hot water. *Chocolat Chaud*. Bread. Morning.

Tomatoes. Chicken. *Gallettes*. Lunch.

Fish. Garlic. Lamb. *Tarte Tatin*. Dinner.

'You will never know,' Phyllis once said, 'how beautiful an old baguette dipped in a water fountain tastes until you have starved for ten days.'

The shame of being found sleeping rough woke Phyllis as early as five o'clock in the morning, when she would fold her newspaper over another dormant soul before defrosting her blood with a sharp walk to the Gare du Nord.

Somehow, Phyllis managed to manoeuvre the morose young man who had relieved the winking nightshift man into releasing her trunk so that she might retrieve her water colours and sketchpad, and then put it back. When she had first asked if he would allow this without her paying twice, the young man had lolled his tongue around his mouth.

'What can you offer me if I let you off?'

'Let me draw your likeness.'

Despite his ugly flat forehead and red bulbous chin that Phyllis presumed had once been the breeding ground for many spots, the proposal seemed to flatter him.

'Please be my guest,' he smirked.

Her pen worked swiftly around his features and softened his disjointed face.

'I like it. That's me, all right! I can see the resemblance. Thank you.'

Her talent discovered, his interest in what might lurk under that dark coat of hers subsided as awe took over.

'If I bring a photograph of my mother in tomorrow, can you do a portrait of her, too?'

'Of course.'

And that little scene was all part of Phyllis's great plan, the one she had carefully constructed so she might avoid Tony until her classes at the Sorbonne had begun. If a few sketches and paintings could bring in some pocket money, she might be able to save enough to rent a room. Then she could turn to Tony and say: 'Thank you so much for your kind offer to sleep on your floor, but you see I already have a place of my own.'

Theirs was often a tense relationship; an unspoken rivalry pulled and pushed Phyllis towards and then away from the brother she had fought so hard to protect as a young child.

At the age of six, Phyllis had fallen ill with scarlet fever during a family holiday in Hungary. Sandor dismissed the doctor's orders that his daughter be kept in isolation and inevitably the fever passed to Tony, a sickly child who was affected so badly that doctors told Sandor and Bella not to expect him to live.

The affection Phyllis openly showed her brother was never

diluted. After all, they were united in a loyal sibling bond; no one else could have ever understood the unsettling and complex nature of growing up with their quarrelsome, emotionally indiscreet parents. Phyllis was not to know that on hearing that his stepdaughter had, as Alfred would say, 'gotten to Paris on her lonesome,' he had offered to pay for her tuition at the Slade.

According to Bella, Tony had then lost his temper, reminding her strongly of Sandor as she watched him rave and bang his fist on the table. 'Why pay for Phyllis? It's not fair! I don't want her beating me at *that* too.'

Yet in Paris, Tony appeared before Phyllis as the perfect Romantic hero; handsome with brooding, Bohemian looks. It was as much as she could do to ride along on his coat-tails. If she ever felt resentment, then Phyllis guarded it well, as she witnessed her precocious brother being swallowed up in the rarefied world of art.

Phyllis's own romantic prospects were nil, yet this time, her family were not to blame. Years before other young women walked en masse into university lecture halls, never mind tour Europe unchaperoned, Phyllis behaved and was treated very much like a boy. She never dreamed of acquiring a villa in Monte Carlo, with glass ceilings, silk carpets, Pekinese dogs, brooches by Boucheron, furs from Reville, chiffon chemises, a tennis court – all the trappings of modern wealth that might be hers if only she could meet the right man. Sandor and Bella never bolstered their only daughter's marriage prospects, probably because they were too tangled up in their own desperate problems. So Phyllis found herself in the unusual position of following her whims, unfettered by any parental pressures to seek out the joys of marriage and children.

It may have been the 1920s but Paris society was squeezing into its literary and artistic élite only a select few females like Colette and the grande dame of Rue Cambon, Coco Chanel. Like clever cats they arched their backs and drew attention to their clever selves. The *bons mots*, the cigarette-holders, the sharp red tongues, the cocktails disappearing as they matched their male counterparts glass for glass.

Swept along on the Left Bank tide, Phyllis attracted some attention with her brilliant eyes, her effortless humour and sharp observations. They let her join in their drunken discussions, the louche, the snide, the slovenly exhibitionists who fell asleep among their wine stains and cheated their models out of payment, the revolutionaries too mean to purchase a cup of coffee, the opium-fuelled writers, whose words stopped flowing once they felt the floor beneath them. Her one mistake, the one thing that kept her from becoming an insider, was that she failed to swoon and pay homage at the feet of the artistic gods. Sycophancy made Phyllis Gross sick. The truth never failed to scurry from her lips.

As an artist, the reception she received from peers and critics never rose in temperature above lukewarm – maybe because she was a woman. Hundreds, if not thousands, of her own bright paintings and sketches were sold in her lifetime, yet art critics defined her talents as modest. To be described as moderate in anything, to be middling or mediocre would have secretly crushed her – it just was not her style.

By now Tony had returned to his room in the Rue des Cannettes and was evidently preoccupied:

I had become friendly with a little scullerymaid who when she came to my room was so tired, the poor thing, that she just rolled over on my bed and went fast asleep. She lived in a fantasy world of her own. She had a boyfriend who had once slit her cheek with his knife (she had a scar) and promised her another scar and a wound for anybody who interfered in her life.

As usual with the Gross family, Tony had skimmed the telegram from his sister announcing her arrival in Paris and promptly forgot about it. It was only after Dick Pearsall had made some remark while picking through oysters at his birthday lunch at Brasserie Bofinger, and said 'When is your sister visiting next?' that Tony had a jolt of conscience. The stained-glass windows Dick said had reminded him of Phyllis and the fainting incident in Notre Dame. The next morning Tony sent a telegram off to his mother.

How much simpler family life might be today if telegrams, the one-liners that cut out the waffle, the elongated discussions and arguments, were still used. For Bella and Sandor and Tony and Phyllis, telegrams elegantly sustained what were already strained relationships. Letters, after all, required effort and time and love. Telegrams simply called for money, brevity and wit.

WHERE IS PHYLLIS?

IN PARIS SILLY WITH YOU.

NOWHERE TO BE SEEN.

LUCKY BOY.

Her presence undetected, Phyllis geared herself up for a smart new term at the Sorbonne. Even though she had spent a month sleeping rough, it would be another few weeks before she was able to afford to rent a room, and she was anxious about her dishevelled appearance. At ten o'clock on 1 October, as Phyllis filed in with the other students for her first lecture, she ducked past the enrolment queue and made straight for the ladies' lavatories.

As an experienced cleaner of toilets, she inspected what she could see was not half a bad job. Above the sink, a huge mirror reflected a wind-burnt nose, bright white eyes, with grooves of charred black below, and brown chapped lips. Pauper cheeks stretched over the hollows of her skull. Try as she might, her fingers could not fork through her knotted plait, which she did her best to tie away from her face.

The brown tiles radiated warmth through to her toes. The water that ran from the taps smelt rank but at least it was hot. She pummelled the hard soap to work up a lather for her face. Splash after splash, the first water that had touched her face since she had arrived from England suddenly made her feel filthy dirty – as if she might never get clean again.

The thought that really tickled her as she peeled off her coat, unlaced her sodden shoes, tore off her navy-blue cardigan, her blue blouse, her petticoat, her black woollen tights that covered a multitude of bruises, her knickers and her vest, was that she might actually smell terrible. All the matrons and nannies who had briskly flannelled her down over the years in a furious effort to purify her skin (and her behaviour), would have shuddered at her present repulsive state.

Her rib bones, she noted, that had previously made do with a slither of skin to cover them, were bursting through to harden her body. She scrubbed at the mottled flesh. Tweaking her thighs Phyllis deduced that one week remained before her legs would be too weak to walk. The passionkillers, as her grandmother called Phyllis's sturdy maroon convent knickers, which had kept her skinny behind from getting chilled, were wrung out under the hot tap. Like all institution radiators, the one Phyllis draped her knickers over were furnace hot and guaranteed to leave scorch-marks. No one would pinch *those*.

'Do not forget your knickers. Do not forget your knickers,' Phyllis chanted to herself half an hour later as she trailed after the other students who buzzed into the echoing vaults of the lecture room, carrying pencils and notepads. Long woollen scarves dangled down their blazered backs, and as she counted fifty heads she smiled at the shiny hair and the expectant laughter.

How new.

How innocent they all looked.

148

But as she pulled out a pencil and a few sheets of paper scrounged from the left-luggage boy, she realised that everyone knew someone.

In those precious hours that ran into weeks, when bearded lecturers such as André Diehl took their students on flights of Byzantine fancy – to soar over Constantinople, examine the treasures of Sophia and marvel at Iznik tiles – Phyllis let herself be released from her tired body and experience a heady thrill more than offsetting cold, dirt, hunger, soaked-through rags and cardboard shoes.

Philosophy swept through her mind, scooping up her imagination and leading it into broader stretches of open land that she never knew existed.

The Good, the Beautiful, the True: which is the most valuable? Discuss.

Try replacing even one word of Hamlet. *There is no alternative.*

As if there was a fire and someone had shouted, '*Appelez les pompiers,*' the students scurried off in every direction after lectures; each one seeking refuge in a café. Still twisting the words just heard into shapes in her head, Phyllis would make her way across the Pont au Change and up Rue de Rivoli to the Bibliothèque Nationale. While the other students gobbled lunch, she devoured the heavy, mite-ridden books, that almost fell upon her as she levered them down from the dusty shelves. The works of Tolstoy, Marx, Proust, Molière, Gide and Homer, in French, in German and in English, kept her body motionless and her mind running. Unlike many of her contemporaries, she realised how precious her time was at the Sorbonne, and gave full rein to her reading addiction.

During one lecture on the use of religious iconography, the skin on her arms prickled under a shaft of light that cut in through the window, leaving a celestial glow on the wooden floors. In her mind she floated outside to the courtyard and sat on the steps underneath the Eglise de la Sorbonne clock, quick fine lines appearing on her paper, and a likeness of the building springing up on the page.

As soon as the lecture ended, Phyllis ran out to fulfil her fantasy. Squinting into the very soul of the building, she barely noticed the woman who tapped her first on the shoulder and then offered to buy the drawing.

'Is that for sale?'

Phyllis jumped. 'Yes, of course.'

'I want to buy it for my husband. He spends his life here, so why not remind him of it some more?'

The air puffed white as the woman laughed and her freckles disappeared as she wrinkled her nose. A Dutch face. Distracted by her red hair, expensively bobbed and tucked under a green velvet hat, the flap of her ten-franc note startled Phyllis.

'I am so sorry, Madame, but I don't have any change on me. I know that is what all artists say to buyers, but it is true.'

'Why would you want to undersell yourself? Your eye is pretty accurate. I shall wait here beside you until you are finished.'

The woman hugged her knees as she chattered. In the remaining minutes of pen-strokes, before Phyllis handed over the sketch, she had enquired as to her background. 'Ah. You are English. May I ask you something?'

'Of course.'

'I wonder if, when you are not studying, for I see you carry the papers of a student, you might like a little Saturday job, selling gloves at Galeries Lafayette. You know it? You would have a uniform, and the pay is fair for Paris. I am the manageress. Hats and Gloves.' She tapped her hat and proffered her hand. 'That's me. Claudine Couperin.'

*

Panthéon. The street of the Gallows. A shudder zipped up her back. The small card inserted next to the bell read: *Madame Delaporte*, written in a loopy black hand. Phyllis pressed the bell.

The woman who opened the door had the face of an angel. Or that is what Phyllis imagined, when confronted with her white-powdered, pink-rouged cheeks and crystal eyes, and before she understood the workings of the mind of the woman who would put Madame Defarge from *A Tale of Two Cities* to shame.

The sing-song voice that trilled from her rosy mouth explained that she was a widow (the worst landladies usually are) as she led Phyllis up the bare wooden stairs. Anonymous walls. The ginger tom cat whose scent hung in the air, coiled his way down the stairs and through Madame's legs. Her guess that the widow was in her fifties was confirmed by the glimpse of blue cheese veins showing through her stockings.

A puff of lavender and the rustle of her crêpe dress as she hummed a little. 'Oh my dear, such a long way up. Oh, I hope you like it. I do so want a young thing for company. The room is tiny, like you. Do you like books? I have plenty in the dining room. We eat our meals *en famille* here. I keep three others, you see. Mealtimes are at 8 a.m., twelve noon and 6 p.m.'

Phyllis passed the bolted doors which hid the other poor captives, locked in their miserable spaces.

'*Et voilà!*'

If Phyllis had only taken after her mother, she would have screamed: 'I've kept my furs in better places than this!' as she turned on her heels and stomped down the stairs.

English reserve permitted her to let out a tiny gasp of dismay, but the graciousness that was often thrown aside by Bella, always remained intact with Phyllis.

'It will be fine,' she said faintly. 'Thank you, Madame. Thank you so much.'

They both stared in silence at the space where it would have been nice to have a window and the grey bed with grey sheets that her dear mother would have described as fit only for a maid.

'The rent is how much?'

The rent was courtesy of Claudine Couperin, who would welcome the young student with a kiss on both cheeks on her first Saturday morning at Galeries Lafayette. Tier upon tier of glass and wrought-ironwork stood either side of a coloured glass dome, which covered a grand central staircase and spanned out into what Phyllis would describe as a palace that faced the rich shoppers on Boulevard Haussmann.

At the department store, Phyllis slipped into yet another disguise, another uniform, this time consisting of a long black skirt with a pleated hem, a white blouse and black tights. Claudine had shown her some little black buttoned shoes in the footwear department.

'Look how soft they feel, eh? The discount is good. I insist you buy them.'

Phyllis allowed her only pair of shoes, so worn that they had dried out hard like pastry even though she had tried to buff them into a shine, to be unlaced and unceremoniously thrown into the nearest bin. Her interest in material things throughout her life was almost invisible, yet after Phyllis had died, her best friend, Dr Esme Wren, discovered sixty-nine pairs of beautiful size four shoes in her wardrobe, most of them unworn. Too many to ever wear, but enough to know that she would never go without again.

'Not so much the student now?' Claudine whispered.

The first few hours behind the counter, Phyllis smiled and waited, shifting back and forth on her new heels, knowing that no customer could match her mother for fussiness and opinion. Years later, she would tell Esme how to put on a glove – *you do it like this* – and she would imitate the Parisian women who would put their elbow on the glass pane, their forearm pointing upward, their hand twisted in a Royal wave, waiting expectantly for Phyllis to ease a glove over their hands. Who would have thought that these kid leather gloves in every shade – primrose yellow, dove white, night black and apple green – and soft rabbit- and fox-fur mufflers would introduce Phyllis to so many people. And that so many people would return home to unwrap the tissued Lafayette box, and comment on the delightful young English-woman serving behind the counter.

Had Sandor known of her success at money-making, he might have withdrawn her termly payments to the Sorbonne. 'Look how easy her life has become now,' he would have grumbled. 'She plays with more money than I could have dreamed of as a young man.'

Unintentionally, Phyllis excelled at one of her father's greatest skills – seeking out small business opportunities with strangers. Financial profit could not be further from her mind though; her longing for friendship was the motive. One day, she had served a gentleman who wanted to find a black fur muffler for his wife's birthday; he turned out to be the playwright Joseph Kessel, author of *Invitation au Voyage*. Taken by the way the young girl swam through and around the hooped French language, he invited her to translate some of his notes at his house.

'Could you bear to teach me also?' he asked diffidently. 'To speak your language?'

Phyllis agreed, and every Friday afternoon after that she went for one hour to his neat house on Rue Christine to tutor him in English and to help out. There, piled on his desk, she spotted a pile of *John Bull*, the British newspaper in Paris.

'I try to read the articles,' Kessel explained, seeing her interest.

'What a good idea. Shall we start off by translating them then?' As Phyllis drew her finger under the dotted word in every sentence, her mouth silently shaped each word, before Joseph took a breath and ran across the line.

'Paris in the autumn is a marvellous place for shopping.'

'Very well done. And the next one?'

'The restaurants are full of dishes you may never have heard of before: omelette, frogs' legs and snails. It may sound rather off-putting but do try it with some of the bread or baguette that the French are so keen on.'

'*Bon!*' Phyllis said, as she thought to herself how easily she might have written such an article.

Exactly one week later, while sitting at the dining-room table in the pension, reeling off an article entitled *An Englishwoman's View of Paris* for *John Bull*, she first set eyes on Vladimir Nabokov.

After shaking hands with Joseph Kessel, following his first English lesson, she had walked straight to the offices of *John Bull*. It was dark and past five o'clock, but Phyllis was not the sort of woman to wait for Monday morning.

'I wonder if I might speak to the editor?' she said. 'My name is Phyllis Gross. I am a writer.'

The French secretary, who had been enjoying the purr of her own typing, scowled through her little round glasses and stubbed out her cigarette as if she was killing a fly.

'The Editor is on edition – we go to press tonight,' she said shortly.

'Oh, I'm so sorry. Perhaps I might wait?'

'No, you cannot. Can I help you?'

As usual she could only be bothered to half tune into the breathless stream of words from the skinny Englishwoman, who had decided not to take up her offer of a chair. Her coffee-coloured dress and coat looked brand new, but the secretary could not help staring at her hard brown hands, that were gesturing enthusiastically. A gardener perhaps?

'. . . and so now I'm here in Paris, painting, sketching, teaching English, that sort of thing, and I thought perhaps I might write a freelance piece or two?'

'Why not? If you deliver it here, I'll be sure to show it to the Editor.'

The secretary watched as Phyllis smiled, nodded, thanked her and briskly left the office. Before now, a sorry trail of young hopefuls had sat on the black leather chaise longue opposite her desk, pouring out their decadent aspirations. Most of them she would never see again. They would promise, as they shook her hand for longer than was polite, to come back, their first feature written. *Why Cubism is the New Art. The Book-Lover's Tour of Paris. The Real Life of a Parisian Chef. The Confessions of a Parisian Lady*. She imagined them stepping outside into the sunlight and promptly falling down a black hole. Making a bet with herself, that this girl with the loud voice would be different, she lit another cigarette.

So now here was Phyllis, her Friday morning Philosophy lecture over and with an hour to go before Madame would serve lunch. A sorry excuse for lunch it would be too; a thin gravy, which she called consommé by floating a few carrot heads on the top, cauliflower or courgette baked with cheese. Meat, on the rare occasions it did appear was always smothered in the same mushroom sauce. Why the delicious pie smells drifted up from her kitchen, Phyllis had only discovered on venturing downstairs to return a water glass she had taken to her room by accident, earlier in the week. There, slumped in a chair, was Madame Delaporte, her fat ginger cat prettily mewling for titbits, as she ravaged what looked like a steaming meat pie, accompanied by a heap of potatoes next to vegetables in every shade of green.

'Shoo! Shoo!' Madame screeched and then raised her glass of red wine to Phyllis and laughed. 'Do you see my lunch?' She laughed through an open mouthful knowing that Phyllis, however disgusted by the meagre offerings she was given, could not afford to move anywhere else.

Phyllis apologised and left. If she had been of a religious persuasion, she would have prayed very hard that night for the soul of Madame Delaporte.

Vladimir Nabokov, the author, was one of the other unfortunates residing with Madame. After leaving his native St Petersburg, he grew tired of Cambridge after graduation and was here in Paris to try his luck at writing. As he walked into what he believed would be the empty dining room, his eyes fell on the back of a girl, the one who had moved into the attic. Seated at the table set for lunch, her dark head tilted to one side, was balanced by two plaits that dangled over the back of her slim red cardigan. Perhaps she was completing some schoolwork. Her feet, he noted, that peeped below the long black skirt, were hooked around the legs of her chair, not able to reach the floor. Her hands seemed as small as her black buttoned shoes, but would her face be as pretty?

'May I?'

Who knows whether Vladimir Nabokov was disappointed or excited as Phyllis turned to face the owner of this richly accented voice. She smiled, stood up and extended her hand to his. 'Heartthrob handsome' is how she described him later. Cruel cheekbones as undernourished as her own. Timid eyes. A passionate mouth. Freshly laundered white shirt, and raggedy cuffs.

He bowed and pulled up a chair. They talked until Madame sulkily served lunch. They rummaged through writers, the latest books, the trouble with the French.

'It is just the two of you today,' Madame sighed, as she dumped two bowls of bouillabaisse in front of them.

They talked until Phyllis began to make her excuses, for she was already late for her English lesson with Joseph Kessel.

'How old are you?' Vladimir stopped her, rubbing his fingers across his eye.

'Eighteen.'

'You look so much younger.'

'Oh?'

'That is no bad thing.' Then, as he leant forward across the table to whisper, he let his forefinger drop to touch her own: 'Would you let me take you to the cinema tonight?'

He did not wait for Phyllis's reply. 'Meet me here at six o'clock. Do not tell Madame.'

Phyllis did not write in her memoirs what the film was, or record any more details about Vladimir. We do know that he could not chase away, much as he might try in later life, his close association with the narrator of his novel *Lolita*, Humbert Humbert, whose preference was for what he described as maidens between the age limits of nine and fourteen: 'who, to certain bewitched travellers, twice or many times older than they, reveal their true nature which is not human, but nymphic (that is, demoniac); and these chosen creatures I propose to designate as "nymphets".'

Maybe Vladimir saw in Phyllis's little girl's body, starved of food and affection, a willingness to please, an openness so different from the intricate ploys of the fleshy French girls. She was, undoubtedly for Vladimir, a nymphet, years before *Lolita* was ever conceived.

What about Phyllis? After her trip to the cinema with Vladimir, she cut off her plaits. Relieved of its weight, her hair sprang into a wavy bob. Her private life was a secret to the end of her days, but she was neither the daughter of typical English prudes nor did she refrain from teasing allusions to her love-life in interviews:

I think I was fairly free with myself if I fell for somebody. I lived on my own – I loved my independence. But I've never led a celibate life. As an adult I was always susceptible and that was part of Bohemian life. Not now, thank God, all passion spent. I would fall for looks, first, then perhaps get bored.

Her face was not the fragile, dolly sort of face that men saw flicker on the screens from Hollywood, but Phyllis emitted a quirky energy which they loved to feed on. A little thing, they foolishly believed, was so much easier to seduce. On the contrary, Phyllis had an almost masculine ability to shake off their affections, to break away from their clinginess and step over (without treading on) them, which surprised and intrigued them. A harsh woman, you might presume – if any of her romantic tactics had been calculated. But Phyllis never went in for her mother's manipulative strategies.

A week after delivery, the first of many articles describing Phyllis's favourite Left Bank haunts was accepted and printed by the editorial staff of *John Bull*. The writer had a grasshopper mind, the editors concluded after tightening up her prose, but what brilliant colour.

'I am a writer and an artist and a teacher and a translator,' Phyllis repeated to herself early one morning as she kicked past the autumn leaves swirling at the church steps of St Germain des Près, before turning into Tony's street. Her new feelings of self-confidence had slowly begun to tempt her into buying her own fresh croissants for breakfast, then curling up in the cosy bookshop, Shakespeare & Co, at number 12, Rue de l'Odéon, where the owner Sylvia would let her leaf through books for hours in the corner. Sylvia, a large, handsome woman, or so she might have been behind her perpetual cloud of cigarette smoke, fussed over poor, withdrawn writers whom she slavishly introduced to one another, above the jingle of her amber bangles.

'Ezra Pound – this is Phyllis Gross.'

'Phyllis, *mon petit* – let me introduce you to Tom Eliot.'

Polite conversation would begin and circle and circle, but as Phyllis clocked the office boys whistling home, she would wonder why, as she spoke to these men, the word 'I' kept hammering into her ears:

'I am, of course, over here trying to get a French agent,' they usually began, 'which I believe I may be able to pull off as some of the English ones have told me I am the *genre au courant*. I don't think I know your work, do I?'

Their eyes would glaze over at the sound of their own brilliance or dart left, right, up and down the bookshop aisles in search of someone more useful.

The ego that nestled firmly and warmly inside Phyllis did not budge. Her fascination with writers would extend to gossip and then she was off, doing her own thing. A queer bunch indeed.

To her surprise, Tony received Phyllis with a little more affection than she had expected. Why, she was almost grown-up, almost a woman, he thought as he kissed her smiling cheeks.

'Guess where I slept for five weeks?'

Tony stared at her. He had never thought to ask. 'Come with me to breakfast at Les Deux Magots,' he offered. 'Bring your sketchpad. I want to see what my little sister can do.'

The round of lectures and café rituals woven into the company of the élite of literary society would immerse Phyllis during three of the happiest years of her life. Correspondence from her parents had dwindled into insignificance. Life, she believed, was rich. Life was beautiful. Sitting between the honeyed twang of Ernest Hemingway and her brother at Café de Flore, through the breaking sun at breakfast and over a long lunch until *les apéritifs* signalled the arrival of Dick Pearsall, or Vladimir, she basked in their conversations, without feeling the need to contribute.

Existentialism. Man and God. Man without God. Art and God. Good God. As each man spoke, in deep ponderous tones, Phyllis would sketch their faces on napkins, and place them next to their wine glasses. Tony's baby sister. What a cute child. And each of the men would chip in to buy her a drink.

'Try him,' Tony turned his sister's face in the direction of the profile of Samuel Beckett. To observe was one of her greatest passions, to capture a face, a stance, a building, a boat in a minimal number of lines.

A coffee cup spiralled and shattered outside on the pavement. Like little hens, the waiters flustered around the man, who kept perfectly still as they whipped away the spilt liquid from his table in napkins and flourished a fresh cup in front of him.

'Tony, who is that blind man? He looks so miserable.'

'That, my dear, is an old acquaintance of mine – James Joyce. I cannot go near him until I've finished reading *Ulysses*, which is taking me an age to get through.'

Carefree though she may have been, the pinch of her darn and mend existence had not changed a great deal. 'Why would I want to burden myself with such a thing as my own flat?' Phyllis would say when asked why she remained chained to the dreary confines of her boarding-house, which incidentally was still good enough for Vladimir, too.

Indeed, her contentment with boarding-houses and bedsitters only ended in 1972, when at the age of sixty-six, Phyllis bought her first home, a flat overlooking the beach at Shoreham-on-Sea in Sussex.

Then one autumn day in 1924, Tony confessed to Phyllis that he was finding the light in Paris drained his energy. The next day, when she went to collect a new set of paints he had ordered for her, the Portuguese cleaner scrubbing the stairs shouted out to her: 'That one he left this morning. Big luggage. Many luggage.'

Tony's whereabouts remained unknown to Phyllis until she received a letter from him in the spring of 1925, in which he revealed that he had spent the winter months making his way through the Spanish countryside on a donkey, happily etching and drawing. *Andalucia*, he wrote, *is where you and I should go for the famous Easter festivities*.

Within days, Phyllis joined her brother in Granada, where Tony began a detailed journal.

The next week we crossed to Gibraltar and as it was Good Friday we ate hot cross buns for breakfast. We caught the boat to Ceuta (North Africa) *and arrived there literally without a penny in our pockets.*

We asked everybody for Señor Bakewell, a friend of Mama's. Nobody knew him. So we hired a horsedrawn carriage and looked for him. This took us along the entire beach and back again to the port. Here we found him rushing around looking for us everywhere. 'Please pay the cab,' (we said) *which he did and took us in and gave us tea. He said Phyllis must stay with him and I would stay at the local hotel. Phyllis played the piano rather well and the next day she played to Bakewell and his English staff. One of them became enamoured with Phyllis. Ultimately we decided to go on to Tétouan* (in Morocco).

En route to Tétouan by train, their carriage was sprayed with bullets.

The Riff War is on. Phyllis and her unnamed boyfriend disappear for hours in the countryside, but their wanderings almost cost Phyllis her life. There was a curfew on and I ran down to the town gates to wait for them as the bell rang. Phyllis and her boyfriend had to run a mile down a long straight road to reach the town before the gates were closed. Once closed the Riffs came under the walls looking for anybody left outside and slit their throats.

A few days later we returned to Madrid and Phyllis to Paris. She had a delayed sunstroke but was looked after by a doctor in her compartment.

The excitement of travelling through Spain lit a small fire in Phyllis; from now on, its embers would burn constantly. Within a few weeks, Paris would leave her breathless, as if its very streets choked her imagination. To travel – in France, in Spain, anywhere – she knew was the antidote.

After her return to Paris, Dick Pearsall took it upon himself to meet Phyllis after she had finished work at the Galeries Lafayette on Saturday. He walked her up to Parc Monceau and, as they wandered through the colonnades, he listened to her stories of Spain.

If he did indeed ever fall in love with Phyllis, then it happened in those few hours. He wanted her enthusiasm. He wanted to have it, to keep it, to throw a blanket over it and call it his own. Phyllis, he believed, would inspire him, she would ensure his success. The day before, he had received a letter from his brother, a postmaster in Cape Town, who had signed off, most likely in jest: *So, old man* (for Dick was thirty-seven now) *when are you going to catch yourself a bride? And where are you going to find one in Paris who understands your hatred of garlic?!*

His irritation with this comment would not disappear. The cure, he knew, was Phyllis.

'I have been thinking in your absence and I wonder if you would do me the honour of becoming Mrs Richard Pearsall.' Dick had interrupted a story that involved a doctor, a fainting nun, some wild dogs and a plate of sausages.

Phyllis turned her head to his, astonished at both his interruption and his proposal.

'Thank you, Dick. I'd like that very much,' she replied.

And that, quite simply, was that. A no nonsense, no fuss proposal, just as Phyllis would have wanted. Why she accepted, without ever having spent any time alone with Dick, is hard to know. Yet for all her struggling with independence, perhaps Phyllis knew that ultimately her future would need to include a husband. If no man had stepped forward until now, then why not choose a man who had protected her, had taken care of her and who had slowly allowed his admiration of her as a teenager to grow into a longing as she reached her twenties?

CHAPTER SEVENTEEN

'Met Him in France, Left Him in Venice'

> Though hills and valleys never meet, it is true that human beings,
> good and bad, often cross each other's path.
>
> 'The Two Travellers', *Grimm's Fairy Tales*

'I'm no longer Pig! How I will miss being Pig!'

Sitting in her nightdress, at the little table on the balcony of Dick's Paris apartment, Phyllis was writing out her luggage labels before their early start.

'Phyllis Pearsall. Mrs Richard Pearsall. I like it, Dick, thank you. I shall keep it. For ever.'

Dick snored.

Phyllis unsealed the telegram from her father again to see if there was anything her mother had missed or chosen not to read out to her. Her father had still addressed it to *Miss P.I. Gross*, and even in the future he never contemplated calling his daughter Mrs Pearsall.

But no. It still simply said: MAKE HAY WHILE THE SUN SHINES.

No love and no luck for me or Dick, Phyllis thought.

This was the first day of their married life together. 1927. Her pen paused. Like every girl who marries an older man, Phyllis flinched at the realisation that her future was held hostage by a

Sandor Gross, Phyllis
Pearsall's father.

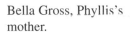

Bella Gross, Phyllis's
mother.

Phyllis, aged six months, with her brother Tony, aged two.

The young Phyllis with her pet elephant Elijah.

Phyllis, aged six, and her brother Tony, setting free some birds in the grounds of The Firs, their home in Surrey.

The war years: Phyllis's sketches
of Wrens at work from her book
Women at War.

A portrait of Phyllis taken in 1940
by the late Sir Henry Turner.

After her plane crash: Phyllis,
aged forty-five, shows the strain
of her ill-health.

In 1936, Phyllis began her A-Z odyssey, overcoming endless obstacles in her bid to give London an up-to-date street atlas. Her first order was from WH Smith's and delivered in a borrowed wheelbarrow.

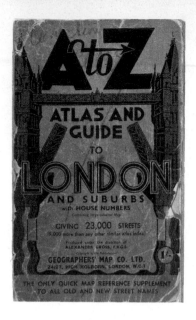

A-Z London is now the market leader and one of many A-Z Street Atlases.

Phyllis was determined to conquer the rest of Britain with her maps.

Phyllis with her best friend
Esme Wren.

Phyllis with Esme
at the Berkeley
Hotel flanking the
portrait of Bella
by Alfred.

Before Bedlam: The portrait
of Bella painted by Alfred,
two years before her death.

Phyllis spent her life recording London and its changes. This drawing from the late thirties shows Waterloo Bridge being rebuilt.

Trafalgar Square from Drummonds Bank.

Claridges: This is Phyllis's last painting, undertaken as a commission for Claridges in 1996.

Government House, Hong Kong: This was painted by Phyllis during one of her visits to Chris and Lavender Patten.

Phyllis painting in France.

Phyllis outside the company she founded in Borough Green, Kent.

wiser being, who would use his own life as a template for her future experiences, and who would never understand how to treat her as an equal. She flicked the thought away. For life? The mess, the misery and the emotional muddle that had twisted itself around her parents' union had left her with a scepticism that was years ahead of its time. To come from a broken home had provided her friends with enough salacious gossip to spread around the world twice. Then on top of that to have an alcoholic mother who had dragged an American lover around before making an honest man of him, and a father who flitted from hostess to hostess, gave rise to steamy anecdotes that became as common as olives at a cocktail party.

Phyllis was not in love. No matter. As long as she had a paint box under her bed at night and her prayers for fine weather were answered, then she could be happy. None of her friends or family ever saw her wear a wedding ring, and if an engagement ring existed, she must have discarded it early on in her marriage.

Love is barely touched upon by Phyllis in any of her writings or her art – except when she refers later in life to the collective love of her company and its staff. Rather than being afraid of commitment, it is as if she has been an unwilling witness for so many years to so many scenes of overwrought and destructive love between her parents that she shies away from what she believes is the inevitable pain that comes with being in love.

Today, her independent attitude would not be given a second thought, but back then, when a woman was defined by the man she married, Phyllis was a feminine outcast. She had not inherited her mother's ability to feign neediness or reel in suitors with endearing signs of feminine weakness, nor was she tempted to do so. It wasn't a lack of anything. She just didn't have the need to feel adored, to surround herself with fawning young men. Yet like Bella, her approach to sexuality was straightforward. At times she appeared coldly indifferent to sex and at others a confident predator.

As a little girl, she had told her mother that when she grew up she wanted a big family. 'Three, perhaps?' Bella had suggested. Phyllis had shaken her head. 'Twelve. I want twelve children, please.'

Even then, Phyllis had seen the tears in her mother's eyes as she retreated into the nursery and quietly shut the door on Sandor's shouting.

'Show me your farm children,' Bella would say, laying her hands on their heads, trying to wobble a smile as she did so. Or she would pull back her skirt to kneel down on the rug with them and hum away as they all sketched pictures in their drawing books.

Mama was always safe as long as she was with us. Twelve children, Phyllis had thought as a girl, would be more than enough protection for me. Yet fifteen years later, she was not so sure that the man she was now staring at, her husband, would be the father of her children.

'Children?' she would say to anyone who asked in later years if her career had got in the way. 'No, they just didn't happen.'

Dick's face, she noted, was as gentle as a baby's when he slept; his frown marks were nowhere to be seen and his mouth lay open and relaxed.

'I have married kindness,' she said to herself.

Yet what a strange way for a young woman to refer to a man with whom she had happily shared a bed on the first night of their wedded life together – but who had made no move to consummate the marriage. Was Richard Pearsall a homosexual? There is no evidence to suggest that he was. Apart from having a strict Roman Catholic upbringing, there would have been no pressure on Dick to conform by marrying, especially in the *laissez-faire* circles of Paris.

A kiss on the forehead – that was all he gave her. Look – no hands, Phyllis had thought. That single gesture only emphasised how alone she felt as she turned in Dick's tumbly soft bed, to face the window. Whatever his amorous intentions towards Phyllis before they married, once they had been made man and wife, he chose to remain celibate.

The biggest irony must have struck Phyllis then. Daughters are traditionally supposed to seek husbands who are the very image of their fathers, yet Dick had none of Sandor's sexual rapacity nor strengths – his arrogant charm, his infectious energy or his passion for attacking life with both hands.

Rivalry with this shy, lanky artist would never have occurred to Sandor. Any man, he believed, who was still scratching around for money at the age of thirty-seven, even worse, making a living as a mediocre painter, deserved to be left behind. His family may have been monied Irish stock, but Sandor didn't understand his sort and for once, he kept that information to himself. In time, eight years to be precise, his daughter would realise that she didn't understand them either.

'Poor Dick.' That's what people would say, long after his dark shadow had faded out of the Gross family photograph. He had found himself rather taken by Phyllis and Tony's peculiar brand of young Bohemian eccentricity in Paris, but unlike many of their contemporaries, it was no affectation. It was a family lunacy.

His eyes could not rest for one minute on his faraway mother-in-law who laughed like an angel but whose smile trembled with fear. Beautiful, he thought, but thank Dear God she is not mine to handle. If Bella ever allowed Dick to interrupt her continuous sing-song chatter, she would stare at the top of his dark hair as if it was infested with fleas, or wander off into another room, humming and evidently bored.

Dick had never stuttered or fumbled with etiquette but there

167

was something about the Gross family that made him do both. No matter that he was taller, younger and better educated than Sandor, he paled in the presence of his father-in-law and so chose to leave any major conversations to his gregarious wife.

Luckily for Dick, Sandor was not the typical British father when it came to the pressure he might have exerted on Dick to keep his daughter in the manner to which she had become accustomed.

'Good money has been spent on the finest education for my daughter. I made my own wife earn her own living – why shouldn't Phyllis? There are no meal tickets in this family.'

Two days before their wedding, Phyllis had flown home to London as she told friends, 'to marry Tony's considerate artist friend Dick, who for long had wooed me.'

Some might argue that their odd coupling was one of convenience. Here he was, a close friend of Tony's, and so by association his character (if not his career) were approved of by Mr and Mrs Gross.

Bella had relayed the story of her traumatic marriage so many times, it was as if it was haunting her and she always ended in a light voice of warning to Phyllis: 'Finding a man one's parents like is half the battle.'

The 11 a.m. ceremony at Chelsea Register Office, Phyllis later described as 'drab' and unlike most brides she never elaborated about the occasion, other than to say that she carried sprigs of white heather. No photos were taken. Indeed, there were no dramas, or tears or hiccups, simply because no family were invited.

It had been Dick's idea, not her own. Keeping them away, out of spite, was not her style. The unconditional love she had for her parents was unusually strong. Even if it meant the likelihood of them running amok on her special day, she would have loved to have turned around to see her father give a wink as he stood upright in his American cashmere suit, and her mother, her head leaning on Alfred's pinstriped shoulder, wearing a gorgeously soft cream hat laden with fresh gardenias.

'Brush your hair. Don't forget a touch of lipstick – but not too dark as it will make you look washed-out. And what about wearing those little pearl-drop earrings your grandmother gave you?'

Bella may not have been there to ease any fears the bride may have had, but that morning as Phyllis smoothed on her new stockings and took her navy-blue georgette dress off its hanger, she heard her voice just the same. It was at times like these – times of significance, when Phyllis could have slammed the door on her future if she had truly wanted to – that in a strange sort of self-punishment, she instead chose to press on and face things alone.

Those moments of solitude allowed her to breathe in composure and to reflect on her loneliness. Lonely and alone were two separate worlds for Phyllis.

'I was never alone. There were friends and, of course, there was always Dick.'

Acquaintances, friends, relatives, neighbours, business clients – somehow people felt the need to wriggle and nudge their way in and out of her life, sucking up her time in the hope that her bright happiness would bury itself in their skin too.

Just as she was about to be invited into another, unknown family, her happiness was weakened by a swelling gloom. If getting married had been the ultimate attention-seeking device, to shake her parents into saying, 'Phyllis, why ever do you want to get married? My, how we miss you! Come and live at home, darling – and stay here with us,' it had not worked.

Had Phyllis truly wanted her family present, she possessed enough driving charm to persuade Dick. This wedding was another Roedean, another Fécamp. Phyllis had accepted Dick's proposal not because she wanted to, but because it was what had to be done. It was what every parent wanted and every daughter. And if not Dick, then who?

Dick had said he didn't want any fuss. So, averse to any disagreements, Phyllis had acquiesced. Just as she did with her father, she tried so very hard to keep him happy and in a gentle mood. Anyway, most new brides would have believed that this was a romantic gesture of Dick's – *let's just do it, you and me.* Sadly, what Dick really meant was, *You are about to become my wife, take on my name and my family. You do not need anyone else now.*

A few months into their marriage, Phyllis saw that, little by little, Dick was prising away her fingers that gripped tightly on to her mother's hand. Of course, had his motives been purely unselfish and he had genuinely fretted about the chaos and distress her parents brought into Phyllis's life, then it might have been forgivable. However, Dick resented the instant magnetic pull that Phyllis responded to when her mother or father needed her help.

After the ceremony, the mistake the newly-weds then made was to walk to Bella and Alfred's house, at 31 Tite Street to announce their news.

Bella opened the front door on the latch and announced in a high squeaky foreign maid's voice, 'Mr and Mrs Alfred Orr are not at home.' She then slammed the door.

Phyllis knocked again. 'Mama, it's me and Dick. We just got married.'

Bella opened the door. 'Thank God. I thought you were the bailiffs. Darlings, get inside quickly – NOW!'

She dragged the pair into the house and fussed with the double lock.

Bankruptcy had thrown the house into chaos. The couple stepped carefully through the hallway where mink coats were piled on top of Sammy the canary in his Regency birdcage, and William & Mary tallboys stood draped with Persian rugs, while silver mirrors, tea sets, cutlery, candlesticks and fruit bowls had been thrown into tea chests.

'We have overspent,' Bella sighed, as she wafted through the treasure. 'Alfred and I have been holding out, but I know they are coming any day now. My poor home made into a fortress. All my worldly belongings to go again . . .'

'Mama, Dick and I got married.'

'Oh, darling, how marvellous! You can both help us out. But first, let's celebrate! Alfred, put some clothes on. We're going out!'

The unlikely foursome of Phyllis, Dick, Bella and Alfred enjoyed a wedding breakfast of spaghetti and Chianti at an Italian restaurant on the King's Road. The bill was paid by Dick.

'Darlings, we are grateful,' said Bella, looking at the empty wine bottles the waiters were removing from the table, 'now we are at poverty's door. This may be our last sustenance in a long while. But please will you help us out and store a few of our possessions at your place, Dick?'

Dick's studio in Clapham was already tightly cluttered. His new wife squeezed his hand hard.

'Of course.'

The next scene was one of such pantomime that it is best kept in its original form. On their return to 31 Tite Street, they found the house overflowing with men scurrying in and out with clipboards. The bailiffs had arrived, courtesy of the foreign maid who, when she realised what she had done, had fled – not to be seen again for a week.

Dick expected his mother-in-law to be flung into an hysterical rage but was rather impressed when she took control of the situation with an award-winning performance.

Bella stood on a chair in the hallway and clapped her hands.

'Excuse me, gentlemen, may I have your kind attention? Let me introduce you to my children.

'This is their deeply moving wedding day. As you can see, we were right in the middle of sorting out their things to take away. The chinchilla cape for the bride, the golf clubs for my son-in-law. All that silver of course, and the mirrors, and the chairs in the corner there. My, aren't you a lucky pair! Dick – why don't you carry out those tallboys, the wonderful present from your father-in-law – who collects furniture, as you know – and we'll all help you load your new things into a taxi-cab.'

Then she turned to the bailiffs and smiled sweetly. 'Why don't you all run along and return in the morning to see what's what then?'

And with that she stepped down from the chair and disappeared into her bedroom.

Phyllis did not flicker an eyelid at her mother's audacity. It was exactly as she had expected. A plan to outwit the lot of them.

'Don't forget to carry your bride over the threshold, Dick,' came a muffled shout from Bella. She had retired to bed.

It needed three taxis to take all of Bella and Alfred's belongings. Two of the bailiffs shook Dick's hand and helped him in with the tallboys. They spent over an hour unloading at Dick's house. Phyllis had left her posy of heather behind, and by the time the newly-weds finally got a chance to sit down, they drank tea instead of champagne. Then they were late for the last flight to Paris. Dick drummed his fingers on the open front door as he waited for Phyllis to finish stuffing things in her suitcase. 'Come on, for God's sake!' he muttered.

They ran into the street and hailed another taxi.

'What a wonderful woman your mother is,' Dick said in the back of the car. 'With what grace she creates problems and meets them and gaily surmounts them.'

Within a few months, his attitude would change towards Bella. Yet Phyllis noticed it had only taken a few hours for his attitude to change towards *her*.

Nothing was shifting. The lazy rituals of life in Paris had lost their attractions for both Dick and Phyllis, who were united by their restlessness. The same weary faces of friends were as familiar as the hard butter and baguettes, and all the cafés seemed identical with their nicotine-stained walls and draughty French panes. People may have been dressed in a red woolly scarf instead of a blue one, or wearing a heavier scarlet lipstick, but the conversations drawn out by red wine that spun round and round on the same point until the light went yellow, were the same. Their noses were dulled by the same smells – of French tobacco, of the waiters, of the patisserie, of the river, and of the city's damp stone walls. Even painting in Paris had grown predictable. The city's brightness had been drained and its sharpness had become blurred. The light that blankly shone on the buildings refused to throw any beautiful shadows.

Before they got married, the couple had discussed how exciting it would be to abandon Dick's apartment, Paris and everything, to go to Spain (for they both spoke fluent Spanish) on a painting tour. A bit like an old-fashioned Grand Tour, but without the grand.

The hours they had actually spent alone together could have been counted on one hand. A piano concert in the Tuileries and *Madame Butterfly* at L'Opéra. Dick believed he had chanced upon his soulmate. Phyllis stood out among those coy, flirty girls who flitted their eyes up and down a man until he asked her if she would like a cigarette and then pouting, she would reluctantly strike up a conversation. Even though he had first met Phyllis years ago, as a gauche schoolgirl, he noted that she gave a slight wince at an arm around the shoulder, or a kiss on the cheek, just as he himself did. If Dick stared at her while she was in conversation with someone else, she might sense it and turn to smile at him, but there was nothing seductive in her look.

Younger girls, Dick decided, were better for one's ego. They adored an older man, and had the energy to indulge one's every whim.

To go off to Spain together was a way, Dick believed, he and Phyllis could get to know each other, without the quips and precious banter of their numerous friends. He also hoped that the dark passion of Spain, with its gloriously strong sun, might work on them both.

'A fresh start,' Phyllis had said.

For if there was one temptation she could not resist, it was a fresh start. So, on their first morning together, they caught a train from the Gare d'Orsay and travelled south, through Biarritz, to Irun. In a figure of eight, they made their way around Spain, sometimes by donkey, sometimes by car and sometimes by train. It was a trip that lasted almost three years, before they settled for another five in Triana, Seville's gypsy quarter.

An account of their ramblings through the Basque countryside was recorded in their book *Castilian Ochre – Travels with Brush and Pen*. With ease and just as her eyes caught them, Phyllis describes the old towns, the women with their plucked eyebrows and hennaed hair, the cool, tall shuttered buildings and fawn-coloured oxen. Spain, she explains, is where nothing ever happens, and when it does, it is unexpected. Their only snippets of adventures are day to day encounters, jokes and misunderstandings with hotel staff, townspeople and local peasants, an

Englishman abroad and a few near-misses of trains. Compared to the lurching unpredictability of her parents' expeditions, the experience must have been a relaxing one for Phyllis. Or was it?

On the cover of the book, Dick has drawn them both sitting side by side, their backs to the reader and with sketchpads on their knees. Rather tellingly, Dick's right foot is slightly raised back on its heel and overlapping Phyllis's foot, as if at any minute it may come down and trap her little shoe.

More intriguing is the fact that the book cover says it is by Richard and Phyllis Pearsall – yet he only did the illustrations. All the text is written by Phyllis and when Dick actually speaks or is mentioned (albeit briefly) it seems as if he has somehow accidentally been caught up in *her* adventure:

Our room was up in a high tower and the window looked down on to the village. It was bitterly cold out as a freezing wind was blowing down from the mountains. The lamps were flickering in the darkness on the balcony of every house, but there was not a living soul to be seen in the spectral square. The village seemed to be completely given up to the dead. Meanwhile the monastery bell kept up its unending tolling, the echo of each boom dragging itself almost to the next.

'Confound that bell!' said Dick. 'It's so damned depressing.'

As they rattled in train after train down through Burgos, south to Valladolid and south-east to Madrid, their friendship became strained. Both could see it was useless, but even so they tried to make the relationship work. To agree on a location to paint. To not make all the decisions. To wait until the other had finished their canvas. To not take the first bath and the last clean towel. To stand closer and speak more gently. To be quiet without seeming sullen, to have privacy without appearing secretive, to be jolly without being annoying. Phyllis would have spun these around in her head, trying to weave them into each day simultaneously.

Passion, at least, had never been a problem for Sandor and

Bella, even when they had stripped down to pure hatred during one of their rows. Whereas here were two artists, each one believing themselves more talented than the other, and who had not so much as poached an egg for another person before, lashing themselves to a near stranger, for life, in the name of love.

A rotten meal, a flea-ridden train, a damp bed, a throbbing head from the late-night chatter of castanets, a lost suitcase, an unsold painting . . . what ought to have been trifling annoyances grew into major causes of conflict.

And for Dick it was obviously worse.

Days and weeks that Phyllis had spent alone in the French countryside with her brother a few years before, had slipped by in a haze of painting, picnics and riverside sketching. Easy and quiet. Any jealousy that Phyllis may have had towards her older brother, evaporated with their peaceful companionship.

On the early starts, to the sound of wood pigeons, they wobbled off on their bicycles laden down with baguettes, wine, rabbit pâté and paints. The only sound was the rasping tyres on the sandy lanes as they pedalled down to the river.

These precious and rare times alone together must have given them both hope that one day, the younger Gross generation might be able to have a family of their own who would exist without fear. The fear of shouting, of failing and the fear of separation.

Perhaps Phyllis had believed that her marriage to Dick would also flow into an undulating blur of beautiful days, each one spent devoted to their own canvas and their own thoughts. Instead, their self-imposed remoteness only made matters worse. Even as early as their first wedding anniversary Phyllis describes in *Castilian Ochre* how she bossily sends Dick off a train during a long stop to buy some alcohol with which to celebrate.

'Lyon!' I said to Dick. 'We must buy some wine here. It's the

*anniversary of our wedding day.' While he went to fetch it, I was left
alone with a man in black.*

In a strange sort of way, the plain manner in which Phyllis
chose to reveal their loveless marriage is a sneaky kind of
testimony, so that if anyone in the future should not believe (or
even blame her) for how ghastly her life with Dick had become,
then there was proof, written down for all to see.

From descriptions in the book and from interviews Phyllis
gave years later, it is obvious that as soon as they were declared
man and wife, Dick had somehow been overtaken by an
irrational jealousy of Phyllis. Within months, his feelings of
inadequacy had given way to an anger that he did not even
attempt to keep under control. Unlike her father, Dick's temper
took the form of silent brooding that might rumble into a
shouting match.

*There was anger, anger, anger, all the time. He wanted me to sell
my pictures but as an artist he also wanted to sell his. But they didn't
sell. He was very jealous of my success and yet terrified about
money. But if I painted it was wrong, and if it sold I was wrong. He
was always finding fault. And if they keep finding fault, you walk out.*

Most couples who pull each other in opposite directions, after a
while submit to each other; the extremes of their different
characters lose momentum until both slowly catch the rhythm of
the other to live and breathe in perfect sync. Dick and Phyllis never
found that gentle harmony, where one could guess what the other
was thinking, or walk side by side, step by step, without speaking
but in perfect contentment. They could not go to a party without
jealousy chasing them. Dick could not relax if he could not spot his
wife, and Phyllis could not relax knowing her husband's eyes were
stalking her every gesture. If Phyllis had taken after her mother,
she would have delighted in the power this gave her, possibly
flirting with younger, richer men, whispering into the ears of her

girlfriends and provocatively walking around the room, a glass in her hand, looking lost and then stopping on her own, knowing that it would only take a few seconds before the handsomest man at the party would come to her rescue.

Fortunately, games were not Phyllis's style. Her mother and father had tricked one another with enough of those for her to see that there were never any winners in games to do with love. Freedom was all Phyllis wanted from her marriage, freedom to paint, to do as she pleased and to do as she pleased without being challenged about it.

Unfortunately, contentment would elude them both. For eight years, Phyllis carried on believing that everything was *her* fault. Just like her mother, berated by her father, the two women were forced by their spouses into believing they were the culpable ones, the ones at fault.

Unlike Sandor, Dick's foul temper reached beyond his marriage. Other people drove him into rages that were almost comical. Phyllis wrote about an incident one night in a tiny Spanish hotel:

A noise of loud talking outside entered my dreams and finally woke me up. Dick was also awake, I could hear his sheets rustling.

'Are you awake?' he asked. I felt I could not keep up my pretence without laughing, though I was sad enough.

'Yes,' I said.

'They have no consideration,' said Dick. 'It wouldn't be tolerated in any other country in the world.' He sprang out of bed. 'I'm damned if I won't try to stop it.'

Dick kept his finger pressed on the bell. Downstairs the bell rang like a fire alarm. The voices continued. I heard footsteps along the corridor. Dick pulled on his overcoat and his hat to hide his uncombed hair. Then a knock at the door. Dick whirled it open. I have never heard such a torrent of Spanish flow out of Dick.

'Certainly, sir,' said the man. 'I will tell them.'

Spontaneity and joy ebbed away from her painting. Her hands that flitted across the canvas became hesitant. Praise over her artistry was something Phyllis did not need, but the scathing undermining of her use of colour and form by Dick worked its charm.

Every time Dick slugged back a drink and slammed the door behind him, Phyllis blamed herself for not making him stay. Pride would have stopped her from writing to her mother, while Tony would never have believed that his friend could turn so sour. Like many ill-treated wives, Phyllis picked apart the little things that she might have unwittingly done to upset Dick, in an attempt to rationalise his behaviour: *I was also rather too popular with some handsome Spaniards, who woke us up at night singing serenades under our window.*

The scurry of rumours exist to this day, at the Geographers' A-Z Map Company and even among Phyllis's most senior members of staff, about her marriage status.

'We always wondered if there ever was a Mr Pearsall,' one director admitted. 'She never mentioned him.' Had she used, they wondered, Dick Pearsall's name for business reasons, knowing that she would be taken more seriously as somebody's wife, rather than as a spinster?

Whatever the truth, it took until April 1935 for Phyllis to realise she could not stay married to such an unreasonable man. But when she did finally acknowledge that she could not take his intimidation any more she left within a week.

'What do you do if they criticise you? You don't say a word back. You just walk away.'

It had been Dick's plan to spend a week in Venice, Casanova's birthplace. He knew it was the perfect time for the spring light to fall on the palazzi giving that sharp desert light that Turner had captured so well.

In Phyllis's mind, a half plan was slowly rolling itself back and forth, growing fatter and fatter, until she tired of it taking up so much space.

Venice might be the place, she had thought.

And it was.

Sickened by Wagner and Chopin and the poets who had swooned over its fairy palace towers and maze of waterways, Phyllis was taunted by the shadowy bridges with their romantic connotations perfect for secret assignations. Oh, bugger Byron! she thought.

Her smile, that had been held fast for so long out of duty, relaxed and became wider. She did not want to unwrap her water colours for the pinky marble palaces, nor capture the sunrise on the jasper-laced church walls. Furious with his wife's indifference and for wasting their money, Dick became even more engrossed than he ordinarily would have been at some little bridge, where seawater from the Adriatic washed an exquisite tourmaline glow on the walls. Phyllis left him there squinting into the distance and dabbling in his oils, for what might have been days.

Titian masterpieces could wait. She did not want to look at art. She walked alone along the sands of the Venice lido and through the noisy back streets. The diamond-pricked water of the Grand Canal shone at everyone but Phyllis. Couples draped like sloths across one another kissed in the rocking gondolas. On the Rialto Bridge, every man seemed to be whispering a promise to the woman he held. Inside every church, decked heavily with ancient ruby velvet, there would be a sightseeing couple, their fingers entwined and he, stopping every now and then, would kiss the top of her head.

Twos and twos. Pairs of people. They made her feel giddy as

they surrounded her in the hum of narrow streets. During the day she forgot to eat. Who knows where Dick ate, maybe at Harry's Bar. At night, she and Dick would leave the Bauer Grünwald Hotel to go out for dinner in the restaurants of St Mark's Square. A thousand candles and a thousand pairs of eyes bright. A knee touching, a cheek blushing, a musical conversation; Phyllis stored every intimate gesture of every man and woman. Perhaps Dick tried to make conversation. She did not see him any more. She could not hear him either. She had already gone.

The following morning was a Sunday. The bells that so bothered Dick at night would not rouse him now. Phyllis knew he would sleep until midday. Methodically and slowly, she packed her suitcase. She counted her money. Enough to return to London. After a bath, she lined her clean and unused paint-brushes back in their box, with her sketch-books. Her eyes ran over the curled body of her husband, who would marry again one day, a girl from Ireland. She noted his grey shirt, trousers and socks dancing across the carpet. His hat. His shoes. She caught them in her head and walked out.

Many years afterwards, in 1990, she told Patricia Mowbray in an interview for the *Sunday Times Magazine*:

After eight years, I thought, do I really need to start each day with someone angry with me and always worried about money, instead of going out and doing something? And I left.

But the leaving wasn't easy. Guilt would trail after her until her death.

In an unpublished interview with Anne de Courcy of the *Daily Mail*, she was once asked if there were any regrets in her life. She answered, *'Walking out on my husband without saying a word. That's the worst thing you can do to anybody. I did it because I can't argue – my whole childhood was spent watching my parents fight.'*

It was the end of another chapter in her life.

CHAPTER EIGHTEEN

'Kiss It Goodbye'

The sound was of fingers drumming. As Phyllis shadowed the frilled and capped Sister down the corridor, past the series of cell doors, she forbade herself to picture what lay behind them, so she locked her eyes on to the ring of keys pirouetting from Sister's waistband. 'Present fears,' she mumbled to herself, 'are less than horrible imaginings.'

The drumming ceased as a scorched voice escaped from the end cell.

'Let me out. Let me out. Let me out. Let me out.'

Phyllis found herself being prodded over the threshold of a red padded chamber.

'Mrs Gross. It is your daughter to see you. I shall return in half an hour,' shrilled Sister after she had clunked shut the steel door behind her.

Unimaginable smells.

'My darling Mama,' Phyllis longed to say, but in reality it is doubtful that her mouth was able to move at all. Ceiling, floor, dead or alive, buried or exposed, wondered Phyllis as the soles of her feet began to sweat. A vision sliced her thoughts of her own mortality, of the choices she would need to make and of the choices that would have to be made for her. But before she could be smothered by her past, Phyllis was scooped back by her mother, hobbled in the corner spewing gobbledy-gook.

'Stupid of them to leave me this,' Bella hissed, her left eye black and bruised, her fingers rain-tapping on the enamel chamber pot. 'Stupid of them to have left me a mirror too!'

With that she flung the pot at Phyllis's head (it was empty and it missed) and chuckled as she somersaulted across the soiled mattresses. She cannot know who I am, thought Phyllis.

The mirror, the staff had informed her, had been unscrewed from the wall by Bella the previous day, while in possession of a pair of tweezers. In this hostile environment, a plain looking-glass was a patient's sole luxury. But it was too, an unnecessary call for vanity and Bella's reflection proved the cruellest reminder of her very real insanity. For without the mirror she might have ignored the distorted jaw, the mouldy bruises and the hoary skin. Now, no matter how ferocious her howling, the reflection mocked Bella as she strained to conjure up the layers of soft brown curls or the plum lips that had once been so pretty for kissing. *You only deserve to behold,* the mirror teased Bella, *the devil's wife, shrivelled, with eyes smote and an engorged gossip's tongue, thick and long like that of a cow.*

'I cannot face what I am, I cannot face my soul,' Bella had mumbled, as she dismantled the glass in an agitated spell between medication. 'I shall bequeath someone seven years of bad luck,' she plotted, 'and then, truly they will know how it feels to be me.'

And so it happened that the very next day, Bella had been merrily swirling up a water-colour seascape on the day ward when Matron had made polite enquiries as to whether Mrs Gross wouldn't prefer to join in with a game of ping-pong with some of the other ladies.

Bella banished the twittering voice threatening to dilute her concentration. Her paintbrushes swooped on to the easel faster and faster and faster. Swoosh with the coal-ash greys, swoosh, swoosh with the malaria yellows into the squally seas.

'Turner, Turner,' Bella flooded her head. 'I paint, by God, like Turner.'

Swoosh with the milky foam on the crests of the waves and swoosh as the salt-spray flecked the clouds.

Matron entreated again.

'*Never*,' Bella shrieked, '*interrupt an artist!*' And with that she had snatched the mirror hidden behind the easel papers and with both hands crashed it down on Matron's frilled white head.

Commotion. Paints and glass shattered, and patients were splattered then scattered in all directions. A scurrying of puce-faced staff to the prostrate Matron at Bella's feet.

Matron apparently did not recall a great deal about the episode but was sent home for the rest of the afternoon.

'Punishment is good for the soul,' Bella would relay to the other ladies as they left her behind to take turns in the rose garden. For Bella it would mean no more meals in the dining hall and no more drawing. Instead, solitary confinement, slops, electric shock therapy, a strait-jacket and one visitor a week became her lot.

And here stood Phyllis, who could hear her own voice tunnelling through her head. '*Oh Mama, Mama.*'

Who is to say how much time slipped away in that cell while Phyllis watched her mother? Certainly the staff would have taken advantage of a family member who could relieve them of their most dangerous patient. In those days, for them to bully or beat into submission a patient writhing with a possessed strength was routine. To stab them over and over with a needle until a hit punctured the flesh and the body collapsed into a weighty carcass was never more than an hourly chore. How else to cope with the mentally ill masses?

There must be some way to reach Mama, thought Phyllis, whose breath had slipped into a shallow quiver and her hands hung damply at her sides. To discover the colour in her hair had fled in panic would have been no surprise to her.

'Take charge, Phyllis,' she prompted herself, and swam to the surface from the murky depths of this present horror.

'Do you remember that time Mama, when I paid a visit to you and Alfred? It was one January,' she began. 'Alfred was painting *Salome*. But he had no model. Then when you opened the door to me you shouted, "Phyllis is perfect!" Both of you made a great deal of fuss around me, and instead of offering me some tea, you pushed me on to the velvet draped chaise longue.

' "There, Alfred," you said, "now paint your Salome!"

' "God dammit, Vernie – my Salome's naked!" Alfred yelled.

'So you came over to me and told me to take off my clothes. I was only thirteen. I was home on weekend exeat. Oh, the tears just ran down my face. I simply could not imagine being naked in front of Alfred. Of course, you said I was making the most dreadful fuss and ripped open my shirt, tore the buttons and everything – do you remember?

'I was crying and crying, "Please, no, Mama!"

'Then you scolded me with, "Surely you did not learn such prudery at Roedean?"

'You made me lie there naked, until – and we had no idea – the maid let in the Savoy Chapel Chaplain, who had been giving Alfred counselling about his drink.

'Do you remember the scene he caused? "Madam, that you should use your daughter for these illicit means and in front of her stepfather! Mrs Orr, I *order* you to allow your child to get dressed and leave this den of iniquity!"

'The shame never left me, Mama, although we can laugh about it now, can't we?'

Phyllis held her breath and waited for signs of a response. Dead still. The high, stretched sound of her own voice had frightened her, but she forced herself to try again.

'Papa has sent me a letter to read out to you,' she said brightly, producing a small note. '"Tell your mother if she'll leave that husband of hers, I'll give her a minimum to live on."'

Phyllis neatly folded it back into her coat pocket and waited. And hoped. And then it came.

Quiet at first, a sobbing and then a roar, 'He and his minimums! Never let him or Tony or Dick or any man steamroller you. They're jealous of our talents. Talents we women are too modest to recognise as worth being jealous *of* . . .'

Bella's bruised eyes never wavered from her daughter's face, as she slunk her head into the side of the glistening damp wall and methodically slammed it against the surface.

'Look at me,' (bang) 'co-founder of Geographia,' (bang) 'a gifted writer,' (bang) 'and what do I have to show for it?' (bang) 'Less than nothing!' (bang) 'Certified and in a loony bin,' (bang) 'after sixteen years with your father.' (*Bang, bang, bang.*) Then Bella slid face down on to the mattress.

Afraid to stop her and afraid to watch her, Phyllis had been transfixed, traumatised by her beautiful mother's crumpled form which lay broken and damaged, dishevelled and grey. A wizened witch, Phyllis thought as she scanned the shocked hair, the vulture shoulders and the stiff bleached gown that hung from the living corpse.

Then Bella had sniffed and hauled herself up on to her knees and lifted her bruised and dizzied head. Phyllis inched forward and proffered a hand to Bella, who had metamorphosed into a crouched catatonic pose. The berry-brown skin on the hand of the younger contrasted with the bloodless skin of the elder. Rivers of grey veins ran where rings had once marked the prettiness of Bella's long fingers, but their strength was undiminished. Spitefully, her mother crunched the hand within her grasp and twisted it sharply. But Phyllis resisted letting out a yell.

It was, she told herself, breathing quickly through the pain, a sign – a good one – of Mama's will, that would surely see her out of this madness.

But this was Bedlam.

Hell on earth.

Today the site has exorcised its past and now houses the Imperial War Museum, but the Hospital of St Mary of Bethlehem had taken in the insane since 1407. In 1675, copying the architectural design of the Tuileries in Paris, it had been rebuilt to attract the crowds. Its reputation, like a plague, had spread from rumour and reality. Such was the fearful gossip about the place that curious Londoners, even educated ones like Dr Samuel Johnson, bought tickets to view the lunatics in their cages – a popular excursion which was terminated in the Victorian era after more enlightened and humane visitors became increasingly disturbed by what they saw. The sentiments of the patients on their public exposure were, of course, never recorded.

'*Let Me Oooooout,*' Bella had grunted finally before slumping into a drugged sleep.

No one else could stomach the experience of entering Bedlam to visit Bella, so it was Phyllis alone who every Monday afternoon made her way across town to witness the spirit being hauled out of her mother, as drugs, electrodes and feeding tubes invaded every orifice. A dribbling zombie is how Phyllis would later recall her mother, subjected to electric shock therapy by a psychiatrist who had pioneered the treatment in Vienna.

The irony was not lost on her twenty-nine-year-old daughter, that this champion of women's liberation, this trouser-wearing libertine who dared her children to roam, speak, and write freely was now shackled to a brick wall. A captive of the State, her once brilliant thoughts were aborted by drugs before they were allowed to form anything coherent. *Clipped Wings*, was the name of the last, unpublished play she had written, and they had done just that.

If Phyllis feared inheriting her mother's mania then she never spoke of it. To talk of such a thing would have exposed her vulnerable side, where faith would fail to keep her afloat, and a side that said, 'I do not want to go on.' And where would that have left her lifelong motto – *On we go*?

High and dry.

According to Phyllis's niece, Mary West, both Phyllis and her brother Tony feared that their mother's madness might be inherited, and this anxiety burdened them heavily.

'What good can come of stress?' Phyllis would argue in later life. 'Why worry when nothing really matters that much? Kiss it goodbye,' she would tell anyone who was anxious about a mistake they had made or something that they felt they had done wrong. 'It is too late,' she would smile. 'Kiss it goodbye!' A philosophy such as that did not just whistle up from dust. It arose from her belief that attachment to anything – be it a place, a person or a situation – would eventually and inevitably result in unhappiness.

Deeply but lightly was how Phyllis loved. For she never recovered from the experience of watching her most prized possession, her heroine and protector, reduced to a snivelling animal.

The deterioration of her mother's mental state, Phyllis had at first assumed, was a mere flirtation with instability, a fantastical attention-seeking device that had in the past reeled in Sandor from whatever affair he was conducting. Yet this time Bella had tripped right over the edge of reality. Now Phyllis attributed her mother's downfall solely to her destructive relationship with Alfred. Like two crotchety children whose combined behaviour was murderous, once separated, their pathetic, drunken rows had depressed the whole family.

The events leading up to this pitiful sight of Bella had been as one might expect from her – extravagant, exhibitionist, and like the true actress she was, played for laughs to a full house.

The return to England of Alfred and Bella after travelling around the world, had been heralded by a fine performance. It was a farce, recorded by Phyllis, that somehow unravelled and spun completely out of everyone's control.

The scene was set in Godfrey Street where Tony and his French wife Daisy were at home with their baby daughter, Mary. They were to host a family lunch which would include his mother, his stepfather and his sister. Turbot poached the French way was to be served by Daisy. In entered the world travellers (empty-handed but seasoned with drink), known to be alive from occasional greetings to their children from around the globe.

Darlings, here we are in Bangkok.

Park Avenue and Alfred is painting in Hollywood next week.

At the top of the lovely tilted many-tiered wedding cake of Pisa.

Alfred then announced to everyone (without so much as a 'How do you do?') that he had dreamt only the other day that he would be commissioned by the Queen Mother, Queen Mary, to paint a full length portrait of her son, King Edward VIII in coronation robes in anticipation of the event in May the following year – 1936.

Bella then took up his rambling tale. 'And indeed Alfred's dream came true, for when I showed some of his sketches to my acquaintance Lord Carruthers, he in turn showed them to the Queen.'

'The Queen, don't ya know,' Alfred interrupted, 'was keen as mustard to encourage her eldest boy to be depicted as the ruling monarch.'

'To discourage,' Bella added, 'his disgraceful infatuation with that ghastly American divorcée Mrs Simpson.'

'But Gawd, you've gotta admire our Yankee style. We just come over here and mingle with your Royals like we were Royalty itself,' slurred Alfred.

Tony sensed that the intoxicated man might benefit from further sustenance and led him into his studio to partake of an apéritif while they waited for Phyllis to arrive.

Daisy, unfortunately, had been left alone to cope with her mother-in-law who was swaying around the drawing room, skimming the shelves and occasionally pulling out a book which she then flung down on to the polished floors while humming 'God Save the King'.

With all the French courage she could muster, Daisy truly believed she could salvage the situation by enquiring as to Bella's health and wondering whether Grandmother would like to hold her granddaughter.

Screams.

Bella charged up the stairs growling. Sounds tumbled out of the bathroom of commotion and smashing perfume bottles. The baby began to bawl.

As hostess, Daisy felt deeply insulted and definitely not shown the respect that was due in her own household.

She paused. She looked towards the studio. The men were inside, oblivious.

She looked towards the front door, ran over to it, opened it and shrieked, '*Phyyllllis!*' Her sister-in-law entered, a few minutes later.

'*Enfin*. Mad. Your mother is *folle*. See to her at once. She destroys my house.'

Crashes offstage.

Phyllis hurried to the scene of feverish redecoration.

'See my black stars like Picasso?' Bella squinted at the mascara

190

in her hand and went on daubing the virgin walls. 'See the new impasto created by her clutter cosmetics?' Bella asked, and then smeared a trifle of rouges, powders and creams in a rage across her imaginary canvas. Her lips chattered and long strands of dark hair quivered away from her lightly twisted bun, a dampness sparkling across her brow.

Phyllis crunched over the amber and glass shipwrecks and reached up in silence to enfold the body that stuck rigid in her arms.

Tears.

'It is sad, my darling girl,' Bella had croaked, 'when one feels it coming on again.'

When the warmth had been sucked out of Phyllis, Bella, refreshed, had wrenched herself free of her daughter's embrace. A tortured wail seared her departure as she flew down the stairs, slamming the front door behind her as she fled into the street.

Phyllis chased after her mother, out of Godfrey Street, down Cale Street then Sydney Street, and on to the Fulham Road.

'I am leaving him,' Bella barked, her upright gait breaking into a steady trot. 'The despicable despot. I've said it umpteen times before,' she continued, 'but this time it's for ever. I'll get back to my own work.'

Mother and daughter arrived, heaving for air at South Kensington Tube station. Passers-by would have seen Phyllis snatching at her mother's arm. 'Mama, please, come and stay with me.'

Bella had been able to detect a noise, a swirling sound blurting from Phyllis's mouth, but she could not decipher the words as wild thoughts stampeded through her head. Her eyes were muddied with tears, her lips, apple-bruised, as she broke down. Yes! But first I shall tell Alfred what I think of him!'

No trains. Bella collared a porter and screeched into his trembling face, 'Aren't you ashamed to work for a company which hasn't got enough trains?' One push and then another, and she nearly shoved him from the platform on to the live rail. A train pulled into the station and just in time Bella yanked him by the collar away from the platform edge. 'Silly man! You'll have an accident!' she scolded him, apparently genuinely concerned.

Phyllis was powerless to quieten her mother as Bella clambered aboard the Tube. She was like a tornado that had gathered a force from the sea.

Bella soon terrorised the passengers. At random she had stomped on their feet, had slapped and punched them and, worst of all – she had screamed. But apart from a few shuffling pages of *The Times* and some muffled coughing, the unfortunate passengers merely shrank a little.

What a relief, Phyllis thought, that no brave gentleman has decided to step in and remove Mama from the train.

They arrived at their stop. To keep up with Bella, to trail her back to Alfred's studio on Cheyne Walk was all that Phyllis expected to do now. Embarrassment, mortification and humiliation were not recognised in the Gross family. You may assume that Phyllis would have cringed, would have cowered away from such uninhibited conflict. But no, this was her own dear family and for Phyllis (who probably stood alone in this belief), love prevailed whatever the circumstance. Yet, as she would discover time and time again – loyalty at any cost has its price.

'*Let me in! Let me in! Let me in! Let me in!*' Bella's scarlet kid gloves battered the black front door to Alfred's house.

No response.

Bella knew that as soon as she had walked out of Tony's house, Alfred would have taken a taxi home to brace himself for his wife's return and blockade their home for fear that she destroy that too.

Bella had picked up a milk bottle. Smash, smash, smash. Now the lion brass knocker. Dudh, dudh, dudh.

The front door had given signs of life. It opened on the latch chain. A flash of red beard appeared.

'Not if you beg for a thousand years will I ever let you back into my house,' roared Alfred, from behind the bottle-proof door.

An Apache war cry rang out as Bella wedged her black kid boot in the door, grabbed Phyllis's wrist and then hurled them both at the solid oak obstacle. Simultaneously, Alfred had decided to retract his hasty decision.

Like silver bullets, mother and daughter shot through into the entrance hall, upsetting two aspidistras and a coat-stand, which hit the hall carpet with a thud.

'Now, let's have a nice glass of champagne, shall we?' Bella suggested as she straightened out her skirt and brushed herself down, briskly.

Phyllis and Alfred exchanged glances.

'Just the three of us. Like old times,' said Bella, who smiled as she took first Alfred and then Phyllis each by the hand and swooped into the drawing room. Neither Phyllis nor Alfred dared to mention that old times did not exist. This was indeed the first of any such occasion.

The maid then entered, tweaking at her apron strings. 'Please, ma'am, may I have the evening off to go to the pictures? *Orphans of the Storm* is on, with Lillian Gish.'

'You live in this house and you want to PAY for entertainment?' shrieked Bella.

The maid's lip had wobbled.

At that moment Bella, who had been wrestling with the cork on a vintage bottle of champagne, which was wedged between her knees and embillowed in her navy-blue skirt, had let the thing go with an OOOPPP!

The maid sniffled and rushed from the room. Bella whooped with excitement as the smoking liquid trickled into three glasses. But after she had daintily distributed the drinks with a little curtsey, Bella fell mute. For all his self-indulged drunkenness, his dry lips and his beetroot cheeks, for all his rages and brawls, Alfred recognised that this was not a good sign.

Not one bit of a good sign, he thought.

Sure enough, later that same night, Bella ran out on to Cheyne Walk brandishing a large kitchen knife, and stabbed a man who happened to be walking alongside the River Thames. Luckily, he survived the vicious attack, but according to Phyllis it took six policemen to restrain Bella who had still struggled even when she was carted away by ambulance.

The system, if that is what you could call the management of the mentally disturbed in the early part of this century, failed Bella. Her death warrant was effectively signed after what became commonly known in Bedlam as 'the Matron and the Mirror Incident'. Bella's presence was deemed untenable. Nothing had ever been done to answer Phyllis's questions or anxieties.

'We don't keep incurables here' was the official final word delivered to Phyllis before the hospital arranged for a transfer. As with many rambling state institutions, only after six months did the urgent deportation of Mrs Gross become a reality.

On one June day, an underfed Bella was taken, shivery and drugged, by ambulance to Horton Hall Workhouse and Lunatic Asylum in Epsom, Surrey. Within a week she had contracted pneumonia and Phyllis was summoned.

A dank and unlit train carried Phyllis from Waterloo to Epsom.

Every noise had jarred, from the ticket inspector's whistling to the rush of steam and wind. A cup of tea from the buffet car had poured itself like hot wax into her tightly drawn throat. Phyllis's thoughts were set adrift in anguish.

'I don't want to be an orphan,' she grieved. 'I have a father, but is it so very bad to ask to keep my mother too?'

It had become evident to Phyllis that an asylum was not a sanctuary or a place of healing, but one where the afflicted and the destitute were sent to rot away. Bleached tiles and death smells greeted her here at Horton Hall. The drone of the insane spiralled down the clicking hallways. The heavy keys, the iron gates and wailing all wrung at Phyllis's guts.

There can be no greater horror than this, she thought, as five senile women and one younger one capered into her sight. This was the Grand Guignol ward.

'Here is your mother, Mrs Pearsall,' the Matron piped up, stopping at a sunken body, covered in the regulation bedspread.

Phyllis knelt at her mother's bedside and placed the chilled wasted hand in her own. 'Has she seen a priest?' she asked.

'Not yet. But he is on his way.'

'Please would you be so good as to fetch me some consecrated wine?'

For all her lack of religious conviction, Phyllis felt compelled to ease her mother's suffering with an ancient ritual.

And with that, Bella rose up in her sheets, her arms out-stretched and her every feature ravaged by the early stages of decomposition. 'I'm frightened,' came a hoarse whisper.

She was only fifty years old. Her own mother had died in her eighties, sitting in her rocking chair at home, preaching the gospel to Tommy, the Crowley family canary. Had it been a happy life-story, then perhaps the priest would have arrived in time, to comfort Bella. She would have gazed into his kindly eyes and the photograph she had kept in her Bible, of her own father as a young man and a priest, would have slipped into her vision and then the soft, smiling face of her own mother would have called her name as she too appeared, standing behind her father, as they beckoned her out of this world and into the next with open arms.

But the priest did not arrive in time. And even the consecrated wine that Phyllis pressed to her mother's lips did not pass them.

'Too late,' the nurse mouthed to Phyllis, whose face was slippery wet with tears.

Alfred proclaimed that he could not paint at all without 'my Vernie'. And sittings with Prince Edward had been reduced to whisky-drinking sessions in which the two men commiserated over their beloved women.

'I cannot live without my Wally,' moaned Prince Edward, and according to Phyllis, Teddy poured out his heart to Alfred.

Alfred never made contact again with his stepson Tony, whom he had encouraged as a student while attending the Slade and to whom he had passed on his painting secrets.

But in spite of this help from Alfred, Tony would write in his memoirs: *I used to quarrel dreadfully with him. He was a good man at heart and his principles in painting were sound. Unfortunately his destruction and my mother's as well was due to the fact that he was a complete alcoholic. He has now long since been dead and my mother too and I hope they have both pardoned me, as I have long since pardoned them.*

'Wretched and bitter' was how Alfred described himself to his friends after Bella's death. He truly believed that to go on living would be an impossibility. Any gratitude he may have spared his late wife's daughter after she had insisted that he keep Bella's ashes had been washed away by his own complete self-absorption.

But when later Alfred decided to scatter Bella's ashes in their favourite place for walking and painting outdoors – Kensington Gardens – he was apprehended and told it was against the regulations of Royal Parks. And so Bella's final resting-place remains unknown.

Forlorn and bankrupt, Alfred's painting of Edward Windsor was to remain unfinished. His ginger beard had grown straggly, his liver could not sustain his high living and within a year, Alfred too had died, far away from his family and homeland, alone in the infirmary at Paddington.

CHAPTER NINETEEN

My Old Man Said, 'Follow the Van . . .' (and don't dilly dally on the way)

Looking back over the past eight years, at her travels through France and Spain with Dick, Phyllis recalled how the bright flamenco colours and orange groves, the scent of wild herbs, blue seascapes and dry white walls had served, as they had done for Tony before her, as sensuous distractions from her past.

The joy of each completed canvas, worked on under the shade of the olive trees in a village square, the easy routine of an afternoon siesta and a night dancing after paella and sangria, and the pleasure of every donkey-ride across the scrubby hills that tracked down to the sea, had led her memories away from The Firs, away from the contented family who had once lived there so long ago.

Only when her marriage had ended did England beckon to Phyllis in her dreams. It was time to go home.

From her scant knowledge of London, Phyllis knew that Chelsea was a pretty place. If she settled there, she would be near to Bella and Alfred. She suddenly imagined herself entertaining them to a tapas lunch (without mishap), or Bella agreeing to sit with her elegantly pinned hair, perfectly still on a stool, as Phyllis sketched her eyes flitting over the busy street below.

But within months of returning to London, and in nightmare circumstances, she had lost her beloved Mama. Phyllis shooed Bella's dying face from her mind. Instead, she recalled the ludicrous, wonderful, beautiful, incompetent mother whose death she would never get over. Before her danced the letter Bella had once sent by mistake to her at Roedean, instead of to the laundry. It read: *Two Milanese silk petticoats are missing*. Much-loved characters sprang up from the children's books Bella had written – Douglas the Daring Dispatch Rider, Mulberry and Merrylegs. Then, the lulling tone that could only come from the voice of a mother, as Phyllis heard her reading from *Tess of the D'Urbervilles* in the library, while she and Tony, no more than eight years old, curled next to the fire, stroking the tiger rug.

Fortunately, the regret and sorrow at her loss never dragged Phyllis down into an inherited dependency on alcohol or other drugs, nor on the creatures that had let both of them down – men.

Sandor, bewitched by his New York life, had begun to publish guides of the city that were selling '*like hot potatahs*' as he told Phyllis with his American twang. New York was swiftly followed by The World.

'Alexander Gross is back in town,' he boasted to his daughter.

Despite their often convivial correspondence, it is an amazing fact that Phyllis did not inform her father of Bella's death for another twenty years. Sandor, of course, was unsurprised that his former wife chose not to keep in touch, nor was he concerned enough to mention it to his daughter.

Phyllis's ability to make and keep a decision like this hints at her formidable wilfulness, yet from her point of view it was based on sound reasoning. Firstly, she would not hear of bringing distress to her father, however necessary, and secondly, that same father, she believed, would only throw dirt and shadows on the memory of her mother.

When she did eventually tell Sandor, it would be in 1955, two years before his death and on a rare visit from New York to London. After a dinner of Beluga caviar and fresh Dover sole, he led Phyllis upstairs to the balcony of his suite at The Savoy to take in the view of the Thames. As she began to speak, Phyllis leaned her head against her father's pitiful face. For once, when his voice trembled, it was not with anger.

'Bella was my life. I never married again, did I? She loved me. Don't forget that, Phyllis. Did she ever tell you so?'

Phyllis could not answer.

Then, Sandor felt the moment shift too much for his liking towards sentimentality. 'You know the reason I'm in Town?' he said briskly. 'I'm here to get backing for a new project. Not really my thing but I'm publishing the New Testament – Jesus, in fifty-two weekly parts, from Mary's annunciation up to Christ's death. And I am also about to start a pornographic comic – you would not believe the booming market in pornography! But I need a title for it, so get your head around that one.'

With that he called room service and ordered himself a whisky. 'You, little lady, must be tired,' he said, holding open his door for Phyllis to leave. And that, apparently, was that.

Sandor flew back to New York the following morning. On his arrival at his apartment he found a telegram:

HOW ABOUT SEXTASY.

He fired one right back: SPLENDID. YOU'VE INHERITED YOUR MOTHER'S TALENT FOR THE OUTRAGEOUS.

Somehow, after Bella's death, Phyllis carried on regardless. The voice in which she asked to be shown around a vacant bedsitter on the Horseferry Road and then the smile she gave as she handed over her rent deposit to the landlady was, for all anyone knew, perfectly normal.

For such an acutely observant person, whose over-excitement at everyday things – the shape of a milk jug, flowers wilting in a window-box, a livid sunset that took away her breath – Phyllis had become strangely monastic about her surroundings. Of course, poverty played a part, exacerbated by Alfred's inability to pay her mother's debts, and his pathetic request that, as her darling daughter, wouldn't it be right for Phyllis to contribute?

But what did it matter, she thought, that her new bed was not wide enough to turn over in, that a chest of drawers had to become a makeshift wardrobe, that none of her wooden chairs matched, while the flimsy lemon curtains were so faded, she could not tell there had ever been a pattern. Money had made her dear parents wretched, yet frequently having none in her pockets in Paris had given her the sensation of total freedom.

Over the months following her bereavement, the rope that tied Phyllis to the present was portrait-painting. Those sitters whom Alfred could not fit into his schedule he generously directed to Phyllis. Clients began to climb the stairs to her bedsitter; after offering them lemon tea, she would perch them on a rickety chair and begin to sketch. Hours skipped away as Phyllis squinted and smiled in turn at the subject, while continuing to paint and chatter away. She did not dither.

'Hop off!' she would eventually say to the stiff bodies longing to stretch. 'All done for today!'

So often artists notched up a reputation as unreliable and ornery miscreants who overcharged for their work, but Phyllis was different. Quite soon, her own schedule was full, too.

At night, a beautiful nothing. Silence. A hot bath. A book – Joseph Conrad most likely, or Henry James. Smoked chicken on toast. Anything and everything, just as she pleased. *I came back to England,* Phyllis wrote, *and oh, it was lovely, not having this perpetual anger.*

201

The years of selflessness dropped away from her. Make no mistake, her kindness and consideration towards others did not disappear, but the effort of constantly trying to please Dick had, she felt, robbed her life of too many years. Unbeknown to Phyllis, she was about to get involved in something new, something all-consuming that would wipe out her nightmares and her terrible sense of loss. That something would reveal itself one stormy night, a few days after her birthday in September 1935.

It was one of those nights when everything seemed destined to go awry. Phyllis had accepted an invitation to dine with one of her more distinguished clients, Lady Veronica Knott, at home in Maida Vale.

Time had already played crafty tricks on her and then, as she buffed her shoes, the light flashed off. Phyllis dashed to the window and could see the rest of the street in darkness. A power cut. After dressing as best she could in what she hoped was her red dress, and knotting a silk scarf around her head, she felt her way down the stairs and then back up again, for she had forgotten the flowers for her hostess. In the street, before she could fully unfold her umbrella it had blown inside out; the monsoon puddles that sloshed around her feet could not have been deeper. By the time she jumped on a bus at Victoria Street, her lilies resembled trodden on leeks and her shoes steamed.

Oh dear.

When the bus chose to choke and rattle and shudder to a stop, apparently too poorly to continue its journey and the conductor shouted, 'Warwick Avenue!' Phyllis hopped down, anxious not to be late. Unfortunately, it was the Harrow Road end, a further splattering walk until her final destination – Bristol Gardens.

Perhaps her spirits were unusually low, remembering how much fuss and fun her mother had made out of rain, but Phyllis could not tweak out a smile. God's wash, Bella had called it.

'Here comes God's wash, children – run!' But now, after years in the arid Spanish climate Phyllis flinched at its all-permeating powers.

Lady Veronica opened the door to receive her battered flowers and battered guest.

'Mrs Pearsall, just you wait there on the doormat,' she said, her voice slightly strained, as she summoned the butler to offer Phyllis towels while she continued to drip quite extensively on to the finely woven Indian carpet. The three couples already poised over their asparagus soup were intrigued by the fiery-eyed, brightly dressed, sodden young woman who breezed into the dining room.

'I am so very, very sorry for being late. Do forgive me, please.'

Then the conversations began, bombarding her with as many ideas as questions.

'Do you drive, my dear?' began one gentleman with a tight little moustache, whose name she thought was Gibson.

'Good Lord, tell me you didn't walk,' interrupted a blonde woman in a shimmering turquoise dress to his left. Phyllis assumed this to be his wife, since 'Gibson' referred to her throughout dinner as 'Silly'.

'No, I'm afraid I just look as if I did.'

'I told you no one walks these days, Silly.'

'One does find it tremendously hard to negotiate London, especially if one is rarely in Town,' chipped in Lady Veronica.

'Yes, but do you not find that unless you are in a taxi, there is no clear way to know how to get to where one is going?' queried Lord Knott.

This conversation would nag at Phyllis all through the remaining duck and brandied-plum courses, and then through the night. The very next morning, she became determined to find a street map of London.

First, she went to Foyles on Charing Cross Road, where she was told, 'The last Ordnance Survey map of London was charted in 1919.'

'I'll take two copies, please.'

As she walked back to Westminster, her mind was whirling with ideas. What should she do next? Back at home, she unravelled one of the maps and put a book on each corner. She hung over it like an eagle, her eyes picking at everything. When the light began to fail, she lit candles, her body casting a mean shadow over the Thames.

'*By the government for the government*,' she murmured, 'but what about me? What if I want to go from here' – she stuck her finger on Chiswick High Road – 'to here' – and she stuck another on Highgate. 'There's no index. No London Underground markings. No house numbers.'

As her artist's eye noted that new roads were nowhere to be seen, she tutted at the misuse of space and the lack of colour. What is more, the map was full of inaccuracies.

'*This just will not do.*'

She knew what Sandor would have done. She also knew that her mother would have laughed and said, 'You show your father, darling. Just you show him what you can do, and beat him at his own silly game.'

'Papa? It's me, Phyllis.'

'It must be rather late there.'

'Midnight. Look – I want to do a street map – of London. There aren't any decent ones, you see. I don't know the place and I keep getting lost, so what everybody else does I have no idea. There's a terrible gap in the market, and I want to fill it – for you, Papa, and for Geographia. What do you think?'

'It's a brilliant idea. But, you foolish child – have you any idea how on earth you would go about it? Leave it to the professionals, leave it to me. I'll see to it that one of my old draughtsmen gets on to it straight away. We've got a nice little money-earner here.'

'No, Papa. *I* want to do it.'

'I give you a week, before you throw in the towel.'

'I think it will take me a year and I'll finish the job.'

'I'm counting . . .'

And with that Sandor Gross hung up on his daughter.

CHAPTER TWENTY

The Scribes and the Fallacies

'Maps are of primary importance because they visualise the mentalities of past ages. They are all subjective. All maps lie.'
Peter Barber, Deputy Librarian, the British Map Library

A blind woman. That is how, for the most part, Phyllis felt as she undertook the mighty and self-imposed task to map London. Blind because, unlike in Paris, she did not have a feel for the city; its shape, its texture or its size. Blind because she had not seen the movement or the workings of the capital for more than a few months. Blind because she had never heard any voices from the city's past, listened to their stories or grasped more than snatches of history.

Her journey would take her over land, by then covered in tarmac and concrete, but underneath encrusted with sliver after sliver of past lives, from AD 50 when the Romans proclaimed it Londinium, capital of Britannia Superior, right up towards the close of the twentieth century, when it would be dubbed the capital of Cool Britannia.

The Romans had constructed a city that was simple to walk around and simple to map. With its neat white, timber-framed houses, laid out uniformly in strong, straight lines from the River Thames to surround a forum and basilica (town hall and law courts), the roads were easy to learn. A long wall flanked the entire city, with six gates used for entering from the west to the

206

east. Their names are still current today: Ludgate, Newgate, Aldersgate, Cripplegate, Bishopsgate and Aldgate.

Phyllis had missed the days of horses grazing in Mayfair, the gallows swinging at Tyburn, the windmill of Windmill Street or the hawthorn bushes tucked around the fields since replaced by Trafalgar Square. She knew little about the expansion of the maturing city, that fluctuated with prosperity, from evolution to revolution, thousands and thousands of times over, like a mutant cell under a microscope.

The inhabitants had suffered from its violent metamorphoses too – even disappearing from the pages of history between AD 457–604, after a Viking invasion that would be named The Great Slaughter. Yet over the months, years and centuries, a stronger city emerged, bearing the scars as a triumphant symbol of its painful past.

Many parts of London are as breathtakingly beautiful as any rural vista, yet the landscape of London was not created through natural means. Instead, its unique face has been created by artifice; vast sums of money have been spent over thousands of years in an attempt to improve on the mismatched looks inherited from previous generations.

Today in London, 34,000 Listed buildings stand defiantly, waiting for the cruel erosion of time and pollution to scratch away at their fragile foundations, until they, too, disappear. Others have been forced out. Marking their passage in history, street-names are the sole reminders of the busy trades that once thrived in close-knit communities; names like Silk Mills Path, Carpenters Mews, Ironmonger Row, Saddlers Mews, Slippers Place, Smithy Street.

Some buildings though, have clung to their birthplace. A Victorian church backs on to a Georgian house, which backs on to a 1970s flat-roofed clothes shop, which faces a minimalist glass-fronted Japanese noodle bar, which lies within earshot of an Edwardian railway line. Every cobbled street, monument, bridge and park, has been planned and built at some point in the past millennium, and with each new construction, the fattening capital spreads its arms a little wider.

At the last count, London sprawls across 610 square miles, heaving under the weight of around 8 million people, 3 million cars and provides sustenance for an estimated 16 million rats.

Yet for nearly 75 per cent of the city's existence, there have never been accurate cartographic records kept. The earliest surviving map depicts London in 1558, during the first year of Queen Elizabeth I's reign. With a mere 90,000 inhabitants, it appears nothing more than a large town, surrounded by the countryside of Spital Fields to the east and St Giles in the Field to the west. The scale is strangely askew. The boats on the river are the same size as a street, while the Tower of London, complete with water-filled moat, appears insignificant by comparison. Unsigned, the hand-coloured map is thought to be the work of Dutch engraver Frans Hogenberg and likely to have been based on a drawing by George Hoefnagel.

Considering that, for the most part, early cartographers produced maps from an aerial view, without the luxury of assistance from either aircraft or photography, their efforts were not half bad. In those days, map-making was not in any sense a structured science; copyright did not exist and cartographers thought nothing of copying and revising each other's maps and then publishing them without checking for accuracy.

From 1550 onwards, a long lineage of cartographers were charged (by the Queen or their patron) to feel for a change in the city's pulse, while recording every spurt of growth and movement. Unfortunately, in September 1666, the Great Fire of London destroyed 13,000 buildings, including over eighty churches. Most existing charts, records and maps, which could not have been re-published anyway, such was the extent of the damage, were lost.

Over the next ten years, rebuilding schemes presented to Charles II by Dr Christopher Wren and John Evelyn provided the foundations for our capital today.

The maps that gave Phyllis Pearsall the skeleton of her *A-Z* were drawn up by a military organisation founded in 1791 which used a corps of the Royal Engineers to conduct scientific land surveys. The Ordnance Survey – ordnance meaning military equipment – was headed by generals until 1977. It had one prime objective: to make 'ordinary maps for ordinary people'. Why the military? The government in the 1790s strongly believed that accurate maps would aid political stability and help the armed forces to prepare for any invasion threats from France.

It was not until 1848 that the OS turned their attention to the capital, in a survey that took two years. Cholera was choking the city and the government wanted to plot the drainage system.

During that survey, for the first time ever, height was taken into account when mapping. Before, tall features such as churches and hills had been shown as flat, which prevented a precise reading. Control points and observatories were constructed on top of tall structures (e.g. the 92-foot wooden tower lashed to the cross of St Paul's Cathedral, and using a theodolite, a scientific instrument for measuring exact angles, the Victorian cartographers took down 900 points in under five months. Then, by taking all the readings of factory chimneys, church spires and the like, the OS team devised a system of triangles which covered the two hundred square miles of the capital. Using a trigonometrical formula, those bearings translated into precise maps. Of course, the maps were not sold to the public, since the scale allowed for five feet to the mile – with the result that the final version added up to 847 separate sheets.

Today, the OS claims that Britain produces the most detailed maps in the world; as the first place to have a complete mapping database, we now have the whole process down to a computerised format. The old methods of cutting and pasting transparent plastic sheets on light tables, of photo-draughtsmen using cutters and strips of bone to paste down changes, no longer exist. Since 1998, surveyors have not touched the tools that had been used for centuries. Wooden mapping boards and set-squares were replaced by touch-sensitive screens that record any feature over eight square metres. Data is not redrawn once back from the field – it is sent straight to the National Topographic Database. It has recorded 321,162 miles of road and about 200 million features, although many never actually appear on paper.

When you know that Harry Beck, the twenty-nine-year-old engineering draughtsman who devised the 1933 London Underground map, received a paltry five guineas in payment for one of the most famous maps in history, then it is easy to see why his forefathers fared no better.

Little is recorded about even the most distinguished early cartographers who depicted London. Few, it seems, were actual Londoners, and more often than not they were foreigners. Cartography was not a respected profession and the rewards were hardly exciting for the months and years spent plotting hundreds of streets, weighed down by a cumbersome 'waywiser'. The latter was a wheeled instrument that calculated miles in revolutions, i.e. for a diameter of 8 feet 3 inches, it was 640 revolutions to the mile.

Like Phyllis and to a lesser extent Sandor, a lack of money nagged at former cartographers. They needed to convince others of the need for maps, and secure financial backers to keep them from the poorhouse until the last inch on the map had been drawn. And that could sometimes take years.

George III subscribed to Richard Horwood of Hackney's map of Regency London when in 1799, he published his original thirty-two sheets in instalments. Horwood took nine years to finish his survey. He attempted to do the same in his native Liverpool, but the stressful years had taken their toll and he died there in 1803, a pauper aged forty-five. Before him, John Rocque, a French Huguenot immigrant who became a Royal Topographer, died in the 1780s with two shillings to his name. Which is quite surprising, considering that he arrived in Soho in 1734 and after working as a gardening surveyor for the landed gentry, had begun to do commercial mapping. In 1746, the public were invited to his print shop on Hyde Park Corner to view his map of London. With his engraver John Pine, he had created a beautiful work of art, approximately 13 feet wide and 6 feet deep, in which buildings, gardens, parks and fields were given careful treatment of shading.

Of course, there is always an exception to the rule. John Ogilby, who was born in Scotland in 1600, saw actual success in his lifetime, and an etching survives of him presenting King Charles II and Queen Catherine with a heavy volume listing the subscribers to the *Survey of the City* map he and William Morgan were preparing. Success only came to him late in life though, at the age of sixty-nine, when he set his sights on cartography after losing his publishing house in the Great Fire of London. Sadly, Ogilby never got to see his great work, as he died in 1676 – exactly one month before his work appeared.

Size and scale plagued the early cartographers: how did one condense an area to master both the details and accuracy? It was not until the late 1880s that pocket street atlases settled on a scale of four or six inches to the mile. As for size – it would be the eighteenth century before maps would appear as one whole sheet. Until then they were published as individual sheets and bound into atlases, such as John Speed's map of London and surrounding areas in 1610 which included 54 regional maps which he combined into a single volume on England and Wales, or used as illustrations for history books and guides to London.

How exactly *did* one consult a map such as Ogilby's, a map which stretched to 8 feet wide and 4 feet deep? Rocque's was no smaller and his suggestion to the customer was to transform the map 'into a beautiful and useful screen' or back it with linen and attach to a pulley for a sort of blind that might be fixed to the corner of the wainscot, so that it didn't interfere with the other furniture, and then 'be let down to examine at Pleasure'.

An advancement came in the shape of linen, such as Greenwood's 1827 map which meant the sheet could be folded and would last a great deal longer than paper.

The simple use of monochromatic tones was satisfactory for most map-makers until the mid-nineteenth century, when mechanically coloured ones were priced at 1s 6d rather than 1s 0d. Until then, hand-coloured maps had been established, using blue for water, green for parks and open spaces, and a beige or yellow for roads.

In the nineteenth century there was a burst of cartographers, from G.F. Cruchley and James Wyld to George Philip and G.W. Bacon, who combined every process of map-making in one place – cartographer, printer, publisher and map-seller. With ballooning the latest hobby, their map to celebrate the Great Exhibition in 1851 was called *A Balloon View of London (as seen from Hampstead)*. The scale is askew although every building is shown in perspective and it is quite an extraordinary map, although it is doubtful that it was really drawn from life.

Map publishers certainly took into account the public's interest in outdoor pursuits – hence the *Cycling Map*, the *Literary Homes Map* and in 1917 for 7d you could buy one of George Philip & Son of Fleet Street's envelope cases that held thirty-two postcard-sized maps, each numbered and charting a section of London.

Of course, Phyllis Pearsall was not the first to take to the streets in order to map London. Yet before the first *London A-Z* was published in 1936, the popularity of maps had been sporadic. They were considered an academic luxury rather than a practical household necessity. In the years before the roads were littered with cars, more often than not a map was not about travelling or finding your way from one place to another; its function was as a social and historical document.

The obsession in Victorian society with class and wealth was exacerbated by the well-meaning social reformer Charles Booth who, in 1889, devised his own *Poverty Map*. A wealthy founder of a Liverpool shipping line, he decided to conduct his own survey of the public's living conditions, eleven years after he settled in London. Gathering a team of investigators, and using seven different colours, he plotted the capital on a 25 inches:1 mile Ordnance Survey map, published by Edward Stanford, a printer and map-maker of Cockspur Street. The extraordinary categories ran as follows: *Lowest Class (vicious, semi-criminal), Very Poor (casual, chronic want), Poor (18s to 21s a week for a moderate family), Mixed (some comfortable, others poor), Fairly Comfortable (good ordinary earnings), Middle Class (well to do), Upper-Middle and Upper Classes (wealthy).*

The findings would reveal that 30 per cent lived in poverty and 70 per cent comfortably. It would also point to how the Prince Regent's favourite architect, John Nash, in building Regent Street in 1821 (and demolishing Great Swallow Street) had separated Soho from Mayfair, and sparked a great class divide.

In 1867, a map alerting the public to the most dangerous areas during the cholera epidemic was published. Another followed in 1899, concentrating on the East End, to show the *Deposition of Jews and Gentiles* across the world.

The twentieth century has seen enormous changes in the map-making process with the advancement of technology, but in many ways the London symbols, such as a red dot or circle indicating the Underground, or a green wash for parks and blue lines for the banks of the River Thames have settled into an instantly recognisable format. Not everyone is happy though. It is as well to know that the world of cartography that Phyllis gate-crashed is as rarefied as the art world to which her brother belonged. Commercially, she stole the show, but her reputation, up until her death in 1996, was regarded within the profession rather sniffily:

These conventional colours are of course of enormous assistance in distinguishing between the crowded details of a London street guide: the difference can best be appreciated when one compares the copy of a cheap monotone guide such as the A-Z *with Bartholomew's or Philip's expensive colour atlases.* (Philippa Glanville, 'London in Maps', *The Connoisseur*, 1972.)

Everyone else, it seems, was taking mapping terribly seriously. If you weren't a scientist, with an academic or mathematical background, then how could you possibly compete? Historians and antiquarians began to add layers of dust to protect those drawn up in the past, instead of celebrating all maps, including the *A-Z*.

Neither the name Phyllis Pearsall nor that of her father were anywhere to be found, in any of my research. It is strange that the very term *A-Z* is as familiar to the public as the brand-names Sellotape and Hoover, yet *The History of London in Maps* and *The Times Atlas of London* included every other conceivable morsel of information, but had quite pointedly left out Phyllis and Sandor. Were they really so dreadful? The fast-food makers of mapping?

Not according to Peter Barber, Deputy Librarian at the British Map Library, who senses that the old traditional view of cartography is slowly changing. The maverick character of Phyllis Pearsall is finally beginning to be appreciated:

'In the past,' he told me, 'snobbery censured map-makers for distorting reality and not producing traditional maps. There is no such thing as an accurate map; there is bound to be distortion, depending on what purpose it sets out to serve.

'Phyllis Pearsall was disliked for being so obviously commercial and instead should have been recognised for starting a trend towards more common cartography. She put a premium on clarity and design over mathematical accuracy, which is much more in keeping with today's style. Until recently, the art of mapping was subordinated to measurement. Phyllis went beyond the patron, to tailor the base needs of the map to a particular segment of society.

'Now if you were to go house-hunting using an *A-Z*, you may find a house but not see any green spaces nearby. That may not be strictly true. You are just looking at the wrong sort of map – for that you should look at an Ordnance Survey one. There is a degree of honesty about the *A-Z*; it distorts reality with a clear objective in mind – to guide the pedestrian and the driver to their destination.'

CHAPTER TWENTY-ONE

A Lonely Journey

September 1935

For a Sunday night I am particularly plagued by the fidgets. The light tweaked my eyes open before five this morning. 'How can you make do with such thin curtains?' my sitters chide, and I reply, 'However should I tell the time without them?' I sprang from my bed with that early start excitement Tony and I first felt as children when we fought to throw goodness knows what from the nursery into a trunk before being bundled into a car and heading for goodness knows where. 'A holiday,' Mama would call it. 'An adventure,' Papa would correct her.

I counted the minutes before the sun rose, leaning on the windowsill and peering down the Horseferry Road. How did that name come about then? Horses could never have pulled passengers across the Thames, since it is too deep by half, so I concluded that there must have been a horse-trader who dispatched horses up- and down-river. My road is a straight one. Easy to draw, no nonsense and no curves, looks the river straight in the eye. Just like Paris. Who ever made Millbank and Whitehall run so wobbly? I shall ask them myself, I thought, when I get there.

Half-panicked because I sensed the work breeding under my bed, none of which I could finish in the time I had left, I fussed over my scrapbooks of drawings and stories and rifled through my canvases and folios. But my commission won hands down. Fine-tuning the portrait of Lady Ashfield ate up all my efforts. A bright day shouts for knock-out shades – bluebell, hyacinth, marigold and rose. Lord Ashfield will not be able to accuse her features of seeming flat and lifeless now.

No need to shed my pyjamas as I had a stockpile of tea and bread here. Tricked by Time again. Perhaps I might have been able to distract myself from my canvases were I to save for a wireless. I had no interruptions, or at least I did not interrupt myself until I heard the clock strike four.

I shall miss my colours. Ever since Alfred showed Tony how to set them out on a palette and he in turn revealed his secret to me, I have never changed the order. Alfred's professor said it was exactly the same colour scheme as Rubens. From left to right – ivory, black, ultramarine blue, veridian green, flake white, light red, cadmium red or vermilion, yellow ochre, lemon cadmium. For the odd occasion cobalt blue, rose madder and golden ochre are used.

Washed my brushes twice after tea. Slowly, I turned them over and over under the cold tap at the kitchen sink, squeezing the colour from the sable until their blood ran clear. The last sweet, tinny smell of paints for a while. The palettes and jars streamed tears so I flooded them with water so as not to prolong their life ebbing down the plug-hole. A solemn burial in their cherrywood box and I shoved them away fast under the bed.

Hiding the canvases required a finer deception. Twenty in all I stacked in the corner, their faces to the wall like naughty children. They felt heavier than usual and no doubt rejected, so as I covered them with an old cotton blanket I promised to be back for them soon.

I then took a sharp knife to my lead pencils until each one might kill an intruder with a single sharp stab to the eye. *Ha! Take that!* I wonder I wouldn't ask a robber if I might draw his likeness first. 'I do,' I should say to him, 'so rarely get the opportunity for new sitters. Would you be so kind . . .'

Kneeling on the floor I packed my kicked-in satchel. In went the pencils, two new blank notebooks, a compass, a rubber and an apple. Moths tickled in my tummy as the sounds of Junior House trickled back. 'Do not let them in,' you say. Don't worry – I rarely do.

Mama knocked on my door last night. I would have sobbed were it not a dream. There she stood, her arms outstretched, clad from neck to toe in her favourite bottle-green velvet dress, her hair finger-coiled around her face and her Ascot hat – the brim swooning from pheasant feathers. But a fuzziness buzzed at the hem of her skirts. 'Mama,' I cried, 'where are your feet?' Indeed, where I might have expected to see her green shoes, there a sulphur-coloured mist swirled. Scooping me up into her arms she hushed me by pecking my forehead with kisses until my breathing rattled less. 'Why, I have given them to you, my darling, for your journey.' And with that, wind sucked me down through a trapdoor and I tumbled in my pyjamas on to a silent Edgware Road. 'Phyllis! Over here!' On the horizon I could just catch her shrouded form. I began to walk as fast as my body would carry me and then faster still. But as I moved towards Mama, the weaker her voice grew and the more distance swam between us. 'Phyllis, come to me,' she sang, until her voice turned into one long monotonous wail. It was the wail of a siren and I ran towards it until my bare feet bled from the sharp gravel.

I wonder each time if I can fool myself into not recognising the signs as I prepare to leave again. It always starts with my hair. On Friday, I took a walk over Lambeth Bridge to the High Street, for a haircut. 'Short as you like, sir,' I ordered Willy Browne, the Yankee barber man. His face, usually circumnavigated by rivulets and creases, broke into a smile. In fifteen minutes he covered Fred Astaire's new movie *Top Hat*, Mr Clement – and he pronounced it *At-agh-leee*'s position as the new head of the

Labour Party, and the aching feet of the shipyard men walking from Jarrow to London. Whatever will be left for his other customers?

The cutting away must be something to do with Papa, I reflected as Willy, pleased that I didn't want fuss or curls, tucked into my head as if it were a box hedge. The British and Americans thrive on their homing instinct. When abroad, their patriotism is as rampant as swamp fever, and they talk of the old country as if it were the Holy Land.

I am the proud owner of the fleeing instinct. It is inherited by the immigrant, the Jew, the exile and on top of these in my father's case – the bankrupt businessman. If Fate was about to hurl the Gross family upon the high seas, then Papa would insist, 'Fate, hold on if you please for just one minute and spare my children the following items: one thick winter coat, one stout pair of shoes and one short haircut. Disguises,' Papa would say, 'are the key to New Beginnings. You see, children, you can become,' and he would turn his back on Tony and me and then whisk around to display a Cyrano de Bergerac nose, 'anyone!' 'But then Sandor,' Mama would gently enquire while walking away from him, 'when can we disguise ourselves from ourselves?'

A telegram from Papa was delivered this morning. The PS gave my spine a shiver. *PS*, he wrote: *Adolf Hitler has passed the Nuremberg Laws – Jews are now second-class citizens.* I can only be grateful that Papa is in America and hail Mary full of grace that Mama insisted on my being Catholic.

Now I ought to cast out my grey cotton painting trousers, held up by string, and the buttermilk shirt that has had more owners than washes. 'A fright, a fright, an absolute fright,' my mother would reel from the threshold as she examined her youngest child perform with a palette. Never mind that she was content to watch Alfred while he was knee-deep in crimson and vermilion oils and bourbon, but her exquisite clothes always stayed out of harm's way.

Starch and a hot iron maketh the outfit. I have a Pressing Engagement. That phrase always reminds me to get out of these dog-robbers and to iron something suitable. Tonight, as the shadows suddenly dropped in, somewhere between pressing the shoulder seam and the jacket hem, I meandered into my thoughts. As I pointed the tip of the iron on to the chasms of loch-coloured wool and then let the metal thud down with an industrial shush which crushed the fabric into a serene flatness, I sensed that no one was with me.

How refreshing, you might think. No. I would rather have been able to report that an infusion of balmy calmness danced around my body to buoy me up before my journey.

I laid my outfit on the sitter's stool. The French navy wool suit should do; the skirt is not too long so I shall be able to stride out. Black woollen stockings. I suppose you might call it a uniform of sorts. From my travels in Spain, my memories lie in a tea chest in the hall and from Paris, only my brown leather brogues have survived and I shall buff those up to wear tomorrow.

I am not running away this time, not walking out or leaving people. I am letting a part of me move ahead, to grow. Let's see if the old Phyllis can catch up.

There are no stirrings from Henekey's pub tonight. Everything is holding its breath for the Monday morning stampede. The moon is in full white shock, and if I lean out to the right from my window I can catch it just about on my face. If I was a seer, the sinister face of the moon would mean to me the enemy light in a world war, the light that failed to guide my plane and the sole comforter of my father on his final passage from Italy to Southampton. But for now my nose is tweaked by the breeze; one sniff and the river tells me to expect a fine day tomorrow.

Excitement woke me at 4 a.m. I lay without light and without sound. Who else will be up now? Just me. No noise from the road below. Then foghorns. Autumn mists clogging the river. Up I get. Up I get. Off I go. *On we go*. Thoughts: none bad, none good. Apprehension: no time. Mind: 'neutral' says the indicator, bordering on 'happy'. I shivered into the bathroom.

If I wake in the middle of the night I do not like to catch my face in the glass. There is something wrong about turning to face the changeling that you mutate into under the spell of sleep. It is that sacred time when a body travels and transforms, from good to evil and back again, when the heart beats to the strokes of another world and breathing becomes shallow and sometimes stops. The night is in death throes at four o'clock.

I turned on the basin taps fast and caught myself. My mouth fell open as if a stranger had thrust a knife into my spine. The glass, blotched black in the corners, gave a funereal silhouette, a death portrait of the sitter and a snapshot. Smile, please. I saw for the first time the little sharp teeth pointed inwards in defeat. I wished my teeth were less timid. Feeble gas lighting gave my shoulders a hunched look and my hair stuck out as uncontrollably as my brainwaves. My eyes sprang up with my smile. Hold it – the mouth has been taught to grin. But it is my eyes, I reflected, that betray me. Behind those infinite blue irises lies an infinite sadness – but that is not what other people see. My fingers began to twitch in anticipation of the day. I ran a hot bath and was out of the house by 5 a.m. sharp.

'You will be arrested for spying, miss.' Those were the first words spoken to me that morning. Despite two hours on foot up and down eight streets, and now halfway through the shambled buildings on Old Pye Street, the only noises to surface so far had been the coal and scuttle, steam and bath ones hissing forth from basement quarters in Victoria.

'Excuse me, miss, I said—'

Like shots fired in the mist, when the deep voice hit my ears I had jolted. My right hand, dead in its navy leather glove, quivered on the notepad and my pencil had flinched across the white paper. Damn.

I twisted round, smiling in anticipation of trouble, to see a young policeman pacing across the cobbles, brandishing a grin, half kindly and half hinting that he might be the sort to give me a good clipping about the ear.

'Might I enquire as to what a young lady such as yourself, miss, is doing out on the streets at this time of the morning when it is customary for only us working folk to be about?' His large and seemingly uncontrollable mouth had not stopped to draw breath, by which time I calculated I might sneak down a few more house numbers.

Forty-nine, fifty-one, fifty three . . . 'I am mapping, sir.' I did not raise my eyes from the hard granite lines.

Mapping. He sighed, turned his mouth towards his boots and directed his glance upwards to the gasping gas street-lamp on which I was leaning.

'Why does that sound like meddling to me?'

Meddling. Now may I tell you there are rare instances in a person's life when the skies may as well have been rent in two as all the wisdom of Job is bestowed upon them. And this was one such instance. I braced up to my full height but still fixed hard on my amateur map executed with my clumsy hand. I understood at once and felt the surge of anger that had thrown Mama in and out of love with her unjust world. Here was I – a woman, unaccompanied and unarmed, who existed in a society where a woman has no business, unless she is a whore or a char, except for meddling.

'I am a cartographer.'

Out sprang the words. My voice had strained. 'Do not ask me to spell it.' I tugged on my earlobe. The skeletal phrase rattled in the air isolated and irretrievable. Sounded like a true profession to me. Lawyer, doctor, professor, cartographer. But then my mind, always primed to goad, turned on me. For there behind the policeman loomed Papa and Dick and Tony and Uncle Frank and Alfred spitting out, 'CART-O-GRAPH-ER!' between howls of laughter. And when their heads weren't rolled back by the seizure of laughter then they were mopping away tears.

'So where's your cart then?' The policeman's voice rescued me. Wet about the ears he was and he most kindly bought it lock, stock and barrel. No notepad appeared. A good omen for my first day out in the field as it were. It was with good grace that I lent an ear to the patter inherited by every bobby on the beat.

'And who do you work for, miss?'

'Myself, sir.'

'In that case, do you think yourself might give yourself a break of several minutes to pass the time of day with a policeman over a nice cup of tea?'

I went, of course. Be open to the kindness of strangers, I had learnt that well enough from my time in Paris. And over the years, I in turn would chatter with and befriend anyone. Because sometimes anyone turned out to be someone and then someone turned out to be of great value.

Constable Peters whistled as he strode into the cramped tea-house on St Ann's Lane. As his conversation meandered across a spectrum of trivia I read his face. Unmistakable cockney eyes. A cockney cobalt blue, the eyes of a rogue. Twenty-seven. A tint of red in his mink brown hair I put down to Irish roots, which definitely accounted for the saintly catholic surname of Peters.

'You want to draw radials out from a central point like Marble

Arch,' he said, thrusting out a considerable wingspan which sent his helmet spinning off the oak bench to land at the wheels of the tea trolley. His face ruddied as he blustered on, 'That's what I'd do all right. Say Edgware, Finchley, Tottenham, Barking, Croydon, Ealing, Harrow and the like.'

Use your common sense, Papa had warned me in his latest missive. Chin out and best foot forward had been my sole plan, but here was a fine tip and the first step in a practical direction. I drained my cup and stuck out my hand. Constable Peters was pleased he had crossed paths with a 'female eccentric', as he would later report to his New Scotland Yard colleagues. Shaking my hand just a little roughly he wished me the very best of very good luck.

And in truth, what exactly was it that guided me through? What was it that permitted me to shun contact with friends and to abandon the nourishment meted out by my palette and my typewriter? I am not able to reveal that to you even here. Craving the company of others was not an addiction, but my insatiable greed for laying my eyes on something unseen, whether it was a bridge, a feather or a new umbrella, I admit was bigger than my belly. And I was taken in by the history too: Blue Anchor and Bleeding Heart Yards, Hanging Sword Alley and Amen Corner. From the muddiest cobbles and dockside squalor to the soft-shoes and automobiles in Chelsea, I witnessed it. Not that I twittered around on a whimsical foreign visitor's tour. Let me rest by saying that my two sturdy feet led me into the darkest alleys in those twelve months, and when not a soul heard me beg for help, then I dug deep into the well of perseverance to draw out just enough energy to carry me home.

Loneliness stalked me after the pubs banged shut for the night, when the huge whale carcasses of buses and trams lay beached in stations and London wound down to a steady pulse. A purpose was, I believed then and still do, set out for me and so I was never left to flounder. This project was all for Papa, for all his hurt, for all his enemies and for every time he told me that I couldn't, that I wouldn't and that I should leave business to him.

I shall not bore you with the countless occasions when I took a side turn off a street and found myself back where I started, or wound up completely lost and had to ask the way. Those first spring months forced my frustration to its very boundary limits as the city cast an alien shadow over hostile and impenetrable buildings that glowered down at me. However dizzied I became by the chaotic fissures of sprawl, my confusion spawned determination to complete the task. *Inconsistencies such as names of houses instead of numbers, unnumbered blocks of flats, churches, continuation into side streets*, I wrote in my diary on 23 May. *I did not falter till 453 plummeted to 35 due to the start of Maida Vale, which ending at 245 plummeted to Kilburn High Road's number 1. Shoot Up Hill started at 27; Cricklewood Broadway at 1 again and when Edgware Road resumed it did so at 329 instead of 455, thus duplicating 126 numbers – differentiated only by Postal District change from W2 to NW2. In fact, every radial supported its own system or lack of it.*

With the goodness of time my method overcame the urban madness. I had purchased from the Post Office all seventy-two existing 6-inch Ordnance Sheets which covered the London County Council Area and which had not been updated since 1919. On plain white paper of the same size, and centring on Charing Cross, I measured out 1-inch squares to the outer margins and referenced them ABC on the top and bottom. I numbered each square down the sides 1,2,3, and added in the nearest station and bus route and bus numbers. After years of spontaneous brush-strokes with a broad interpretation of colour and shape, here was I struggling to master mathematical exactness and precision.

The parasites of rolls and scrolls of paper bred avariciously in the warm den that had once been my bedsitter, and each one nestled in its own patch on the floor. When briefly loitering outside a house to jot down markings in the street, I often pictured the interior, perhaps capaciously cool and linear grand or perhaps a moth-eaten tomb of decomposing books. *Happy or sad?* I would ask as I read their windows. *What works of great importance are stirring within your walls?* Had anyone, I wondered, ever peeked down from the cosmos to dissect my little ant building and spied me crouched over a maze of lines, squiggles, figures and abbreviations? Spread before me they would have seen the whole capital in my far from neat hand-writing. How my sturdy fingers had burned from manoeuvring thousands of individual letters into a Lilliputian space. Night-mares, Mama had led me to believe, ought to feature past lovers returning to haunt their victims, but only the fear of drawing the wrong abbreviations in ink popped up in mine. Should C denote Close, Court or Crescent? M mansions or mews? Then the distinction between Abbey Roads and Streets, Aberdeens, Acacias, Addisons, Adelaides. And that probably said a great deal about my choice of lovers.

Mercifully, the body has little memory. No matter the size of the blisters stinging my ankles or the exhaustion burrowing into my calf muscles after an eighteen-hour day, I would greet a new morning with as much confidence and optimism as if it was my birthday. After midnight, if my eyes caved in with fatigue or felt dry from simply looking at too much, then I rubbed Mama's gold wedding band against my lids. I realise this remedy is as much an old wives' tale as leaving my shoes upside down underneath my bed at night, but it gave me comfort.

I was lulled like a baby in a hammock by the reassuring rhythm of routine. The morning ritual was brief and I shot out of the house within thirty minutes. First came a harsh scalding bath if my nose felt icy on waking, or a cool shower if the night had been spent thrashing about for summer air. Assam in a pot, if you please, plus the Delft cup and saucer (chipped but does the job) and a little milk. Since frequenting workers' cafés for respite, suddenly lemon in my tea no longer suited my surroundings as it had done in Paris.

'A laaaymun?' a steamed pudding of a waitress had screeched when I had ordered a cup of tea *au citron* in the Embankment station café. Well, I wasn't truly English, was I? 'You want to try a drop of cow's milk, love.' At least I entertained all the customers who took the opportunity to look up from their newspapers to gawp at me.

If condensation kissed the inside of my windows, on went the grey lamb's-wool cardigan – a donation from the Communist neighbour – my vest and navy woollen stockings. I avoided wearing hats, even in a blizzard (on that occasion I opted for a silk headscarf) for they were liable to hold the water if it rained. This I learnt to my cost after the grey beret I started out with fell limp after a severe April storm and so I donated it to the centuries-old flower lady on Lambeth Bridge. 'Fine day for a grey beret,' she would chirrup as I nodded and passed her stall. Her face dimpled into smiles that day when I proffered the battered felt. 'Take these Michaelmas daisies in return, miss, won't you?' How I itched to paint those white flowers.

Breakfast was never allowed until 7 a.m. after I had two hours and thirty streets under my belt. Not that I needed to do so, but a poached egg on fried bread was a treat. 'I can't quite place you, miss,' said the Greek proprietor of Daphne's Café in West Hampstead who puffed between tables in a red pinny, gesticulating with a stripy tea-towel in one hand and a row of plates dancing up the other arm. 'So are you a teacher then, miss, or a governess?' he asked, stopping to wipe the steam from his spectacles and casting an eye over my notepads. People never quite settle until they can label you; they do not feel comfortable with a stranger, or someone who disrupts a daily pattern. To sweeten me up, the proprietor profiled his regulars.

'He in the corner is the vet from the High Street and he's been coming here for his bacon butty since 1925. And those two there,' he nodded towards a brace of schoolgirls in dark green pinafores, 'they're my nieces – twins, doin' their homework.'

When I volunteered what I was up to, he smiled at me and squeezed my hand. 'Young lady like you should be at home,' he said. 'Gotta husband?'

'Left him in Venice.'

I am sure he didn't quite believe me. And I had never said the words before. But there they were. And that was that. Poor Old Dick.

There was a thrill at moving amongst the different tides of humanity who surfaced in any given twenty-four hours. The noiseless industrial workers seeped out early on, trailed by the cooks, the roadsweepers, the doormen, the laundresses, the newsmen, the milkmen, the undertakers, who without fuss went on their way, treading lightly so as not to wake up the rest of the world. Gentlemen arrived on the scene by eight o'clock, whistling, carrying their light briefcases and starched to the eyebrows. The speed limit for automobiles stood at 30 miles per hour. Off they went with their feminine passengers, slugging along the Brompton Road, depositing their charges outside Harrods. Now the trams and buses began to ooze with small children, housewives and secretaries.

Wherever I happened to be at around noon, I would seek out a bench in a park and pull out a sandwich from my satchel. A tranquil spot sprang up without fail; like the Garden of

Remembrance next to Marylebone Church, or St John's Square in Clerkenwell. A tightness knuckled down on my chest as I ate; I was never quite able to master the art of relaxing when there was so much work to be done. Like clouds that skitter across the sun, despite my baseline cheery disposition, my mood might slip from melancholic to benevolent to angelic and back again within the course of eighteen hours.

The mechanical walking took over my body by about six o'clock in the evening. That was when I could look down at my feet moving one in front of the other at quite a lick and know they had a will of their own. In the sweet summer months this was my favourite time. Birdsong mixed with children's voices, and if I was truly fortunate, with the scent of stocks and sweet peas. My biggest indulgence was to close my eyes for a minute and to keep walking with only my senses to guide me. In the winter months when the chill clung to my winter coat, my breathing slowed, my systems shut down as if in suspended animation and the foggy breath from my nostrils warmed my lips. The tissue-paper skin on my face felt as if it might tear if I smiled, and tears ran in the wind and sunshine. I could barely move my mummified toes, encased in wool and leather. Chilblains and chapped fingers were part of the job.

Make no mistake, there were things that I loved. Turning the key into my bedsitter after midnight and the kettle calling for my attention. Then the milky warm suds of Pears soap as I wallowed in the bath, rubbing the street out of my stockings. That first rush of air on leaving the house that pinched my nose and face and stole my breath.

If I had been a fan of cameras I would have wanted one there with me on that September morning when I clambered to the top of Primrose Hill as the sun rose. Below me I watched horses, steaming under the weight of their handsome riders, smartly ascend from Regent's Park Barracks.

They would not have known how significant they were to me – the people who threw an extra dollop of sugar into my porridge because they thought I needed feeding up – or Mr Freddie Baxter, the furrier from Mayfair who invited me to the theatre and offered to have someone else complete my journey if I might like to accompany him to Monte Carlo. The Norland nannies in Holland Park who ambled past and let me peek at their little charges and who giggled as if they had nothing other to worry about than the young men who took them every week to the pictures in Kensington. The gravelled faces and battered bodies of those who felt the pull and shove and strain of early morning market trading, who made me feel free and alive.

But for now I eased my stiff body between the sheets on my little wooden bed. Slowly the scenery in my mind ground to a halt. I did not count the streets completed or those I had left to draw. You see, I just had to keep going until I was finished, however long it took me.

'It is a far, far better thing that I do, than I have ever done; it is a far, far better rest that I go to than I have ever known,' I puffed before a canopy of sleep spread across my face. It was a rare night when my body, as leaden as a corpse buried at sea, did not list and sway down and down into the deepest depth of sleep.

CHAPTER TWENTY-TWO

From Abberley Mews to Zoffany Street

WHY?! WHY?! WHY CAN'T YOU EVER DO WHAT I TELL YOU? !!!
BAD ENOUGH WHEN YOU DON'T THINK! BUT WORSE WHEN
YOU DO! WHAT A DUNCE TO SUGGEST SO ABYSMAL AN
ALTERNATIVE! WHAT CUSTOMER'S GOING TO HAVE THE
NERVE TO ASK A SHOPKEEPER FOR THE FIRST AND LAST
LETTER OF THE ALPHABET! LUDICROUS! HE'D BE LAUGHED
OUT OF COURT. WHEREAS 'OK' IS ON EVERYBODY'S LIPS.
SYNONYMOUS WITH 'FINE' INFERRING EXCELLENCE. WITH-
OUT FAIL YOU'RE TO USE THE ENCLOSED COVER DESIGN I'VE
HAD ESPECIALLY DRAWN FOR YOU. AT MY PROMPTING THE
ARTIST HAS PLACED THE LETTERING – *The* OK *Street Atlas &*
Guide to London OVER AN OPEN TOWER BRIDGE, TO SYMBOLISE
THAT THE OK OPENS UP LONDON TO THE PURCHASER . . . SO
BURY YOUR MALAPROPISM, AND LET THIS BE THE LAST I EVER
HEAR OF *A-Z*!

The telegram must have stuck fast in her memory, for even
many years later, Phyllis could remember every spitting word of
it. Yet despite her father's ferocity, she flatly ignored his
instructions and went her own sweet way instead. And for once,
it would be the making not of Sandor Gross, but of his daughter.

Stubbornness, the Gross family trait, had, at last, grown strong
in Phyllis, like a thick weed that has pushed up through hard soil.

Even though Sandor may have toughed out twenty years in the mapping business, Phyllis knew he was completely wrong about her new map. Wrong about the name, and wrong about the design on the cover. Yet, however strongly she may have felt about resisting her father's orders, Phyllis was obviously uneasy about her first rebellion. *Unlike my mother,* she wrote in her notes, *I am neither married to my father, nor emotionally, mentally or financially dependent on him*.

What she had failed to recognise is that, like it or not, she would always be emotionally and mentally bound to her father. But Phyllis convinced herself that his forceful attempts to intrude on her career had less impact, because of the distance between them. Now her late mother's warning seemed pointless.

'Never work for that megalomaniac. He'll use you as a drudge and then destroy you. You'll end up a wreck like me. He's competitive in everything he says and does. Most men resent successful women, but that Hungarian father of yours – he's the worst of the lot.'

No one, Phyllis had thought fiercely to herself, cares about getting this map right as much as I do. So much so, that for over a year, her neighbours barely caught sight of Mrs Pearsall, while her friends had tried to entice her away – from what they weren't quite clear, 'some sort of street atlas, you say?' The smart white invitation to dine with Lord and Lady Ashfield (*to see your beautiful Pembrokeshire landscape hung*) the following Saturday, remained exactly where it was, alone on the mantelpiece, wilting at the edges.

Nothing wrong with smoked haddock and peas, Phyllis had thought about her alternative Saturday-night supper, although some lively conversation about art would have been preferable to that huge pile of paperwork.

How many times had she let her eyes fall on the canvases that were stacked, unclaimed against the walls? The grey, wizened face of Chelsea Old Church was hiding among them somewhere. It hadn't been an especially grand choice as her final painting before starting the *A-Z*. Indeed, Phyllis had decided its very ordinariness would distract her from the realisation that there would be no other mornings alone with her easel, standing in just one spot, captured by just one subject, for a long, long while.

The smell, that was what she craved so much now, the sweet smell of the oil paints, those clues to a new work and another life. The temptation to unwrap her palette was as cruel she believed, as it would be for Alfred to catch sight of an unopened bottle of bourbon and not reach for its warm comfort.

'But I am not a dabbler. I cannot start what I cannot finish. So you will all have to wait,' Phyllis said aloud.

Unfinished, half-chewed, whimsical projects that had simply not worked out did not exist in the Gross family, and the most despised characteristic of all – becoming bored – had never been an option.

Unlike her father and mother, it wasn't the prospect of a golden bank account, wardrobes stuffed with couture clothes or friends who knew the right people, that had enticed Phyllis to compile the *A-Z* map.

Phyllis had already marked her own life's path as empty. A brood of her own would not be travelling alongside her. There would be no little ones whose curly heads fought over their first poster paints and colouring pencils. There would be no birthday presents, no nursery teas, no waiting up for Father Christmas or *Just William* stories at bedtime. If maternal instincts had ever tugged at her sleeve, then by now, aged thirty, she had shooed them away. Warmth and affection from Phyllis would never be physical. Of course, as a good woman and a tremendously kind one, it could be found in her thoughtfulness. One memory that her nephew,

Jean-Pierre Gross, has of his Auntie Phyllis is after she kindly intervened when as a teenager, cycling along Hove sea-front, he had crashed into a parked car and tumbled over the roof, suffering a gash on his chin. Angry at the dent he had left, the driver insisted he sign a paper, confirming that he would pay for damages.

Phyllis rose to the occasion. She wrote the man a letter, outlining her nephew's good conduct and ended by saying, 'I'm not questioning his responsibility, but your humanity.'

But since she had banished her sentimental and emotional life along with her first husband, she was not the sort of person you would naturally confide in with a problem.

'Just get on with it,' she'd say. 'That's the ticket. On we go.'

With the humiliation of one failed and unconsummated marriage behind her, and at such a sensitive age, for she was neither fortunate enough to be a grand old lady, nor felt young enough to be whisked into marriage for a second time, she must have come to the conclusion that it was, as an institution, not suited to the Gross family.

For Phyllis, the stigma of divorce back then in 1936, apart from Wallis Simpson giving it a touch of glamour, made it unmentionable. To be a spinster did evoke more pity, but she certainly thought the freedom of being unattached was worth it. Small restrictions like an arm firmly coiled around her waist and nuisances such as the suffocating noise of someone else's breathing in the night or the splitting of grocery bills had bothered her in the past, and now were gone for good.

So what if there weren't any signs of a dinner service, or Irish linens to show for her eight-year marriage? From her wooden bed to the enamel mugs and rough blue towels from Woolworths, Phyllis had purchased everything in her bedsitter she could lay her eyes on. This is all me, Phyllis had thought when she had first unpacked her belongings.

Not since she had been a youngster, perhaps eight or nine, tearing around the grounds of The Firs with Tony, knowing that her beloved Mama was writing at her bureau, within skipping distance and there for the hugging, had Phyllis slept so deeply.

To outsiders, her carefree and nomadic life in Spain with Dick must have sounded enviably Bohemian. Yet it wasn't until she had stopped, right here in London, that Phyllis had noticed how wearing it had been and how even a sickening routine crept into a rootless life.

I can forget it all, she thought thankfully.

Forget how to befriend each new proprietor, charm every donkey-owner and chambermaid, acquaint herself with the temperature of the hot water and how many minutes it took to run a decent bath, to remember not to stub her toe on the unforgiving bedpost, to outsmart the rattling window-pane, to work out the coolest place in each room to take a siesta and how her senses had been immersed in the sharp odour of fly paper barely masked by wood polish – and both overpowered by garlic.

Now she could hang up her clothes and know that she would not be folding them into a trunk or bag the next day. Thank God! Her shoulders relaxed a little. Her wounds had almost, but not quite healed.

Pacing back and forth in the darkest pit of her memory, Phyllis was aware that she lacked two vital elements of self-esteem that ought to have been rounded up and handed over to her by her father. Respect and recognition. No matter how far she needed to search for the errant pair, no matter how long the journey, Phyllis was prepared to hunt them down.

What would Papa admire?

Vast canvases of her own fantasy paraded through her mind – gigantic ones with broad strokes lashing up strong, abstract forms, or surreal landscapes broken down into jigsaw-puzzle fragments. Yet she knew that no number of lively paintings or brilliant portraits could have prompted the praise from her father that she so longed to hear: 'Phyllis, what a wonderful imagination. What a good eye you have. My daughter is indeed an artist, you know. You must keep going, Phyllis – for painting is quite obviously your calling.'

In her own small way, Phyllis took on her father and walked straight into his own territory – map publishing. Confronting what surely was her biggest fear – failure – head on was particularly brave, considering that should she indeed fail at producing a map, she would be doing so at the very feet of the man she needed to impress most.

Strangest of all is that her suitability (like her father before her) for mapping was laughable. You only have to look at her exuberant brush-strokes and quivering line drawings to gauge the sheer speed and spontaneity with which she completed her work. See the fidget, the chatterbox, the wit and wonder how she wrenched her fabulous mind into a confined space, as small as one of the squares she had to draw. Precision, with the exception of her dead accurate eye when it came to painting from life, was not an attribute she either possessed or aspired to. Pinning herself down to the crushingly steady work of mapping must have been torture.

Her knowledge of how to actually produce a map was unbelievably vague, and her unmethodical mind carried her in such a roundabout way, that what ought to have been a complicated but logical process, came together in a totally haphazard way.

First, she corresponded with her father by letter in America: *I am beginning with the London County Council. For that, I have decided is the correct area to cover.*

You will have to buy a lot of 6″ Ordnance Sheets. I'd say about sixty or seventy.

Where does one get those?
Don't you know? Stanfords of course.

The staff at the OS counter at Stanfords had been suitably amused by the young lady who requested enough paper to stack twice as tall as she. 'Seventy-two, you say, miss?'

'Yes, please.'

'What will you be using them for?'

'Oh, just a map. A sort of street atlas. Of here – of London.'

'Which poor soul is going to be doing that then, miss?'

'Me.'

'Goodness gracious. Now there's a thing to keep you quiet.'

Like a person with the extraordinary surname that needs to be spelt out each time they give their personal details, or the person whose sports car has a particularly thrusting engine – after a while, Phyllis stopped counting the number of people who either rolled their eyes or tut-tutted with scepticism after she had revealed her map intentions. Wait and see, she thought. Just wait and see.

With the sheets carefully bound into taped rolls, Phyllis staggered on to the bus under the weight of her dangerous weapon. I am carrying the whole of London, she thought as she leant against the wall while she dragged the bundle up the stairs and through her front door.

Next she tracked down her father's top draughtsman, one Mr Fountain, to his top-floor flat in Maida Vale. Still heaving the seventy-two sheets about, she thought her two early morning bus-rides would end, as she would say, in triumph. With all her raw data collated, she had expected that as an experienced draughts-man, Mr Fountain could run up a map in next to no time. She would hand over the result of her 3000-mile journey: her twelve precious hardback notebooks, each one filled with small sketches of streets, their names and house numbers.

But disappointment awaited her.

When Mr Fountain finally opened the door to Phyllis, he turned out to be a tall man in his sixties, dressed in a smart brown suit, his face dour and his hair obviously dyed a flat ebony.

'I understand from my father that you are still keen to do some mapping work,' Phyllis said to Mr Fountain.

When there was no response forthcoming from his stony features, she persevered, 'I wondered if you would be at all interested in helping me. From what Papa tells me, you're exactly who I need to talk to. I'm going to do a map, you see – of London. They're so out of date now and I can't quite understand why anyone hasn't thought of it before. With the buses and trams and new streets and everything . . .'

'I see what you're getting at. So long as you understand I'm not used to dealing with amateurs. I'm a professional draughtsman. And I won't be doing any favours. I'll charge my normal rate.'

'Thank you. I'm delighted you've agreed.'

And with that, Phyllis grabbed and shook Mr Fountain's heavy hand. His gruffness she hoped was not on account of her being a woman, although to be employed by a female half his age, she realised, might have made him feel a little piqued. Confidence did not escape her, though. Next to her own dear father, whose temper was legendary among every printer in London, Mr Fountain would be sweetness itself.

As they stood there on the threshold, for he did not have the manners to invite her inside, he unrolled each sheet to check her purchase.

'You will need stick ink and tracing paper. Run along to Hunter Penrose in Farringdon Road. Then you will need to go to Norton & Gregory in Castle Street.'

Each map, he explained to Phyllis, needed to be reduced. The reduction bromides then had to be sun-copied and a dozen of each pulled on good white paper.

One thing Phyllis had learnt as a little girl was that to admit to her father – or to any other man including Dick for that matter – that you had absolutely no idea what they were taking great pains to explain to you, simply enraged them.

I can always ask somebody kind to help me, Phyllis thought as she wrote down his orders. I can't even ask him any questions I'm so confused.

At her first stop, Norton & Gregory, things began to slip into place as a junior assistant talked Phyllis through the process for sun-copies, which went something like this:

'The tracing original is put on to sensitised paper and then fastened around a hollow glass tube with a strip of canvas clipped around them. Next, a high-powered light descends inside the glass tube, casting an image on the sensitised paper. When the light is turned off, the canvas is unclipped, and the original and paper image are removed; the sensitised paper is put face down on to a canvas-backed jelly bed and rubbed by hand. The paper is then peeled off, printing ink is rolled on to the jelly bed image and copies are pulled on cartridge paper, by hand.'

Phyllis could hardly bear to watch the minute-by-minute process happening over and over again. She could not imagine ever acquiring such a skill, since it required a laboured precision. Magical, but slow. As the whirring smell of chemicals clogged her throat, the only way to escape was to imagine herself out in the street, in fresh sunlight, painting a juicy green tree and a gorgeous white Georgian house. Where will I be? she wondered. Ladbroke Square, perhaps, or Chepstow Villas.

After nearly an entire day, Phyllis lugged the sun-copies back to Maida Vale on the bus in the early evening rush-hour. Her spirits were high as she tap-tapped on Mr Fountain's front door, but she found that even with her first few tasks successfully completed, his humour did not seem to improve.

'Leave those with me and return in one hour,' he snapped. And with that he shut the door.

Sixty minutes later, Phyllis climbed the stairs again.

'Now you need to index these.'

'How?'

He pulled out an example. On each of the seventy-two sheets he had marked up 3⁹⁄₁₀-inch squares. Across the top and bottom margins he had run the letters A-N, and numbers 1-17 down both side margins.

'Off you go,' he said. 'And don't come back until you're done.'

At home, in my amateur fashion, Phyllis wrote, *I tried the impossible. Simultaneously to alphabetise the places (with their references) while listing them on writing paper. Until no longer able to squeeze new ones between each other, nor by littering the margins with arrows to where they belonged, I appealed for help.*

Help came in the form of her next-door neighbour. Too impatient and too proud to send a telegram to her father, she tentatively knocked on his door.

He was, by all accounts, first and foremost a Communist, so Phyllis revealed little about him – apart from the fact he had a brilliant mind and once gained notoriety for taking a group of unemployed men to lunch at The Ritz. Later on, he spent time in prison where his punishment for a variety of subversive activities was sewing mail bags.

'May I trouble you?' Phyllis asked him. 'I'm quite sure you must be wondering why I've been keeping such strange hours. Well, let me show you what I've been up to.'

She ushered him into her room where the evidence covered every spare patch of table, parquet floor and bed.

'My, what a pickle.'

She handed him the indexing draft for inspection. He frowned at the pages with Phyllis's writing scrawled like a rash over each one.

'I know. It looks a fright.'

'Before you even start on such an index, my dear child – I suppose you have checked all the new developments and plans, in case of any LCC changes?'

'Er . . . no.'

'Ah. Well, now you know what to do next.'

Indeed she did.

It was definitely her father's strict influence that made Phyllis, despite all her independence, happy to take instructions from a man, whereas Bella would have lashed out at any helpful suggestions and resorted to her own plan.

A few years before their marriage soured, when Sandor recognised that Bella had outgrown his admonishing phrases, he was lucky enough to have his own children to practise on:

'Do as I say, children!'

'No one is asking for your opinion.'

'How dare you question whether I am correct!'

Even now, Phyllis did not challenge her neighbour's thinking or even question if there was a better way of going about things. She just got on and did what he said.

The very next day, Phyllis set off just before 9 a.m. to visit all the Borough and County Surveyors within the London County Council. She did the same the next morning – and the next – until she had trotted in and out of every LCC building. Seven days it took to pin down every relevant piece of information she needed.

This was where her lifelong hatred of bureaucracy began. To gain access to what should have been quite straightforward, public information, she was forced to use her winning smile and lightest voice over and over again, to squeeze past minor pen-pushers, who looked at her askance when she requested access to any recent records of road developments for her new street atlas.

'Why would you be wanting to draw up a new map, when there is a perfectly good one available?'

'Does it not bother you that the map is over fifteen years old?'

'My, you have bitten off more than you can chew.'

Fortunately, most of them said, 'Good luck with your map – a new one is certainly well overdue.'

Ushered into their quiet offices, she was allowed to view the new Ordnance Survey maps, updated by hand. Developments, construction, new houses, road alterations, cropped up in every postcode.

In a world that had yet to experience the wonders of the photocopying machine, Phyllis scanned the lists; her eyes plucked out the new names and she adjusted her own landscape. By her own admission, she drew the scale, shapes and grids awry. Soon the scenery was filled in with the silent extras – the crucial but rarely acknowledged water and gas mains, fire hydrants and street lamps.

For the next three months, a complete rectangle dangled in Phyllis's head. Cut into tiny squares that made up a grid, it became a template for the real map, as the hundreds of streets she had jotted down swarmed around her consciousness in search of the right direction.

Top pressure concentration, Phyllis wrote in her notes, *lulled me into a false sense of security and a growing fascination with London's history implicit in its many names.*

The distraction of her imagination wandering off into the history of Farmer's Road, Hangman's Acre, Houndsditch, Terrapin Road, Fossil Road, White Bear Place, Paternoster Row and Charterhouse Square, where Carthusian monks were burnt at the stake during Henry VIII's prosecution, inevitably added days to an already gargantuan task.

One by one she printed the letters according to their position in the reference squares. Using a fine black pen, she executed each tiny word, the size of a thumbnail, with exacting neatness. Phyllis hummed aloud the first letter of every name as she spelt it out. Santos Road, Cromford Road, Mexfield Road, Galveston Road, Schubert Road, Manfred Road, St Stephen's Gardens, Cavalry Gardens, Kendal Place, Oakhill Road.

Ten names in one hour. Hypnotised by the mindless concentration, it was two weeks before she calculated that going at such a miserable speed, the map would take twenty-seven weeks to complete.

Let's run a bit faster.

Stepping up the pace, Phyllis took daily short-cuts and added up the figures in her head. Breakfast, lunch, dinner, bath and sleep = six hours. Mapping = eighteen hours. Laundry, correspondence and household chores became delegated to *Unimportant For Now* status. Windowsill geraniums grew listless. Unopened mail multiplied. Sundays turned into Mondays and weeks turned into months; shirts were swapped for sweaters, lightweight trousers swapped for corduroys. Who needs a hairbrush?

The kitchen clock ticked for no one. Birdsong chased the light and fog chased the dark. The larder shelves, overcrowded at first with tins of corned beef, smoked chicken, peas, beans, tapioca, pâté, Earl Grey tea, Stilton and fruitcake, gradually emptied.

Over the weeks that Phyllis took to separate the piles of streets into As, Bs, Cs . . . which she then subdivided into second, third, and fourth letter piles, the name *A-Z* flashed up in her brain. She could hear her mother sing the words. She could hear Tony asking for a copy in a shop. She could not quite hear her father asking for one. She pictured herself giving him a beautiful, first edition.

'Why, the *A-Z*! My first choice for a name, you know, Phyllis.' He smiles. He likes it.

And thus, she wrote, *did I become addicted to the* A-Z.

Phyllis gathered and shuffled a thousand blank postcards. Twenty-six shoe boxes donated by her neighbour became makeshift homes for each letter of the index. Paper-cuts crisscrossed her fingers, but just like the knots that spun together in her neck, she hardly noticed them as she spread the giant game of Patience that kept her mind locked until her eyes swam in darkness. Like a swimmer deep underwater, Phyllis became oblivious to every sound except the chatter of her own mind. She lost the strains of the accordion at the St Patrick's Day party held in the flat upstairs, the daily trundle of traffic in the streets outside and the scraping of chairs next door. When black spots darted into the skirting boards – that was the signal for her to stretch and yawn and tiptoe through the giant piles and crumple into bed. Sometimes she would dream that the wind had stolen into her room, had lifted the cards into a gentle whirlwind and tossed them up into the sky, never to be seen again.

Then, as quickly as it began, it was all over. Or so Phyllis thought.

Carefully packing up the sheets, she delivered them to Mr Fountain, who remained unimpressed by her marathon compilation.

'I've finished,' she announced, and handed him her index list.

He flicked through it and sniffed, 'Come back when you've written it out legibly. I cannot possibly read your scrawl. Look at the mistakes: D for O, C for G, P for R. Use serifs, too.'

'What are they?'

'Look it up.' And with that he shut the door on Phyllis.

Most of us would have sloped off at that point, spluttering with curses as months of hard work had been shredded before us in seconds. Yet there is never any mention in her writing of Phyllis actually getting cross. Of breaking down in tears of frustration out of sheer exhaustion.

'Never mind. What's the use in worrying? Don't fret, don't fret, don't fret,' she said aloud to herself as she went down the stairs, trying to calm her runaway heart.

All the tears in the Gross family had been allotted to Bella and all the shouting to Sandor. None had been left over for either Phyllis or Tony, and neither were inclined to ask for their share.

Instead of sulking, Phyllis found the nearest Post Office and sat in a corner for over five hours, rewriting each page of her index on a new A4 notepad with tiny, square letters, her right hand cramped with the pain of her efforts. Her second visit that day to Mr Fountain brought scarcely more joy, however.

'I need the index printed in 10 point and on good white paper.'

'Who will do that?'

'The City twenty-four-hour Service Trade Compositor.'

'Where are they?'

'Off Fleet Street, of course.'

It was ten o'clock at night before Phyllis had the new index ready.

'*Please, please, please,*' she chanted aloud on her final ascent to Mr Fountain's home.

'That's more like it, young lady,' he said approvingly.

Her project off-loaded, her head lighter than a fairy bubble, Phyllis hadn't realised she had walked home, taking the Edgware Road, then Park Lane, Grosvenor Place, Victoria Street and finally Artillery Row. She couldn't feel her feet and all she wanted to do was breathe and breathe and breathe in the fresh air she had deprived herself of for so long.

Once inside, she opened the sash windows and watered the geraniums. She pushed the French net curtains to one side and took in one last heave of breath before climbing, exhausted into bed.

That night, the wind did steal into her room and it lifted and twirled the cards into a gentle twister. Phyllis felt the breeze on her hair as the sounds of early morning traffic roused her. There was another sound, too – of rain pattering on cardboard.

NO!

Phyllis sat up and saw her raw data – the 'T' box – tip and spin and empty out of the window. She rushed over and looked out to see white cards free-falling in the rain. Some landed on car bonnets, some landed on the pavement (face down) or in the gutter, and one slipped on to the top of a bus.

Phyllis raced down two flights of stairs. *Stop at the lights. Stop at the lights. Please, bus, stop at the lights!*

Phyllis darted in front of the bus, paused at the traffic-lights. But it surged forward with the other vehicles and she found herself forced back on to the pavement. Like a refugee gathering rice bundles from a helicopter, she swept up armfuls of cards.

Breathlessly, she counted and recounted from *Tasso, Taunton* and *Templar* through to *Tower Hill* and *Tyler Close*. She could not sense that any had actually gone astray, except the one that escaped on the top of the bus. But she was determined to spot the mistake in time, *before* Mr Fountain's proof went to the printers.

CHAPTER TWENTY-THREE

Those Who Trespass Against Us

'A dirty Jew polluting our country. Every one of you with a drop of that iniquitous blood should be exterminated. What's more, I'll start the great purge now!'

This diatribe had been unleashed from a certain Mr Namier, a fat-bellied pig of a man, who was also a shop buyer, as he prodded the object of his fury – Phyllis who, at half his size, could only hold up a copy of her *A-Z* as protection.

A series of almighty crashes could be heard around the building as he gave one final shove, so her body bumped and thumped its way down the flight of stairs leading from his office to the door on to the street. He had snatched up her satchel and hurled a copy of the *A-Z* after her. Thud. Thud. Another copy of the *A-Z* bounced off her back.

'Get out!'

Burning with shock, Phyllis lay motionless and hunched at the bottom of the stairs, before her leather satchel was thrown on top of her with a final slap.

'Don't ever dare set foot in any of my shops again.'

After she had collected up the *A-Z* copies and disappeared into the street, Phyllis caught a flash of herself in the glass of a shop window. He could tell, she thought dazedly. He could tell by the hook of my nose, by the blackness of my hair, by the olive tone of my skin.

Phyllis had never stood face to face with a Mosleyite before.

247

The hair on her arms had prickled, some months earlier, when she had witnessed the Blackshirts march in formation through Whitechapel towards her crowd of anti-fascists. In their eyes flared blind hatred of such intensity that she knew it to be wrong. She remembered squeezing tighter and tighter the hands that were linked to hers, and shouting louder and louder the words that her neighbour, the day before, had invited her to chant: 'They shall not pass. They shall not pass. They shall not pass.'

The mounted police had charged at both sides. With the rest of the anti-fascist mob, Phyllis had fled, running until the sound of horses' hooves disappeared.

I was there as an anti-fascist, she thought. Not as a Jew. How naive. So now I must defend my heritage too – even if it is not my faith.

Before the stairs encounter, and before most Londoners had thought about eating breakfast, Phyllis had wedged twelve copies of the *A-Z* into her satchel and set off to sell, sell, sell, quite convinced that buyers of the large department stores would praise her ingenuity.

It wasn't smugness exactly, that allowed a smile to cross her face as she walked up Park Lane towards Selfridges, but the belief that London had been deprived of an up-to-date street map for far too long.

Fortunately, the personal hostility that Phyllis would come across, the simple rejection and ejection from most stores, did not so much as scratch at her heart. Her skin gleamed with the thickness of a rhinoceros hide. Thanks to Roedean and years of belittling from her father, she simply smiled and said, 'Thank you very much for your time.'

If anyone had challenged Phyllis and told her, 'My dear, that is *not* how one goes about business,' she would have laughed at them and asked, 'How else are you supposed to do it?'

Unbeknown to her, it was how Sandor and Bella had first sold their world maps. Like her mother before her, Phyllis assumed that her happy, winning self alone would persuade the buyers to purchase her wares. What did they see? Her accent was smart all right. Her raincoat and scarf were not new, but well-pressed. Shoes, polished but old-fashioned. Smile, handshake, gaze – firm. However, her innocent type of assertiveness disconcerted or irritated many of the male buyers. New to the trade and a lot to learn, most concluded. And who buys maps from a skinny young woman carrying her samples in a school satchel?

At Selfridges, on Oxford Street, one needed an appointment to see a buyer.

'Who are you from anyway?' she had been asked.

'I'm not. I'm Phyllis Pearsall. My father used to own Geographia.'

'We only deal with large companies.'

Hatchard's were more concerned with dispersing the crowds gathered to see Queen Mary.

'Not today,' she was told irritably. 'The Queen is here. One glance says it looks terribly amateur, miss. Did you draw it yourself?'

Phyllis turned her back on the sneer and made her way to Foyle's.

After half an hour of waiting, she was shown through to Mr Foyle's office.

'Please, Miss Pearsall, do sit down.'

Like an examiner studying a candidate's paper, he slowly thumbed his way through the pages in silence. Phyllis kept perfectly still. He sighed. He frowned. Finally, he passed judgement.

'May I give you a word of advice? The map trade does not like change. It has been undisturbed for years. We – or should I say they – will not let someone, an outsider like yourself, or anyone else for that matter, upset it.'

'Thank you, Mr Foyle, for your help.'

From Charing Cross Road, Phyllis walked east to Mr Larby's warehouse in the Old Bailey. It had been a tip-off from Mr Duncan, one of her father's former draughtsmen who had passed the advice to Mr Fountain.

'I've only got five minutes, gel.' He ran a grubby finger down the index and the ink smudged. 'Bleeding ink! And look at this, the last letter in the third column of the index, guillotined off. Get it right next time, gel, and we'll have a think about it. And don't go bothering me with your business, speak to my assistant Nancy.'

That night, as she soaked her bruises in the bath, Phyllis did not reflect on the spite she had run into without warning. From the most important sales directors, to the commissionaire at Bumpus on Oxford Street, who had confronted her with, 'Trade round the back, missy,' they had not seen her as anything more than a nuisance. Such was her belief in her map, that Phyllis could not even whistle up any scorn for the buyers' secretaries, who had not even opened the map or bothered to show it to their boss in the next office, because their stocky little calves, in their cheap little heels, were too tired to shift themselves.

Known names might have been too high an aim, she wrote later. *Yet faith in my wares intact, I combed the suburbs. Only to be perpetually turned down. Or even shooed out, as pitilessly as a gypsy.*

The second day would be better, Phyllis told herself. Her tactics were to move south. She dunked her head under the sudsy water and held her breath. But the second day was *not* better. Nor was her third. Or her fourth.

At Barker's on High Street Kensington, the woman buyer peered over her reading glasses to scan the cover. 'What does WC stand for in your address?'

'West City?'

'West Central. You appear not to know your own map. Why would I want to buy any? Good day to you, madam.'

At Simpkin Marshall's the buyer smirked at the light cover of the *A-Z*. 'Handled once, they will be soiled. It needs a redesign.'

Mr Toler of Toler Bros laughed at Phyllis and slapped the table. 'Well, I don't know. Whatever next? I will make you a promise. When the Great British public asks for a map of London, I will buy your *A-Z*.'

By now, Phyllis sensed the trail go cold north of the Thames, but even as the air began to chill, she had walked across Battersea Bridge, headed down Latchmere Road and across The Avenue on Clapham Common. Small bookstores and newsagents were her new targets.

The first person ever to buy an *A-Z* map would be one Mrs Naylor, a most unlikely candidate. A naval widow, she ran a newsagents on the corner of Clapham Common South and Cavendish Road.

Mrs Naylor was standing, arms folded, behind her counter, sucking hard on a liquorice sweet that had blackened her already frightening teeth. 'Can't you read?' She pushed her glasses up on her nose and pointed to a scruffy cardboard sign in the window that read NO HAWKERS NO CIRCULARS. 'And don't try to preach to me neither. My husband was lost at sea, so I know all about God.'

To her surprise, the young woman did not make a move to leave, but was clutching a book that she had pulled out of a satchel. That smile, Mrs Naylor thought afterwards, that smile of hers was ever so sad. I'm glad I helped her. She won't last a minute.

'I am so sorry to trouble you,' Phyllis said brightly. 'Would you be interested in purchasing an up-to-date street atlas of London?'

Mrs Naylor popped another sweet in her mouth, and sucked

noisily. As if the heavens had revealed a wounded saint, she let out a long, sympathetic noise.

'*Ahhhhhh* now. You can't read, can you? *Ahhhhh*. Never mind, ducks.' She thumped the cash-register drawer and raised the counter flap.

'Here you go, love, take a bob for one of your street atlases. Won't be able to sell it myself, but customers get all sorts of lost around the Common. Come out the back and have a spot of dinner and I'll set you wise about retailers.'

In the tight squeezed kitchen, Phyllis sat at a rickety table, while Mrs Naylor worked miracles with chump chops. The Players Capstan advert that hung above the mantelpiece picturing a smiling, white-bearded sailor; apparently it was the spitting image of her late husband.

Phyllis hardly touched her meat, potatoes or cabbage and did little better with the junket and cream pudding, as Mrs Naylor relayed the tragic tale of her heroic submariner who was lost in November 1917.

'Keep the white ensign flying without me, old girl,' he told me. The handkerchief she had been petting her nose with, disappeared up the sleeve of her blouse. 'Right. That's enough of that!' she said bracingly. 'Us ladies do all right, don't we? You are a clever miss – cleverer than I thought. But remember this. Never interrupt a man busy on a job, and never expect an order to be placed at the first call. Keep at it. Go back again and again. Why not have a go at wholesalers?'

The following day was a Friday. Not a good day for new business, but that would not have stopped Phyllis from putting on her navy-blue suit and walking along the Strand and behind the Aldwych to Portugal Street, towards the head office of W.H. Smith & Son.

Determined not to get a short, sharp shrift from the tradesman's entrance, her plan was to make her way undetected through the main door, and then ask to be shown straight in to Mr Smith.

Inside was a microcosm of the world, and staring up into the dissected three floors, her eyes blinked at the hundreds of employees, carrying files, books and briefcases, all walking and discussing what seemed to be urgent matters.

'My name is Phyllis Pearsall,' she told the porters. 'I have an important street atlas I'd like to offer Mr Smith.'

Weeding out tradespeople was obviously a speciality of the smart uniformed gentlemen on the reception desk. As if they were speaking to the Queen herself, they gently guided the young woman into a dark passageway and ran off a list of directions that quite evidently would take her in the direction of the trade and packing rooms. 'The Subscription Office, ma'am, is what you require.'

'Why, thank you so much, sir,' said Phyllis sweetly, as she allowed herself to be ushered into an echoing corridor, the dark door slamming behind her.

Past lifts, staircases, magazine binding rooms, hurrying men directed and redirected her. 'Keep going, keep going,' Phyllis muttered, trying to sense the direction she was coming from and going to – and then, as it always did, the door she had been searching for appeared.

She knocked. The door was locked. She read the faded sign: REPRESENTATIVES SEEN 9 AM TO 12 NOON.

It was a minute after midday. Just missed it. Better luck next time, Phyllis promised herself.

At 8 a.m. on the Monday morning, she had arrived too early, but by 8.30 a.m. the tiny, stuffy waiting room had filled up with sales representatives, gossipy-looking men who all seemed slick to the routine. They offered one another cigarettes, they winked, they laughed and they ignored the woman – a secretary, they had decided – standing in the corner.

'Mr Cruise will see the first of you!' a young office boy shouted out from behind a counter, and he ushered through a tall man with a bulging suitcase, who handed back his cigarette to a ginger-haired man.

'Next!'

'Next!'

By a quarter to twelve, Mr Cruise had seen nearly everyone. Phyllis realised that democracy was not in working order outside the Subscription Office.

She approached the office boy. 'Excuse me,' she ventured.

He whistled loudly, ignoring her. Then after he had checked the clock on the wall, he smiled and yanked down the blind. 'Beats me,' he shouted, 'what a woman is doing here anyway.'

For seven more days, Phyllis truly believed that if she arrived early and waited patiently in the queue, eventually Mr Cruise would see her. It is curious what will happen if a woman is squeezed into a packed room of men. Her skirts were far from short, her suit did not hint at cleavage and her flat lace-up shoes were hardly a come on, but still Phyllis found herself pestered, patted, and chatted up by men, some just passing time and some looking for a quick fix. Women with less experience might have run out, distressed by the pub saloon smoke and suggestive banter, but Phyllis was inured to her father salivating over young women and she had watched Dick's eyes slowly work up and down a girl before. There was no anger. This was what men do.

Resistance was easy for Phyllis, but her smart rebuttals left a nasty taste in their mouths. Groping might not have occurred had Phyllis worn her wedding ring, but groped she apparently was: *They hadn't seen women reps and just asked, starting to fondle one,*

whether I was beddable. I said I was too busy doing maps to be
beddable.

'I hear a woman is haunting the place.' A head had poked
around the corner of the office door. A tall man, with a tall man's
voice, spoke directly at Phyllis.

The smoky waiting room, empty of reps as the clock once
again had forged on to midday, had only one visitor left.
Memorising the index had seemed an efficient way of diverting
another day's disappointment, and off she had travelled as far as
Blackbird Yard, Black Boy Lane and Blackburne's Mews.
Surprised by the recognition, she rushed forward to shake the
hand of Mr Cruise.

'What can we do for you? Whose secretary are you?'

Phyllis pulled out a copy of the *A-Z*. 'These, all of these,' she
held open her satchel, 'they are by me. I know nothing about
publishing. I know it's bled. I have done my best to be accurate. I
compiled the information myself. I walked every street to do the
house numbers too, and you won't find that on any other map.'

Luckily, her keen outburst did not fluster Mr Cruise. 'Come
into my office. A lady representative? Most unusual, I must say.'

With genuine interest, he scanned page after page of the *A-Z*.
He turned it upside down. He closed it shut, with a snap. Slowly,
he opened his Subscription Order book, and carefully penned
what seemed to Phyllis to be a gargantuan order and then
presented it to her.

1250 *A-Z Atlas* @ 1/-

500 Standard Guides @ 6d

250 Printed on Premier paper @ 2/6d

50 Printed on Premier cloth @ 5/-

'Thank you, thank you, Mr Cruise!' If her head was light from
excitement at her first major success, it was also light with panic.

'Before you thank me, do you know our terms? The discount

for wholesale is 33.3 per cent. The order is on sale or return. Payment will be assessed at the end of the year. Our managers pay thirty days from invoice. Here is a list of WHS wholesalers, shops and bookstalls for you to call on.'

'Do you think they will sell?'

'If anybody thinks he knows what will sell, he doesn't know the trade.'

As Phyllis stepped out into the street, her mind had already run ahead with a plan. A hand barrow from her local pub, Henekey's, could be wheeled through the streets, carrying the copies, direct to Strand House. Time did not allow for celebration. The first 10,000 copies had cost £250 to publish and she calculated that even if they were sold at five pence each, it might take months to break even.

In the following weeks, Phyllis pushed herself physically hard, as it had never crossed her mind that anyone other than she might manoeuvre the heavy loads back and forth. She woke up earlier and earlier, sometimes four o'clock in the morning, to keep up with invoicing, packing and delivering in bundles of ten, as many copies as she could to the mainline stations of Paddington, King's Cross, Marylebone, Euston, Waterloo.

Panic never swirled around Phyllis, as she blocked it with action. Not even when stations telephoned with same-day repeat orders. Within seven days of receiving their initial batch of *A-Z* copies, Victoria station requested a delivery from Phyllis three times a week. 'Young lady, you have got a map on your hands. These are selling faster than I can put them on the shelves.'

Her coolness was quite unnerving. In later years, she would accept very little praise for her extraordinary effort. 'It was the map, dear', she would say. 'It sells itself. I had no control over it.'

It was still too soon to contact her father. Phyllis restrained herself from telling him until her next mission had been secured.

Mr Prestcott, an energised American with rolled-up shirt-sleeves, met her at F.W. Woolworth & Co Ltd in Bond Street House.

'They say this *A-Z* is already out there. Now I'm not keen, honey,' he told Phyllis, as he flicked the map to make a whizzing noise over and over again, 'I'm not at all keen. But Muriel, my secretary, tells me she can find her mews in it – what's it now, Muriel? St George's?'

Muriel appeared from behind a filing cabinet. 'Yes, Mr Prestcott.' She smiled at Phyllis, snatched the book from her boss and with the tip of a very red-nailed finger, she pointed out her house in Primrose Hill. 'You see. There it is!'

'So there you go. Muriel's happy, so I guess I should be happy. I'm giving you our usual trial order of six dozen for each of our three main stores, which will turn into all our London stores if the public go crazy over them, but I'm not holding my breath, little lady.'

CHAPTER TWENTY-FOUR

Drawn to Make Maps: The Motives of Map-makers

Make no mistake, Phyllis Pearsall was no Luddite who hung on to the old-fashioned tracing paper and ink rituals of a bygone era. To keep their hard-fought place as one of the largest independent map-publishing companies in the UK, Phyllis realised during the 1980s that heavy investment in technology was essential. Computers would not be allowed to disrupt the sociable office atmosphere, but nevertheless she embraced the introduction of expensive software systems and was impressed by the speed at which they reorganised her company.

The greatest thrill for Phyllis was to see how computers removed the chore of alphabetising hundreds and thousands of streets. Until 1991, each street name or village required a record card, describing its exact location on the map, the county and postcode. These would then be alphabetised by hand, before being input on a page format for inclusion in either a book or on the reverse of the sheet map. In 1996, The Geographers' A-Z Map Company Limited produced its first electronic street map of London and the M25 on CD-ROM.

The not so bright local girls, who had spent twenty-six years flapping and folding the hard map covers and concertina boxing the map sheets, would eventually be replaced by a £40,000 machine. Today, 95 per cent of company production is undertaken digitally, and revisions to existing maps are no longer done by hand, but scanned and manipulated in Raster format. This is astonishing, when you remember that the glory days of mapping were less than sixty years ago. Back then, the mapping process could take weeks, as several technical staff worked on a drawing, before the sheets were stuck together with cow gum, sent to the printers and bound with traditional stitching. It was a time when a task that took hundreds of hours to complete was appreciated for its skilled perfection, whereas now we scoff at such laborious methods which prevent instant availability.

Even then, printing had spread its talents; maps were no longer sent out to one firm only. Some specialised in monotone printing, others preferred their presses to use the four- or six-way colour process, when each one would be printed over the next – yellow, red, blue, green, brown, black. Up to four hours could be spent for 'make-ready' when the ink was put into the print ducts, matching the colour to the copy and getting the register as good as possible. Wash-up was even more crucial. Each press had to be spotlessly cleaned for at least another two hours, or else a run could be ruined if, say, traces of yellow were left in the press when red was printed.

The estimates given to Phyllis varied from firm to firm. According to Phyllis, some, such as Gordon & Kerensky, or Greycaines & Weiners, nudged costs higher and higher, knowing that a woman – and an inexperienced businesswoman at that – was less likely to challenge their expertise.

When they pulled out their printers' rule and claimed there were too many windows or columns to a page, Phyllis was made to see how an area would have to spill over on to a new page. More pages increased the size of the print-run dramatically, and immediately elevated the cost. However, gentlemen were still in abundance in North Acton, at Lowe & Brydone, where Mr Williams considered Phyllis a long-term customer, teaching her rather than trying to blind her with science and fiddle her bill. Pin binding, he advised her, was cheaper than stitched binding; what's more, she should ignore litho printing and instead stick with the Letterpress method, which The Geographers' A-Z Map Company still use today. Now, because there are over 250 titles, ranging from sheet maps and atlases in black and white or full colour, to large-scale street plans of towns and cities, and small-scale road maps of the whole country, several private contractors are used, each specialising in different types of print such as sheet-fed, small-format black and white, large-format four colour, web-fed black and white, and web-fed four colour.

At Lowe & Brydone, they hinted to Phyllis that it would be prudent if stereos of each page were kept. A stereo is a papier-mâché mould taken of each page when it is clamped by 'furniture' – pieces of wood or metal that are fitted around the type and into blank spaces to keep the page firm. A charge, they told Phyllis, would be made for leaving the metal standing, but then if future alterations on the map were needed, the reprint would not look uneven, as the presses would not have been repeatedly used.

Paper provided by the printers had an extra handling charge, as Phyllis discovered to her cost. With 15,000 sheets to a run, tonnes rather than reams of paper were required. But she would only ever make an expensive mistake once. Was it cheaper to buy direct from a supplier? Who was the best in the business? Mr Brown of John Dickinson. Croxley white, from Croxley Mills, would be Mr Brown's choice of paper, and a finer, more expensive thin-scrim (loose woven cotton, with forty threads to the inch) for the cloth-lined editions. He delivered promptly to the printers, allowing the paper sufficient time to be stacked, hung and acclimatised to the temperature and humidity. The printer's nightmare was paper that shrank, or stretched before the job was done, as they would need to repeat the order – free of charge.

After the phone call from Lowe & Brydone telling her that the galley proofs were ready, Phyllis followed her usual routine; she took the Central Line to their offices in Acton, where she would sit for hours and hours, correcting the proofs. That is where the professional proofreader had queried the 'T' index.

'Is Trafalgar Square left out deliberately?'

As with all trades, each area of speciality reserved a healthy disrespect for the other. The draughtsmen sniffed at the sometimes shoddy efforts of the printers and only gave them a sun-copy to test out the accuracy of their presses, the printers bemoaned the quality of the paper after the client had sifted through estimates for each one and selected the cheapest and most efficient contractor.

In the early days of the *A-Z*, after World War Two, Phyllis took on seven good draughtsmen: Wally Cooper, Dan O'Shea, Jimmy Mayo, Ernie Sheed, Cliff Brown, Den Walker and Ron Davey.

This was the era when an apprenticeship was not a half-hearted stab at keeping school-leavers off the streets. Five hard years the apprenticeship lasted, so those boys who had left school at fifteen and stuck to the daily practice of lettering had already proved themselves steady workers by the age of twenty-one. They would be able to letter ten street-names in an hour, in any style, drawn with a 290-gillets nib. Did they work too slowly for mistakes? No. If the wrong letter was drawn, it was carefully scratched out with a sharp scalpel knife, so as not to tear the paper.

Many found their hands were not steady enough, that their eyes ached too much or, having been demobbed, felt confined by a deskbound job so they dropped out. By then, the drawing office was kept busy with updating the *London A-Z*, while finishing work on the Leeds and Birmingham ones too. Those who succeeded, according to Fred Bond, a draughtsman who joined the firm in 1950 at the age of eighteen, knew they were like gold-dust, and were rather pleased with their wage of sixty-two pence a week.

It took a special sort of brain to scrunch up the top half of the body day in, day out, to focus a beacon of energy into a pinpoint of concentration and depict an inch of a city or town, on a window-pane-sized drawing board. Draughtsmen are a breed who live in their heads. Unlike Phyllis, those who produced the *A-Z* maps were not fuelled by words or speech, but were content to perch like empty, angular carcasses on high pine stools, until lunch, or a friend persuaded them to join in with a tea-break game of whist in the club room.

Many say it is a science, but old-fashioned cartography has the feel of an ancient craft. You can tell this from the dry workshop smell of fine crisp script and the rustle of tracing paper. A blind person would derive as much sensual pleasure from the map-maker's surroundings as a sighted one. Reams and reams of woody-smelling parchment, stacked without a breath of room between them, slightly rougher to touch, and more matt on one side than the other. How heavy and stable a ream feels, compared to a single, fragile sheet with its sharp edges that can slice into thick-skinned fingers. In the air, a blind person could trace the distinctive iron scent of pencils, sharp and slatey, and the vinegary smell of inks.

To the right of the drawing board, lined up neatly in their place as the draughtsman would expect to find them – for draughts-men, like surgeons, rely on the ordered precision of their instruments – are compasses, pin-thin black ink pens, brushes, erasers, rulers and set squares. The severe edges and blades of the tools are sharp, and bring back the memories of geometry lessons. That is until the chubby pots appear, gobbling up coloured pencils, paint-brushes and pens, which thankfully take the map-makers from the coldness of the technical world into the reassuring domain of artists and craftsmen.

CHAPTER TWENTY-FIVE

There's More to Lose than Getting Lost

Through a crowded street, Phyllis chased a man. Sometimes he looked back and she caught sight of her father shouting, and sometimes he would stop and slowly twist his face towards her, revealing the dry features of Mr Cruise. Just before waking up, Phyllis would feel a rise of panic as the man ran ahead, dropping copies of the *A-Z*, one at a time, and as she bent down to pick them up, she found their pages blank and the cover muddied and ruined.

In her sleep, Phyllis could never catch up with the man, and when she awoke, was confused as to whether her legs ached from running in her sleep or from the strain of the day before. Fortunately, the anxiety that tried to smother her at night was kept at bay during the day by constant activity. At speed, Phyllis navigated every twist and turn that each hour, day and week would bring to her new enterprise. The smart navy suit and corporate smile were swapped for a rough pair of cotton trousers and a light shirt. She did not need a watch to know that it took exactly twenty-one minutes to wheel the barrow, fully-loaded with copies of the *A-Z*, from Paddington to Euston, and another eighteen to King's Cross.

In the same day that stockpiles of *A-Z*s grew up the walls of her bedsitter, so too would they shrink within hours. Selfridges and

Harrods had heard about the atlas, and told their buyers to sign her up. Sales of the *A-Z* soared in such a way that it made Phyllis laugh with astonishment, but what was *not* funny was the challenge of actually getting the maps out there to the customer. Money could not stretch to a delivery boy, so from morning to night, unbeknown to them, the stores relied on Phyllis, wheeling copies around London on foot.

Efficiency did not extend to the drudgery of paperwork. The concentration that Phyllis had poured on to the indexing had now all leaked away, and she dreaded facing up to the monotony of form-filling. Stacks of order forms lay in a huddle under the tea pot, and on the kitchen table, until the secretary at Woolworths summoned Phyllis for a meeting.

'Order forms!' she barked. 'You *must* get the hang of these, Mrs Pearsall, or else you will go broke. First, get our printer to do labels for each of our London stores. You may send us invoices for his work. Then you will send us a written receipt for each order as soon as you get it. If you do not follow the rules, we can no longer buy from you. Good *day*, Mrs Pearsall!'

As the rest of her building lay asleep in their beds, Phyllis drank endless cups of tea to fuel her battle with basic accounting that would drag on until two or three in the morning. While pencilling columns in a sixpenny cash book from Woolworths that read MONEY IN and MONEY OUT, figures and pounds, shillings and pence were pushing her beloved painting further out of reach.

'Be patient,' she told herself.

Profit and Loss, Mrs Naylor had warned her, were the two most crucial elements to keep a watch on. 'Do not let your Loss overtake your Profit. Do not borrow a penny, not from anyone.' Phyllis had paid for the printing, publishing, packing and expenses out of her own savings. Personal spending had dwindled to a meagre diet of bread, milk, jam, fresh salmon and potatoes. But to take a salary? It had honestly never occurred to her.

The humming background noise that had spurred her on as she heaved packed bundles downstairs, into filthy goods lifts, dusty warehouses and newsagents, was the urgent reminder that her father would be arriving in London in less than two weeks' time.

If she was expecting praise from Sandor, then Phyllis was a fool. In New York, his own newly established mapping company was expanding to nourish his greed. Why, wondered Sandor, could his own daughter not work for him in America? As with his wife, he would have had no intention of paying her. How much harder it was, he had discovered, to keep an eye on his daughter at this great distance. No one knew the trade like he did, and for all he could tell, Phyllis could be bringing his name into disrepute, although the name of Gross had long been forgotten by the mapping fraternity.

Whether he was loath to admit to her talent, or was blind to it, as Sandor set sail on the *Mauretania* from New York, he already had plans to buy her business. The memory of his bankruptcy would not be shaken off, and no matter how much the Americans warmed to his quick buck success, Britain was where he longed to be accepted back into the business world.

On his arrival, the warm hugs and proud cries of, 'Let me look at you!' – greetings from a father who had been absent for seven years, never happened. Seeing his tousle-haired daughter waving, smiling and holding out her offering of what he sensed would be a disaster of a map, such niceties became irrelevant, as his temper slid out from beneath him.

The A-Z Street Atlas of London. Produced under the direction of Alexander Gross FRGS.

'Look at these pages, bled!' he ranted, outraged. 'Look at these outlays! You will be the ruin of me. How *dare* you conduct business from a tawdry bedsitter. I'm a member of the Royal Geographical Society – what are you trying to do to my reputation?'

Whether Phyllis was being sincere when she agreed with him is unlikely, but agree she did.

'I am so sorry, Papa. You are right. It's been fun, but I am no good at business. Back to painting for me.'

Year after year of doing wrong (according to her father) and saying the wrong thing (according to her father) had inoculated Phyllis against the rejection and scorn conveyed in Sandor's wrath. Was she hurt? No. As she saw it, her best effort was simply not good enough. But her sweet calm voice caught Sandor out. Frightened him. Who else would secure his name in London? Who else would follow his advice, orders and care so little for financial reward?

'Wait,' he said hastily. 'You must rent an office. I will found the company for you. The Geographer's Map Company – how about I give you half? You are too airy-fairy to run it on your own. It needs a man – I'll bring Tony in. Let's see if you can put all your mischief right.'

True to his word, within two days Sandor had secured two offices for £1 a week, above a café in Napier House, 24–27 High Holborn. It had, Sandor revealed to his daughter, all the modern conveniences: central heating, telephones, a caretaker, a lift and lavatories. He hired the voluptuous Miss Hemelryk as secretary, the equally beguiling Miss Fox as filing clerk, purchased two desks, four chairs, a Remington typewriter and a filing cabinet. The most useful addition to the *A-Z* team was one seventeen-year-old delivery boy, Gordon Lester, whose gangly frame contained enough energy to distribute packs of *A-Z* maps all over London from morning to night.

'You are here at the beginning,' Sandor declared to them on their first day, his arms wafting across the newly painted office, 'at the start of something great. Work hard, for your reward will be employment with the most excellent map publishers in the world.'

The staff looked at their feet. How, they wondered, could a two-room amateur outfit go anywhere? They were small fry in a city of big fishes. All the enthusiasm in the world could not make up for a thin pay packet every Friday, and within a year, Miss Fox would tire of the cramped office and be lured away to the more frivolous world of lingerie at the department store, Gamages.

'Who is paying for this, Papa?'

'You are. Efficiency is bound to increase turnover.'

Of course, Sandor could never actually be gracious enough to tell his daughter that he was abandoning his half-share of the company and that she could do with it now as she pleased, but Phyllis knew that restoring his pride rested on her coaxing the business into life. Only truly dedicated hard work, she believed, could bring success and without panicking about the enormous task ahead of her, Phyllis plunged her heart, soul, time and money into the uncharted territory of *A-Z* mapping.

Secretly, she must have felt pleased that once again, her mind, always quick to turn away from emotional confrontation, had been genuinely diverted.

Within another twenty-four hours, Sandor had left for New York, his mission completed. What really irked him was that his son could barely raise a smile at the offer of running a family business.

'I'm an artist – what has this got to do with me? Count me out, Papa.'

Instead, Sandor had left his silly daughter in charge. Keen but incompetent, albeit solvent at the moment, he believed it would only be a matter of weeks before she disgraced herself and he would have to step in.

The disgrace never came. In sole charge of four members of staff, including a draughtsman, Phyllis no longer needed to steam through the streets with deliveries. Instead, she used the time to manage the office, to get to grips with the accounting, the selling and updating the index.

A more experienced entrepreneur would have fretted about the state of finances, which ran (as Sandor had done once too often) close to the edge. As far as Phyllis was concerned, there was either Solvent or Bankrupt, and every weekday she would arrive long before the café below the office had opened its doors for the first fry-up, and would stay at her desk until ten or eleven o'clock at night, to ensure her company remained the former.

Was she lonely? Walking away from her friends the year before had not proved as painful as she'd expected. Side-lined and side-tracked, their presence became irrelevant. A man, or relationship with a man had become unthinkable, unwork' *Whatever would I want one for?* she thought. She would make the mistake again of relying on another pers(happiness – especially not a man.

In a strange way, Phyllis found flirting with the wo business quite exciting. The challenge of being a single wo trying to be taken seriously by difficult men had not dissuaded from moving onwards. After all, some men were charming had given her more than her money's worth of free advice. ' initial test of mapping London in her memory had gone lil dream, printing disasters had been averted and now her l A-Z hobby had stepped up a gear into a genuine full-occupation.

Her beloved painting was still squashed away at the bacl

mind. Creative release would burst free at weekends, when rather than catch up on sleep, Phyllis would take the first train to the Borders of Scotland to paint in solitude, or stay in London, painting the river, or go down to Hove to paint the sea. Holidays she considered an unaffordable luxury until ten years later, when she would be forced to take a long physical and mental break.

Diligence can only make up for so much, and with no one to advise her, mistakes were inevitable. 'Meet your problems head on,' Bella had always declared, before hurling herself into an argument with her husband. The first serious mistake to touch her collar was the Inland Revenue waving a red, Final Demand.

For months, Phyllis had persuaded herself that the long, tedious forms might wait, so she went, in person, as Bella would have also chosen to do, to plead for assistance.

'If you do not understand the forms and you do not understand the rules, then we suggest, Mrs Pearsall, that you make use of a good accountant.'

'How does one go about that, sir?'

'How does one conduct a business, madam?'

His rudeness prompted the memory of one of her wealthier, Hyde Park clients, Amy Binder, who had talked about her husband, BH, as she sat for her portrait. He was a self-made man, she had proudly declared, rising from a Nottingham railway booking clerk, to a partner of the chartered accountants Binder Hamlyn & Co. in the City.

There was her accountant. But even an accountant could not save her from the ignorance that a copy of the *A-Z* had to be donated to the British Museum and other libraries, or that the Ordnance Survey were owed substantial royalties.

I am not taking a salary, she wrote in her next letter to her father, *until I am certain that every aspect of the finances has been taken into account.*

270

As her appetite for money was poor, the financial burden that she single-handedly carried did not stop her from sleeping at night. But the human burden did. In an interview with Anthea Hall for the *Sunday Telegraph* in September 1986, she recalled: *'Very early on, and I had been responsible for the index, a doctor wrote to me saying that one of his patients had died because of a mistake in our* London A-Z. *I hadn't the courage to look it up for ten whole days. When I did, I found it was his error, not mine. There were several streets with the same name and different postal districts. We make it clear to everyone who works in the company that lives depend on us.'*

Before the end of 1936, Phyllis was called to task again, with a serious warning from her father: *'Have you seen King Edward with his fancy woman? Magazines here have photographed them on a cruise, in the Adriatic. I know that look. He is not giving up this woman for anyone, crown or no crown. Stand by with a Coronation route.'*

When on 11 December 1936, King Edward VIII abdicated, the map for the Coronation of his brother, George VI, had been in preparation for over a month and required a further three months to complete. Two print-runs of 20,000 maps were delivered to newsagents and stationers all over London in May 1937. At 6d each, the maps sold out in two days and the profit was quickly spent on the salary of the first *A-Z* sales representative, an ex-vicar by the name of Mr Norton.

On the Warpath

War is inevitable. What are you going to do about it? Have you prepared a map of Europe for the Daily Telegraph? *Why do I always have to explain the self-evident? Too much painting, I presume.*

The short letter from her father in July 1939 had been opened and read, then left face down on the kitchen table. The anger in his five-day-old words could not seep into Phyllis's mind and twist themselves into a worry. It was a Saturday after all, she thought to herself, and anyway, Lady Ilchester was expecting her early that morning, to begin a painting of Holland House, in Holland Park. The war could wait.

Now that business matters were running more smoothly, Phyllis treated herself to a lengthy painting session every week-end. It was the perfect antidote to her other life. Anxieties accumulated during the week were rubbed away by two whole days devoted to painting whatever she fancied. The Saturday before, she had travelled to Tenby Bay in Wales and painted the lifeboat slip; the one before that, she had spent working on a water-colour commission of the Ministry of Transport in Whitehall.

Now in the cool morning light, as she became absorbed in mixing a russet colour for the red-bricked Tudor façade, a feeling of foreboding wove its way into her head. The war, it seemed, would *not* wait.

Stocks of the *A-Z* had recently run quite low and once, while up in Pembrokeshire, where she was painting a view of Saundersfoot bay, Phyllis had felt so uneasy about supplies that she had sent a telegram to Miss Hemelryk (who had taken on the additional position of part-time Major with the Terriers – the British Army's Territorial and Volunteer Reserve): A-Z LOW. REPRINT TEN THOUSAND.

The jitters had shaken Phyllis quite late on. For the past year, ever since Neville Chamberlain had delivered his nervous 'Peace in our Time' speech, the government had criss-crossed the capital with air-defence plans and built air-raid shelters.

What a shame, Phyllis had brooded, after an unproductive meeting with a Ministry of Defence official, that they think my air-raid shelter map of London too risky. It had been her own idea, to distribute thousands of them as a free public service to offices and homes. Instead, after a cup of weak tea and an hour kept waiting, she was informed that despite being a map publisher, she would not be party to any classified information.

'I suggest you keep your eyes above ground,' she was told. 'What is more, Mrs Pearsall, in the event of war, a defence regulation would prohibit the sale of maps on or over one inch to a mile which is, I understand, the exact scale of your *A-Z*.'

Her painting of Holland House had somehow built itself on the canvas, while Phyllis had been deep in thought. She was interrupted by the sound of Lady Ilchester's voice.

'My dear, you have not eaten all day,' said her hostess, suddenly walking into her vision, carrying a plate of cheese and biscuits. 'Do you realise it is late afternoon? Please, dear, don't feel you have to finish today.'

Time, from then on sprang in distorted leaps and bounds. No one could have foreseen that over the next six years, Phyllis would produce eight perfectly timed war maps that sold out each time. Of course, there was competition from other publishers, such as

Sandor's former firm Geographia, which had been bought for less than half a crown by his competitors, but like a blinkered race horse, Phyllis did not see anything except the finishing line.

The newspapers had not yet printed reports that Germans were massing on the Polish frontiers, and it was not until 3 September that Britain declared war on Germany. However, as Phyllis walked home to Horseferry Road via Kensington High Street, Sloane Street and down past Victoria, a strange sort of anticipation fizzed through everyone she passed, as if something as destructive as a war might actually spark up their daily routine.

The minute Phyllis shut the door of the flat behind her, she telephoned Mr Fountain. 'I'm going to buy a Stiehelers' *Hand Atlas* and send you the relevant pages,' she announced. 'We urgently need to do a map of Europe. On it we must include the autobahns, the railways, and both the civil and Luftwaffe aerodromes.'

His melancholy voice could not even raise itself in a time of crisis. 'You'd better get the information to me fast. You are just like your father, Mrs Pearsall – thinking I can do this in no time. Well, I can't. So you will have to wait.'

What Phyllis did not know was that Mr Fountain too had a very bad feeling. So bad, that he worked until dawn for several weeks, in order to draw up an additional map, that of the Western Front, highlighting the Maginot and Siegfried Lines, with semi-underground forts and anti-tank defences.

Sandor was right. The then *Daily Telegraph* editor, one Mr Pulvermacher, invited Phyllis to his Fleet Street office as soon as she had asked his secretary for an appointment.

'Let me see your map of Europe, Mrs Pearsall. Unroll it, if you will.'

A tall man in a black suit, Pulvermacher held the map up to the sunlight at his window and scanned the lines back and forth.

'Let me know when you're ready with a dummy – paper, cover paper, map folded and tipped in. Give me a quote for runs of 100,000, 250,000, 500,000 and 1,000,000. Now you must excuse me . . .'

As Phyllis took the usual route home past Whitehall, her feet trod a little quicker when her eye caught the sickening additions of sandbags, barbed wire and sentries.

To occupy her mind as the dummy for Europe was put together, Phyllis spent hours sewing black serge linings into curtains for the office and her bedsitter. I'm too near the river, she thought as she hung the heavy drapes in her bedsitter. I must move. Then she saw to it that every window and glass door was stuck with strips of brown tape to prevent glass splinters, should bombs go off.

Exactly one week later, Phyllis was shown back into Mr Pulvermacher's office, holding the new map.

'As you will see,' said Mr Pulvermacher, his face unsmiling, 'I already have a map in front of me. It has been drawn by Geographia, your father's old firm. It was already under way, you see. We could not let you cream off the market, nor could we publish without your additional information. I'm terribly sorry. I'm afraid this map will be on sale tomorrow.'

'No, no,' said Phyllis, smiling as she always did at painful moments. 'It's my fault, I'm the sucker.'

Without pausing to waste her time on anger or disappointment, she moved on, her next stop *The Times*, who turned her away, followed by the *Daily Express*. Here she was told: 'We don't believe it will come to war, Mrs Pearsall.'

Finally dispirited, Phyllis trailed over to Mr Fountain. 'All your hard work has gone to waste,' she reported miserably. 'Nobody wants it. I've been a terrible fool.'

For the first time ever, the morose fellow actually smiled at his employer. 'I've done *my* job,' he said. 'Now you do yours. Go and sell them *this*.'

Stubbing out his cigarette, he unrolled on his drawing board a magnificent, detailed map of the Western Front.

This time, the editor of the *Daily Telegraph* could not print her map fast enough, and gave it a half back page in the Saturday edition.

The *Daily Express* agreed to see Phyllis on the afternoon of Friday, 1 September. Out of the whole of Fleet Street, their building was the only one not to be bolstered by sandbags and tape. 'We're not jitterbugs here,' the editor said, showing Phyllis to a chair. No sooner had he put on his spectacles to examine the Western Front map than voices gathered in the corridor outside. A news editor burst in without knocking.

'Hitler's invaded Poland!'

'Sandbags!' shrieked the editor. 'Get me rolls of sticky tape. Our policy's changed to war! War, everybody! *War*!'

Phyllis did not warm to his business style. How could she under such conditions?

Apparently unnoticed, she slipped away.

On Sunday, 3 September, the afternoon was bright and sunny. The day before, Phyllis had removed the invaluable map originals and the *A-Z* index stereos from their safe-deposit box in the Holborn branch of the Midland Bank. This was a timely act, since in the winter of 1941, the bank took a direct hit from a bomb, and the *A-Z* originals would have smouldered in the rubble.

As Britain declared war on Germany, Phyllis was being driven in an open-top sports car to a friend's house in Peasmarsh, Sussex. There she carefully packed her precious cargo into a steel-lined safe built under the garage before returning to London.

'I do wish you would move out of the centre, Phyllis,' another friend, Joan Walker-Smith, had said to her on the telephone that morning. The two had been at Roedean together. 'Why don't you come and stay with me here, while my husband is away with his regiment? You know how I would love the company.'

Lonely air-raid sirens wailed as if they would never stop, when Phyllis arrived back in Town. It was past midnight, and the empty black streets seemed to shut her out. Suddenly the thought of staying with Joan in Golders Green seemed the most comforting prospect imaginable. Like so many others during the war, Phyllis made instant decisions, for there was no time to analyse things and mull them over, although like everyone else she realised that one wrong move, in any direction, could cost her her life. Without stopping for a break, by candlelight, she packed the furniture from her bedsitter into a taxi and then unloaded it in her office, before heading off to Golders Green, carrying one small suitcase and a paper bag stuffed with tea, potted ham and flour.

In her diary, on 27 September she wrote: *Today Poland's resistance collapsed. A sorry day. My stomach turns with guilt, knowing that our map sales of the Western Front have run away with themselves. I am making money out of slaughter.*

Pandemonium, from six o'clock in the morning until midnight, by wire, by telephone and by mail, the orders and re-orders flood in. Time is playing tricks again. I need more hours. My hands know the routine of invoice, pack and label. I'm a factory girl! Lester delivers from dawn until dusk, never without a cheery whistle. His mother makes us both corned beef sandwiches and once the sirens start, we listen to big band music on my wireless, as we sort out the deliveries for the next day. Did I ever ballroom dance? No, but somehow such a frivolous thing now seems the most beautiful thing in the world. My atlas is still bedtime reading by candlelight. Painting could not be further from my thoughts. I dream of maps. I dream of Hitler's armies marching on and on. But I cannot bring myself to order a map of Great Britain, for fear that it will bring Hitler closer to an invasion.

On dark winter nights as a student in Paris, Phyllis revealed in her memoirs that she had often huddled against the radiators in the Bibliothèque Saint Geneviève and read the German High Command apologias for losing the First World War. Now she retrieved the information; the fault did not lie with the Schlieffen Plan, but the Germans believed their circle of attack began too far south and ought to have begun in the countries north of Belgium.

Could Hitler's moves be anticipated? Using the sharp instinct inherited from her father, plus her own historical knowledge, Phyllis instructed Mr Fountain to produce large-scale maps of Scandinavia, The Low Countries and Northern France. However fast he worked, though, Mr Fountain could not keep up with the next burst of developments, as Italy almost immediately declared war against the Western Allies, and twelve days later on 22 June, France signed an armistice with Hitler. Then came a telephone call from Mr Prescott of Woolworths.

'OK, now tell me that you have already thought about this one. What we need right now is a *War Map of the World*.'

'Give me two days, Mr Prescott,' Phyllis said calmly. 'I have three thousand flat sheets on standby in the office. I need to fold them down and tip them into covers. What price are you looking at?'

'I can do sixpence. But we'll process the branches, Mrs Pearsall.'

An experienced professional would have taken the originals and printed a trade edition on cheap paper. But to her cost, Phyllis put speed above profit. Telegrams of orders flew in: REPRINT 10,000. Such was the demand, that although profit eluded her, so did losses. 'Next time,' Phyllis told herself, 'we use the cheap paper.'

Next time would be a mere two weeks later, when she realised from the wireless news bulletins that the Mediterranean was shifting into focus but had not been charted effectively.

'Mr Fountain, I'm sorry to do this to you, but with everything moving south, I'm thinking of Italy and Egypt. Can you do me a *War Map of the Mediterranean*?'

On 4 July 1940, a statutory order arrived in a brown *On His Majesty's Service* envelope at Napier House, prohibiting the sale of the *A-Z* atlas. Phyllis had always known that one day soon, her favourite map would need to be withdrawn for security reasons. During a mad week of trips by tram, bus, Underground, train and on foot, Phyllis and Lester retrieved 20,000 copies from every wholesaler and retailer. As they wrapped the bundles in flood-proof plastic, before locking them in a rented Clapham ware-house, the strange sadness of leaving behind her atlases, that held between the covers years of her effort and strength, overwhelmed Phyllis.

'On we go,' she told herself shakily. 'On we go, Lester.'

'Wilco, Mrs Pearsall.'

The public binged on titbits of information and were greedy for more, which Phyllis hastened to provide. The *War Map of the Mediterranean* reached the stores, but the *War Map of Russia* never did. The sinking by German submarines of merchant ships carrying timber, meant that paper was severely rationed and prices became too exorbitant.

Phyllis sent telegrams to her father, who had happily repro-duced each of the maps so far that his daughter had forwarded to him, and thereby made a tidy sum, to see if the war had strangled America yet.

NO PAPER HERE. HOW ABOUT YOU?

GOOD HERE. KEEP GOING. DON'T STOP MAPS.

Sandor did not understand. His imagination, caught up in the sparkle of profit, had for once lost track of the reality of life in London.

Darling Papa,

You must understand me when I say that I cannot carry on the business here. One takes an order from a shop; and say by the evening or next morning when I might deliver it, the place is more than likely just a heap of suffocating rubble in a partly demolished street. Jagged ruins of windowless houses, with a bath or a fireplace hanging out of an open floor. London is a macabre parody of a stage set. One has to step through the chaos of hose-pipes and broken debris. Ambulance crews, firemen and neighbours dig out the dying and injured buried alive.

Anyhow, I have been called up for Government Service but cannot reveal any more to you than that.

Your loving daughter, Phyllis.

For three nights a week, Phyllis enrolled for Civil Defence duty and undertook fire-watching from the Napier House roof. As she watched the blips and bursts of lights and flames that shrieked above the city, Phyllis could not bear to think of her streets being wiped out. Like most Londoners, she wished there was something she could do to protect the capital.

On the first four nights of the Blitz, the systematic night-time bombing of London by the German Luftwaffe, between one and two thousand Londoners lost their lives.

Phyllis had long since been able to function on a minimum amount of sleep, but she found the real strain came from the deafening noise – the incessant rap of anti-aircraft gunning, the drawn-out drone of aeroplanes and the sneering whistle of bombs.

There was one particular incident on which Phyllis would not be drawn. She and the caretaker's wife had been crouched on the roof for fire-duty when a bomb dropped on High Holborn. Both women were blown down the stairs by the blast, but their tin hats stopped them from getting more than bruised legs. A silence crushed them before they heard screams out on the street. A direct hit on a packed evening bus heading to Islington had scattered limbs, heads, shoes, torsos and hats, among shards of glass and metal, for a few hundred yards.

No doubt Phyllis and the caretaker's wife were soon in the thick of it, leading injured and dazed strangers into waiting ambulances, and working alongside everyone else in that nightmare scene before locking themselves in the office for a tea break.

Now early in the mornings, Phyllis walked from Golders Green to the deepest of all Tube stations, Hampstead, where she would take the Northern line south to Holborn and the Censorship Bureau.

As she picked her way through the pot-holed streets, careful not to catch her shoes on glass or to disturb rubble, Phyllis kicked over and over in her mind why the government had assigned her to a tedious job in the clerical Civil Service, when Tony had become an official war artist, with the rank and uniform of a Captain. Off he would trek to the Normandy Landings, Burma and Egypt, while his sister was confined to faceless offices where she could hardly breathe for restlessness.

Typing reports with two fingers on troop movements in the North of England was hardly a sage use of her skills. Phyllis longed to be outside, to be helping those made homeless by the Luftwaffe. The bureaucrats, she believed, cared nothing for the families with children, who settled down every night in the Tube stations, with their blankets, Thermos flasks of tea and bloater-paste sandwiches. They had not breathed in the stench of unwashed bodies, urine and disinfectant that hung in the dark tunnels, nor had they sat next to someone with scabies, who scratched incessantly.

It was now that Phyllis began to form her own ideas of what good management should be. She could not conceive how the Civil Service could blunder on like this: it was so unproductive. Individuals were lost in the hierarchy of over-staffed departments, nobody seemed to take responsibility for their own actions, and the general public were deemed nothing more than a nuisance.

'The Civil Service was so completely dead, even in war-time,' she told *Telegraph* journalist Anthea Hall, in 1986. 'We once received a note saying there had been a cloud-burst in the Peak District and men were freezing and starving. *Take no action*, a memo instructed. *This concerns other departments*. A colleague and I (you couldn't act alone or they'd think you ambitious) had a plane taking up food and clothes within an hour. A memo came back, warning us: *On your own head be it.*'

Phyllis did not fit in. If truth be known, her wilful ideas of how to go about things made her a dreadful employee, and she simply couldn't fall in with the team. It took the Civil Service a whole two years to recognise this – even discipline took a roundabout route – and in 1944 Phyllis was transferred to the Ministry of Information, Home Intelligence section, under Lord Stephen Taylor.

'What can you do?' she was asked by a rounded man with receding hair, who rather than look at her was sketching on his blotter. 'Can you write?'

'Travel writing, yes, but as a map publisher I can draw. I mean I can draw and paint rather well.'

The man looked up. 'Very well. The Ministry of Labour needs illustrations for its leaflet on the conscription of women. I will see that you get access to the various munitions factories. I suggest you stick to sketching the women. We will do the words here. Make sure you check in with me every week or so – my name is Graham Greene.' Then the man who would later become a best-selling author, stood up and produced a broad smile as he shook her hand.

'How do you do, Mr Greene.'

It was the perfect assignment for Phyllis. How easily she slipped in and out of factory floors with a pen and a sketch-pad. Mothers, sisters, daughters, wives – in their faces Phyllis recognised her own tenacity. For weeks on end, she would travel up and down the country, chatting to women in boiler suits, drawing them in their cumbersome Army and Air Force uniforms. They joked about how easy it was to snag a hairnet, how the tin hat *ruined* one's waves and how the muscles in their arms had grown quite firm from lifting weaponry; but never, ever did they complain about missing their loved ones.

Inexplicably, the drawings were never used by the government. However, in 1985 and 1990, Phyllis published two books privately, entitled *Women Drawn and Overhead* and *Women at War*. They reveal witty, sensitive sketches of women who were determined to remain feminine-looking and still tackle a man's job. These ordinary women were, like Phyllis herself, desperate not to be leading ordinary lives.

CHAPTER TWENTY-SEVEN

Was There an Alternative Route?

KLM DAKOTA CRASHES IN LONDON FOG
HOLBORN MAP PUBLISHER ON CRITICAL LIST
New York Times, 6 November 1946

The ancient words that soothed the throb of her bleeding head were whispered over and over in Hebrew. In her mind, Phyllis felt the presence of the small, Jewish man who had once sat opposite her on a late bus from Chalk Farm to King's Cross. She saw again the *Torah* held inches from his nose, comforted by his continuous swaying back and forth, the sounds forming without him seeming to breathe. Sounds that echoed back through the centuries, the beginning and the end. Her eyes flickered into consciousness and she heard a woman scream.

From the details that Sandor scanned in his *New York Times*, Phyllis should not have survived the crash two nights earlier of a KLM Dakota flight from Schipol Airport in Holland to London. From a clear, cold path across the Channel, the plane had bucked and jolted in a sudden wrap of fog, which disorientated the pilot so much that they hit a steep bank on the edge of woods near Shere, in Surrey.

Those who pulled her broken body from the wreckage saw a woman without a nose, blood streaming from her head into her eyes. In a biting wind, they wrapped her in a thick overcoat and laid her in the frozen grass until the ambulances arrived.

'Help that poor woman,' Phyllis whispered, for she could still hear that terrible scream, like the high-pitched cry of a vixen. It was months before she realised that the terrifying noise had been coming out of her own shocked body.

There at the scene, without anaesthetic, they stitched her fractured skull and bandaged her crushed nose, cheekbones and strapped up her broken back.

'I've got to get to my office,' Phyllis had mumbled, but that was something she would not be able to do for three months.

Like Bella after her riding accident, forty-year-old Phyllis would never be quite the same person again following this traumatic event. After plastic surgery to her face and a painful, slow recovery, traces of injury, such as a limp, would drag her energy down for the rest of her life. Shingles, two strokes, glandular fever, pneumonia, ulcers, septicaemia and black-outs would add to the dull persistent headaches. And like her mother before her, the heavenly barbiturates that numbed all pain would eventually become an addiction.

Such was the frailty of her spine, that doctors warned her against a second marriage. Sex, they inferred, was out of the question, as of course, were children.

'Endeavour to lead a quiet life, Mrs Pearsall,' they said, smoothing her hand. 'Try to ease up a little on your workload.'

'How refreshing to shake off bureaucratic shackles for the stimulus of having to earn money one spent; of having to get things done by piercing brick walls, of never giving up, of producing something tangible and needed – to resurrect our A-Z maps.'

It was 8 May 1946, six months before her accident, and her excitement was due to the fact that despite her tricky behaviour, the Board of Trade had offered Phyllis a permanent, well-paid senior Civil Service position – which she had great delight in turning down. Maps were her future. Her temporary future, of course, until she might wriggle in more and more days spent painting. The restrictions on the sale and purchase of maps had been lifted in January 1944, but Phyllis, like many other printers and paper manufacturers, had been wary of restarting production.

As with every other Londoner, it was as if, for the duration of the war, her life had been suspended while she journeyed for six surreal years through a terrible dream. This had inevitably led to Phyllis's enthusiasm chilling a little, and now it was time to warm her hands on the Geographers' Map Company once more.

Not everyone had fared so well. Joan Walker-Smith, with whom Phyllis had lived throughout the war, had lost her husband in action and was keen to sell her Golders Green home, so Phyllis moved on.

After the dark days of the Blitz, the idea of taking the Underground was so awful that Phyllis moved further into Town, within walking distance of the office. With few spare properties to rent, after a three-day hunt of Bloomsbury and Marylebone, Phyllis was lucky to find an attic flat at 9 Robert Adam Street, off Portman Square, for an exorbitant £5 a week.

Londoners had scoured their mangled streets for souvenirs of war. The *Dig for Victory* banner that had hung across the colonnades of the Royal Exchange disappeared. London Underground posters declaring *The Proud City*, showing Chelsea power station lit up by searchlights, were carefully removed from stations and pasted into scrapbooks. For Phyllis the war already echoed as history, as a story of street heroes and unrecorded selflessness. Memories of her father's financial tricks and dealings with money seemed obscene, his motives now more callous and futile than ever.

Slowly at first, she and Gordon Lester unwrapped and

removed from storage the massive stock of 1939 maps. As she revealed their pristine faces, the same sadness lay on her head as while sorting through Bella's things after her cremation. The folded piles of petticoats. The square boxes of kid gloves. Of shoes, of hats. All waiting for someone who would never return to them.

But Phyllis *had* returned to her beloved maps. And how dated they looked! How clean and innocent. She flicked through the useless pages where the East End streets and docklands had been flattened and decimated.

'Let's start again, Lester. We'll need to do a new atlas, with a brand new cover.' Suddenly, Phyllis could not wait to get rid of the old *A-Z* copies.

Within a few months, servicemen from all around the world, who were struggling to negotiate the war-damaged streets of London, happily parted with their money to have an '*A to Zee*' as the GIs called it.

Napier House suddenly felt too cramped and too despondent, Phyllis decided. Instead of saving some of the £10,000 sales profit to treat herself to badly-needed items of clothing such as stockings, underwear and an overcoat, she blew the whole lot on refurbishing the huge top floor of 21 Gray's Inn Road, rented for £1 a week.

Phyllis admired the way it stood alone, defiantly, while numbers 19 and 23 had been blasted to rubble. With Lester's help, she scrubbed the dusty floors clean and laid linoleum. A stock and packing room was set up, and workbenches were run along the windows for Mr Fountain and his team.

Mr Nolan was only too glad to return to his sales job, and a Mrs Ford was hired to cover book-keeping and correspondence, as well as an extra draughtsman, Wally Cooper. The war had trained all their minds to such a high pitch of concentration that they would work happily without a break, through the day and late into the night. When extravagant food parcels of turkey, game pie, pickles, caviar, fruit cake and cheeses arrived from her father, Phyllis would spread it all out for a staff picnic, atop a tablecloth on one of the desks.

Mr Fountain and Wally Cooper tutted and shook their heads as they cut in the alterations to the original *A-Z* maps, highlighting the bomb damage around St Paul's, the City and the East End. In the Blitz alone, 18,000 tons of bombs had been dropped on the capital. Irrespective of wealth, nearly every district was scarred and the second time around, Phyllis assessed that a daily schedule of careful indexing on foot, would take over eight months.

In October 1945, she noted: *The curiosity which entices me up every street, alley and road in the worst affected areas is different on this journey. As I approach a corner, or bend, I wonder what lies in wait for me. How my heart turns to witness the remnants of gracious homes and buildings that have withstood centuries, shamelessly demolished.*

They say that nearly 700,000 children were evacuated. Most, I see, are back, more shabbily dressed than before, with dark shadows under their eyes like me. My feet are not so light. I am nearly ten years older. I cannot wait for Zoffany Street . . .

Yet as she walked, Phyllis could not help turning over the problem of paper shortages. By the time government restrictions on paper had been lifted her map might be out of date again. Print runs were limited to 5,000 but cost as much as a run of 250,000.

Early one evening, when she arrived back at Gray's Inn Road, Mrs Ford announced that two gentlemen were waiting to see her. One of them, Eliot, had suffered alongside Phyllis the monotony of report writing in the Ministry of Information. The other, an unsmiling Dutchman with a droopy moustache, was the British agent for an Amsterdam printers.

'I've got a book that I would love you to print, Phyllis,' Eliot said, opening pages to reveal texts from the New Testament on each right-hand page and an Old Master painting on the left.

'Eliot, I'm afraid you really need a fine art publisher, not an old map one like me. And anyhow, no one can print anything for the time being. There's no paper.'

'Not so, madam,' said the Dutchman. 'By special arrangement with the British government, everything that we at Van Leer print, can be imported here.'

'If that is so, gentlemen,' said Phyllis, 'we may have a deal on our hands.'

The next morning, Phyllis arrived before nine o'clock at the Board of Trade, and her request was granted for an appointment with the official in charge of Imports.

Leaning back in his leather chair, he dunked a ginger biscuit in his tea and listened to Phyllis. 'Sorry I can't offer you a biscuit,' he interrupted, grinning through a mouthful. 'I've only got two.' Preoccupied with his munching, he did not begin a response until his tongue had greedily ensured that every last crumb had disappeared.

'We are, Mrs Pearsall, helping the Netherlands recover some of their economy, but only by permitting our paper dealers to export to them. Now, about maps . . . I think I am correct in saying there is an import exemption and open licence for, let me see . . .' He unfolded a leaflet on his desk and ran his finger down the page: 'Yes – winkles, gold nuggets and maps. So if you choose, madam, you may import maps of London by the hundreds of thousands.'

'I love life. And I love luck,' Phyllis hummed to herself as she walked back to the office. Under her instruction, Mrs Ford stopped her ledger-writing and brewed an especially large pot of tea, before cutting the angel cake Phyllis had bought to celebrate.

'I have some very exciting news, everyone,' Phyllis announced. 'Van Leer will be our new printers in Schipol, Holland. I propose that we boost our pre-war order of 10,000 per run to 250,000. It is a gamble but I think the Geographers' Map Company can do it.'

'Will we have to write *Printed in Holland* on them?' asked Mr Fountain.

'Yes. Yes, we will.'

The gloomy cartographer rolled his eyes.

There was no partner or deputy with whom Phyllis could talk through her doubts. There never would be, for Phyllis was not that sort of person. Although she was conscientious and hardworking, her need for absolute control would, in the aftermath of her plane crash, nearly bankrupt the company. Everyone knew their own job, but no one knew, like Phyllis, each single detail.

As much as it pained her to contact her father for reassurance, that night she sent him a telegram.

PLACED ORDER FOR HALF A MILLION A-ZS. WHAT DO YOU THINK?

DON'T EXPECT ME TO BAIL YOU OUT.

DOING FINE. ON WE GO.

At night, her sleep was sound. In the mornings, her eyes smiled back at her confidently. Like Sandor before her, when it came to making decisions, Phyllis despised procrastination.

Within seven days, Bliss & Son, in Cursitor Street just off Chancery Lane, were hired to tackle the expanding accounts, and six more draughtsmen joined the team.

Delegation, however, could only go so far with Phyllis, who insisted on personally accompanying the original *A-Z* stereo plates and the tons of paper transported from Liverpool Street station to Harwich, then into the ship's hold and on to customs at Hook. After a few trips, Phyllis knew which customs officials to smile at, and when to raise her eyebrows at others. There was no question on the Export and Import papers she could not answer, but still they took delight in holding up the tons of Mechanical Newsprint paper for the *A-Z* for hours.

For the return collection of six 35x45 bundles that arrived in East London Wharf in Bow, Phyllis hired one Mr Noakes of the Rapid Van Service, who helped her stack, pack and deliver orders all over London. He handled large zinc plates from Lowe & Brydone, and black plate and transfers made by Van Leer.

'Mr Noakes, how do you fancy coming on board? If you do, I will buy you a white van with our insignia on it after a year's service.'

'Count me in.'

In the autumn of 1946, Phyllis had begun flying to Schipol and back twice a week, for meetings with Mr Van Leer, in war-time Dakotas still unadapted to civilian flights. In her diary she wrote: *My greengrocer in Chancery Lane had kindly supplied me with used wicker boxes and wrapping paper for the increasingly large orders I had to pack. First reports from accountants show a margin of profit. New coat for me.*

CHAPTER TWENTY-EIGHT

Stepping Back

The pretty sprays of roses, tulips and snowdrops that friends and colleagues had fussed into vases for her bedside at home, went unnoticed. Daylight even in the low points of winter made her eyes weep with soreness and the darkness of the black-out curtains was a blessing. Walking was reduced to a dizzy shuffle and her muscles had wasted away to skin. 'A simple journey today,' Phyllis would say to herself, as she talked her way to the bathroom and into a hot bath. 'On we go.'

Sometimes, if the heat swelled her head, she would crawl, wrapped in her towel, straight back into bed. On other days she would harness all her energy to pull a brush through her runaway hair. In the mirror, her eyes swam, her nose looked borrowed and her cheeks bitten.

Sandor, despite boasting to his friends of his daughter's miraculous survival, did not think her state serious enough to merit a visit. He even sent her a typically brusque telegram, which was tinged with self-pity: HURRY UP OUT OF HOSPITAL. YOU CANNOT RUN A BUSINESS FROM BED. WHY MUST MY DAUGHTER ALWAYS BE SICK?

Fortunately, Phyllis's isolation, among a mountain of blankets for weeks on end, unable to read, to talk, to listen, did not depress her. Outside, the drilling noise of traffic reminded her of the speed of the world beyond her bedroom. In the third week of March 1947, those same cars came to a standstill in one of the worst blizzards of the century, but Phyllis did not notice. The barbiturates that fogged every sound and smell, took care of that.

Phyllis could only allow herself to think about the office for a couple of minutes before her head kicked with pain. How was her little family coping without her? She pictured the arguments, the sulking, the petty rivalry, those who clocked off before 4 p.m. and those who arrived later than 10 a.m.

The reality was far more serious. In the months that had elapsed since the accident, Mrs Ford had panicked about wages, and took it upon her flustered self to pay everyone too much. The new *A-Z*s had arrived, been sold with a solid profit to cover overheads and a reprint, but the original map plates travelling in the hold of the KLM plane had been damaged beyond repair and had to be replaced at great cost by Lowe & Brydone, wiping out any profit. On top of that, the company bank balance had allowed over £10,000 to seep out from under its gaze, lost to extra print runs, expensive paper and temporary staff.

When Mr Bowman, Phyllis's Bedford Row bank manager, paid a house visit, clutching a small box of chocolates, even she gauged that matters must be getting out of hand.

'Do not worry about money, Mrs Pearsall, not one bit. We will allow a good customer such as yourself an overdraft of £8,000, should you need it.'

The panic that now flashed to the front of her mind, was the date of 13 February. That was the deadline for delivery of the latest index for the *A-Z*, that had to be with Van Leer in time for the next 40,000 print run.

'Only I can go,' she muttered to herself. 'It must be me.'

On 11 February 1947, Phyllis hauled herself out of bed before lunchtime. She pulled on corduroy trousers over her pyjamas and put on a cardigan. Six hours later, she was ready and telephoned for a taxi. For an extra fee, the driver carried four heavy packages of index cards and original sheets into the car, and then went back for his passenger.

The slightest movement or jolt to the head caused sickness and pain. The palms of her hands sweated and trembled as she huddled in the back of the taxi.

'Here we are, love,' said the taxi driver, as he pulled into Liverpool Street station. A hammering echoed in her ears as she rattled coins from her purse.

'I'm all ready for the night-train,' she said, winking at the taxi driver and showing a peek of her pyjamas.

'Mind how you go now!' he shouted after the woman, wobbling her way to the ticket booth.

There were a few lost hours to follow. From fragmented accounts, Phyllis collapsed before boarding the ferry at Harwich, but was carried to a cabin by three sailors. At Hook, she caught the correct train but when Mr Groen of the Van Leer printers did not meet her at Nijmegen station, she collapsed a second time.

The ambulance driver who met Phyllis at Liverpool Street station on her return was sickened by the light weight of the woman who was carried on to a stretcher.

'You don't speak much, do you?' he joked as he lifted her on to her bed at home.

Phyllis shook her head. *Not any more.*

He emptied the dead flowers from the crowded vases, and washed the cups and saucers in the sink, but was unable to tempt Phyllis to some soup, while waiting for the doctor to arrive. The latter, after examining Phyllis with a variety of disconcerting sighs, issued a stern warning.

'I must tell you, Mrs Pearsall, that you are in need of some quiet and a good year's rest. Should you return to work, I would not like to be held responsible for the consequences.'

Most of us would have listened to his words, and reluctantly accepted his advice. But there are some people like Phyllis who walk away from the predictability of safety. Their lives seem precariously rerouted, diverted, plucked within seconds from dangerous situations, only to hasten them on to the next, equally disastrous one. They exist at a constantly heightened pace, apparently one step ahead of the rest of us. Infectiously energetic, people like her seem to be ahead of their time. In fact, they are just trying to beat it.

On the Monday morning, Phyllis greeted everyone from her desk as they arrived into work. She ignored their astonished faces, which confirmed how shocked they were by her ravaged appearance.

'Good morning! Good morning!' she said briskly.

In the first couple of hours, Phyllis had instructed representatives from paper merchants to make appointments with her. Letters were issued to Van Leer, to confirm their printing contract of the *A-Z* for a further five years, despite the paper restrictions lifting. Lowe & Brydone would win back the sheet maps and the *Greater London Atlas*. Her shrill voice was higher than before, more insistent and more determined.

Mrs Ford gave her a wrapped package of duck pâté and a jar of home-made gooseberry jam. 'I feel better now you are here, Mrs Pearsall. So much better.'

'So do I. Thank you.'

Over the next few months, the financial concerns nipping at her ankles were kicked away. She remembered her father's words of Expansion Equals Efficiency and hired a new draughtsman, Fred Bond, and a sales representative, George Elston.

'In the next three years,' she announced to the office one morning, 'I want us to spread out from London, to cover all the major cities. First we will do a new map of England and Wales.

To be followed by the quality editions – or Premiers – of Leeds, Birmingham, Manchester, Coventry, Glasgow, Wolverhampton, Walsall and Bradford.'

Her eyes were still too sore to read, or concentrate on reading proofs, so she asked Mrs Ford to read out account figures. If she heard an inaccuracy or an extravagance she would shout 'Stop!' And then, 'Sort that out, Mrs Ford.' The weak energy resource Phyllis had tapped into could only supply power to her brain. Her body ached and the very thought of walking, or lifting packages, made her hands tremble.

One morning, Wally Cooper approached Phyllis and waffled with embarrassment: 'I know, Mrs P, that what with you not being so well, that you might like help indexing and well, you see, my wife Mary, who has worked on telephone indexing, could perhaps help you, if maybe you thought it might be a good idea?' He flushed.

'Why didn't you say so before? A husband and wife team – I like it. But we need another office boy, too. Any ideas, anyone?'

On 6 April 1948, Nigel Syrett took up his position as office boy, after Phyllis had interviewed his father, Jack.

'My boy is only fifteen, but he is no good at school. Don't pay him a wage and don't give him a holiday,' the man had admonished.

Nigel would prove to be one of the company's best acquisitions. Energetic and cheerful, he knew every short-cut possible for deliveries. His agility and practical thinking reminded Phyllis in her memoirs of her younger self: *Mustard-keen he darted through London's Underground with mounted board maps larger than himself, dodging in and out of coaches. He unloaded heavy Dutch consignments and carried them up and down the dicey office stairs and to and from the rat-infested basement. His mission efficiently and promptly completed, he asked: 'What's next?'* A fortnight after he began, Phyllis offered him a permanent job at one pound and five shillings a week.

His boss was, according to Nigel, as tough as old boots: 'Phyllis looked incredibly frail but she had the most fantastic mind. She was ambitious too, not for herself, but for the company. Her whole life involved the Geographers' Map Company and it was hard to know where the business ended and her life began. Phyllis knew there was no potential for a get-rich-quick business like today. It was plain hard work.'

Month by month the finances not only stabilised, but thanks to the dedicated office team, they steadily improved.

However, the frustration at not being able to sleep at night, to walk more than a mile, or climb a flight of stairs without difficulty, had started to grate on Phyllis's mind. Despite the comfort they gave her, the painkilling drugs were making her drowsy, slowing her down; even preparing her paint palette at weekends seemed an incredible effort.

Progress may have been limited, but she would be knocked off her feet, just after her forty-second birthday, by the first visit from her father since the war. Phyllis recalled his arrival in October 1948 at 21 Grays Road, completely unannounced, and how in front of the staff, he openly savaged her.

'Good Lord. What a fright you look. Haggard. Crippled. Barely past forty, and like an octogenarian! Imagine what it's like for me. To be afflicted with so decrepit a daughter is too much! Aren't you ashamed? Can't you put make-up on? Your mother never let herself go like this, even at death's door. You look ghastly!' On the verge of fainting, I reached for a chair and heard him from afar: 'Take off my shoes, can't you, instead of sitting there! Here's my jacket – hang it up.'

The spite and jealousy that spouted from Sandor had been provoked by irritating comments from Mr Cruise, the buyer at

W.H. Smith & Son, who had, in a passing telephone exchange, commented that Phyllis produced better quality maps than her father.

'Betrayed by my own daughter!' he thundered. 'You want to corner the market here, do you, so I can never return?'

'You know very well that I have done my best for you, Papa. All of this is for you. All of it.'

Tears did not fall down her hardened face and Phyllis remained seated, trying not to pass out as her father paced the office. Mrs Ford spotted her red fists clenched in anger and saw her left eye start to twitch as Sandor moved in on the filing cabinets and flung papers to the floor.

'Is this any way to run a business? I don't think so.' With that, he stormed out of the office and shouted back up the stairs, 'Meet me tonight at The Savoy. Dinner. Eight o'clock. Do not be late!'

CHAPTER TWENTY-NINE

Lo! I Am With You Always, Even Unto the End of the World
Matthew, Ch. 28, v. 20

The waiters in the Savoy restaurant thought it was a lover's tiff.

A small woman in a blue suit would not stop crying. 'How could you? How could you?' she wailed.

The man beside her, a smarter-looking, older gentleman in a cashmere suit, was turned away from her, but still raised his voice to hiss: 'For God's sake, Phyllis, how dare you make a scene! Everybody is looking. Be quiet now. How can I have *two* demented women in my life?'

'Now I know what drove Mama insane,' the woman shouted.

If anyone had been able to eat their beef soup or rabbit pie up until then – well, now their hushed voices fell to an absolute silence. It was, they believed, perfectly acceptable to put down their cutlery and stare as the woman accused her companion of being a philandering adulterer, a devil and a megalomaniac, before throwing over her chair and running from the room. She flounced past the bellboys and out on to the street, and for the first time in two years, Phyllis walked, sobbing and sobbing, until she could sob and walk no more.

The dinner had started off civilly enough, but then Sandor had insisted on pulling out his favourite topic – women – as he perused the menu. Hungarian wives are so much more accepting than English and American ones. They forgive peccadilloes as long as one doesn't desert them, whereas Englishwomen demand monogamy.

In her mind, Phyllis could see her poor, bandaged Mama, paralysed after the riding accident. She could feel her hand stiffen in hers, as Sandor threw insult after insult at her pathetic form. All Bella had ever asked for was his support and love.

Some might say Phyllis's outburst was connected to post-traumatic stress disorder after the plane crash. Others, that Phyllis came face to face with her own mental fragility. But that night, it seemed to her that Sandor had been employing the same sadistic, demoralising tactics in the office and in the restaurant, that had eventually robbed Phyllis of her mother.

The next day, Tony received a letter from Sandor, a copy of which went to Phyllis. As an artist, Tony could not rise to any of the family squabbles about business. He skimmed through his father's letter, but found himself untroubled by what he felt was petty. He had no interest in maps, in production or in being a company director. Whether his father's actions were legal, given that he had handed over the reins to his daughter, is also questionable today.

I write to say that Phyllis thrust convulsive scenes upon me in a restaurant this evening, where I am well known. She hurled abuse at me and her hysterical eyes were those of a madwoman, her voice shriller and louder than I have ever heard.

I therefore have no alternative but to give you full control of the Geographers' Map Company. *I shall issue further shares in your name. I advise you to look into the accounts. She has to be watched.*

Your loving father,
Sandor Gross.

PS On receipt of a copy of your will, I will take the necessary legal steps.

That night, after receiving her copy of the letter, Phyllis had a stroke.

For two months, Phyllis was blind. The shock of her father's wrath and her own vulnerability had snatched away her sight. Sandor had already flown home to New York, but on hearing the news from Mrs Ford, he sent a telegram. DO NOT WORRY. RETHINK. GET BACK IN OFFICE ASAP.

His cruelty at tearing all her hard work out of her hands in one swipe, and handing it back in the next, had sickened her. Tears flooded her face as she curled up alone at home in her bed, realising that she was one step nearer her beloved Mama. She did not dare believe that her sight was gone for ever. She did not dare feel that her business would flounder and sink without her.

To keep herself occupied during the day, she dictated stories to Mrs Ford about her travels in Spain. These would eventually be published in *The New Yorker* in 1955.

After weeks of darkness, Phyllis awoke one morning and a mottled vision of the ceiling came into view. She could hardly breathe with excitement as she blinked and blinked, and out of nowhere, her sight flickered back into focus. It was, Phyllis would say in later years, like the Road to Damascus conversion. Having been an atheist, from that moment onwards she conducted her life and her company as a Christian – born again, in the true sense of the meaning. Whether it was in the quotations from the Bible in her Christmas cards, to references to the Bible in her company manifesto, her enthusiasm for Christianity would become as keen as it was for maps.

As her sight grew stronger, she scurried for writing paper. The first thing Phyllis felt compelled to do, was to send `letter to her father. Animosity would not be allowed to wear away at her. Forgiveness, she felt, was only fair for him, her dear, darling father. She would try to understand his own loneliness with acceptance and kindness. The relief that came with the release of her own, albeit contained, bitterness, coincided with her call to Christianity and it is around this time that Phyllis wrote of her vision of Christ:

I had the strange sensation of an opaque membrane being peeled from my eyes. Without emotion, I experienced God, as a living, all-powerful presence. 'Let not your heart be troubled,' were the words, 'ye who believe in God, believe in Me.' And there spiritually He stood. In my heart, closer than hands or feet.

For the rest of her life Phyllis, albeit not a churchgoer, would believe that although her own human father had abandoned her, God had lifted her miraculously above all her troubles and held her tight.

What Phyllis could not foresee was that, despite her forgiveness, her father's life would only stretch for another six years. After a series of heart attacks in New York, he let business relax as he took a succession of holidays in the South of France. In August 1957, Phyllis received her final telegram from him on the *Queen Mary* bound for Southampton.

MEET ME OFF THE SHIP PLEASE. 30 AUGUST.

That same night, Sandor was found dead, sitting upright in an armchair in his cabin after dinner, his heart having stopped without warning. The letter then, that Phyllis wrote as a reply that same night, in her firm, looped handwriting, he would never get to read:

My Darling Friend and Father,

I cannot wait to see you. I know that I should thank you for all your help with my business affairs and I truly know how wise you are.

Lovingly and gratefully, Phyllis.

To be greeted then at Southampton dock by a body bag and her father's suitcase would ordinarily have shattered his daughter. But her faith had allowed her to understand that her family, scattered to the heavens, were no closer than the family at 21 Grays Inn Road.

Back to 1952, and the time of Phyllis's conversion to Christianity. A strong will and a strong faith now carried her wherever she wanted to go but when her weight fell to less than five stone, her colleagues pleaded with her to check into a Sussex rest home, founded by Dr Octavia Wilberforce, in Backsettown, Henfield. Here, in the Tudor rooms with their views of rolling pastures, Jersey cows and orchards, Phyllis found a haven that she would retreat to often over the next ten years.

Backsettown, read the brochure, *supplies a Rest Pause, under special conditions, to the efficient women in every class whose activities are threatened or impaired by the stress of modern life.*

There teachers, nurses and academics were cared for with lavish attention, in the comforting surroundings of an old country manor. Phyllis was ordered to rest in bed and fed up on roast dinners with fresh vegetables from the farm, and soggy puddings covered in cream from the Backsettown herd.

When her body plumped up to its usual eight stone, Dr Wilberforce started to reduce her painkillers.

'I'm afraid you've been over-drugged for too many years,' she told Phyllis, 'and the process for withdrawal is a gradual one. But you will succeed because you want to, unlike those poor unfortunates who use drugs as an escape.'

The initial three-day roaring nightmare of withdrawal took Phyllis back to her mother's cell in Bedlam. But when she saw the grey skin on her own flinching face in the mirror, Phyllis vowed she would not linger there.

Through intense prayers and light strolls through the woods and across the downs, Phyllis began to breathe in a happy peace. The emotional race that she had pushed her body to run over the past twenty years, was beginning to feel meaningless.

For once, enjoying the freedom of her own solitude was not as agreeable as passing the hours with the female companions she made at Backsettown. Over a cream tea at the fireside or under the cherry trees, she would paint or talk. It was here that she was introduced to a friend of Octavia's called Dr Esme Wren, a brilliant heart consultant. The two women became the best of friends. They shared a sociable, intelligent wit, a love of travel and a greed for books. As for chatter, they could talk about any subject until the Backsettown cows came home. In later years, they moved to be near each other in Shoreham-on-Sea, and it was Esme who cared for Phyllis in her final days.

CHAPTER THIRTY

A Path for My Family to Follow

Protection and strengthening of the weak. This demands impartiality; no self-righteousness; but readiness to listen, kind firmness and definiteness; and the generous and patient imparting of one's own knowledge and experience. Even temper and no moodiness; praise for good work and gently constructive criticism.

Paragraph D in Phyllis Pearsall's letter of intent to trustees on foundation of The Geographers' Map Trust

From the very beginning, the atmosphere that Phyllis had created at the Geographers' Map Company gave her staff a powerful sense of her leadership, whether she was present or not. It was a superb management technique, for although Phyllis had a desk in the office, according to her staff, from the late 1950s until she died, little time was spent there, as she trailed around Europe with Esme, painting to her heart's content, and it would often be covered in maps ready for packing.

Like her mother, Phyllis had realised that if she could encourage and motivate her staff, and keep them happy, then they in turn would be diligent and loyal.

Like all successful company directors, Phyllis knew every single detail of all the map projects that were being worked on, and every piece of company gossip. With each Annual Report, Phyllis became aware of the passing of time. Like any parent, she felt it vital to protect her family, especially as she had witnessed so many firms being bought out by brash upstarts who fired old-timers and employees not considered profitable.

After years of research and under the guidance of Sir Bernard Miller of The John Lewis Partnership, Phyllis consulted the company lawyers and in 1966 formed a trust – The Geographers' Map Trust. Instead of giving every employee shares, there is just one joint share to protect them against takeover bids and safeguard their jobs.

Although Phyllis had never received a huge sum from the company, by making this decision she would legally lose all profits and earnings from it. However, a unanimous vote kept her as Chairman until her death in 1996. Any profits, she made clear, must always come second to the welfare of the staff and their families.

'In some small way I am banishing the memory of my father's two bankruptcies by establishing an unshakable and peaceful environment for those who have shown me the kindness of their loyalty and commitment.'

It was the ultimate gift to her staff, and an acknowledgement from Phyllis that they had warmed her life with their love; the very thing that she never received from her parents.

CHAPTER THIRTY-ONE

In the End is the Beginning

'The older I get, the happier I become. When you're a baby, you're the centre of everything. But as the years pass, you're no longer standing in your own shadow.'

When it came to choosing the right spot for her painting, Phyllis behaved like a small child; she lacked the self-conscious inhibition that frequently stops adults from doing what they would truly love to do. There she would be, sitting on the pavement in Grosvenor Square, or huddled on the steps of the Bridge of Sighs over the River Cam in Cambridge, as if setting up home with her easel and paints.

The anxiety that taps old age on the shoulder, did not dare approach Phyllis, who ignored her own physical deterioration and her vulnerability. If she ever set off on a day trip alone, Esme would worry terribly that she would be mugged, or worse. 'Don't worry, Esme,' she would call out. 'Never worry.'

For sixty years, curiosity and the need to achieve had driven her onwards, whereas old age, Phyllis discovered, offered all the contentment and freedom she could desire.

'The odd thing was that from the moment I had started in business I stopped worrying about what my painting was going to look like,' she once said. 'I didn't care about the result any more, I just enjoyed the act of painting and stopped making comparisons with my previous work. This turned out to be an enormous joy and freedom. I can't ever achieve a painting as beautiful as what I see, but I simply don't compare it; and this is something I would recommend to other painters.'

The weather, apparently, was never allowed to dictate whether it was a suitable day or not for painting. It was always good weather. Even if the rain rapped hard against the windows, Phyllis never moaned or cursed the heavens. Instead, she would look rather pleased and say, 'Look at that beautiful rain. This is the day the Lord hath given us. Let us rejoice and be glad in it.'

Unable to sleep more than a few hours each night, Phyllis would manage to set up camp on Westminster Bridge, to paint the Houses of Parliament, by six-thirty in the morning. Oblivious to early morning traffic and commuters, her hands would hurry and scurry across the paper, trying to catch those first glimmers of sunlight that would cast the Gothic stone in gold. She might have been perched on the Champs Elysées painting the Café l'Alsace or sodden under a dripping umbrella for *Rain over Dartmoor*, but when Phyllis unlocked her box of paints, the world around her disappeared. There was no pain in her back, no headache, no past, no present. Her face became grave as she fell into a deep concentration. Passers-by who clustered at her shoulder to watch an image appear, could not distract her from a trance that would last hour after hour.

Early one April morning, the eighty-two-year-old had driven up to London and parked her red BMW at the Speaker's Yard, courtesy of her friend, Jack Weathcrill. Next, she lugged her equipment for forty minutes, past Downing Street and all the way up Whitehall to the Haymarket. There, the little figure in waterproofs, a Liberty print scarf at her neck, with one paintbrush tucked in her shock of hair, painted the grand colonnades of the Theatre Royal, until early afternoon. With only a few touches needed to complete the painting that would later be presented to actor Sir Peter Ustinov, she paused for her first break, to eat a banana.

'Excuse me,' a tourist asked her, 'can you tell me the name of a good hotel?'

'No. Go away. I'm having my lunch.'

Rare flashes such as this, betraying some sort of temper, are quite refreshing. After all, who doesn't want to believe that underneath the sunny charm of Phyllis Pearsall, a more ordinary woman existed, plagued with foibles like the rest of us?

In this last stage of her life's journey, Phyllis did indeed do exactly as she pleased. An inheritance from her father kept her comfortably off, although she never received money from the company.

Time, she understood, would not let her drag her heels. Sleep would become irrelevant as her obsession with the day in, day out reality of painting overtook her. Still the Chairman and Joint Managing Director of the company, her role was now honorary and at last her art was no longer a morsel of luxury, to be sneaked in around interviews and board meetings. It was time to catch up on all those years, when her brother had run away with his talents, while she had tied hers together and diverted them into business.

A final surge of energy fired through her last twenty years. Her output increased and in 1980 her entire Brittany water colours were bought by a private collector, as were the Scottish Border water colours, three years later. Since 1984, her informal commissions had been overshadowed by more elaborate and corporate ones: *Speaker's House* for Lord Weatherill, 1984, *The Houses of Parliament* for David Mitchell MP, in 1986, *Shoreham Panorama* for Sir Richard Luce, 1992, *The Peak, Hong Kong* for Chris Patten, Governor General, and in 1995 *Trafalgar Square* for the Royal Bank of Scotland, Drummonds Branch, and *Edinburgh Castle* for John Menzies.

Those who knew Phyllis never expected the tight girth to slacken on her modest life, despite her quietly hidden wealth. The materialism and emotional avarice that plagued Sandor and Bella in their own lives, had thankfully not inflicted itself on their daughter.

Even if she had not become a devout Christian, Phyllis would never have frittered away her money. Phyllis wisely counted every penny in and every penny out. Wine, bought for presents, was sent down by the crate from Berry Bros, in St James's. Lacking a sweet tooth, she never indulged in chocolates, cakes or biscuits. She preferred a simple diet of fresh fish and chicken, speedily cooked in a microwave oven. Her money might have been invested in artwork, jewellery, a seaview mansion or a new BMW every year. Surprisingly, for such an acutely observant woman, aesthetic beauty was irrelevant. Home was a sunny, spartan, one-bedroom flat, with polished wooden floors, bordered with Portuguese tiles, that housed hundreds of her paintings.

Her sole indulgence was travel, so that she might paint wherever in the world she desired.

'What about Paris, Esme?' Phyllis would throw into the conversation every now and then.

'That sounds a wonderful idea.'

Packing, for Phyllis, took minutes and weeks of planning were tedious. So by now, Esme was unfazed to find herself booked on a flight the following day.

In Paris, their favourite haunt was the smart Lancaster Hotel on the Rue de Berri, off the Champs Elysées, where Phyllis became something of a fixture with her easel, painting the façade furiously, day after day.

'Would Madame care to sell the hotel one of her exquisite paintings?'

'Absolutely not. They are for an exhibition.'

'Would Madame like to be a guest of the hotel, another time, so she might paint a picture for us at her leisure?'

'Madame would be delighted.'

Often, after a week or two, the friends would drive further south to the Loire Valley, and stop wherever Phyllis spotted her next conquest. Set up on a long grassy verge she might be absorbed by the Château Chenanceaux, the shadows of a bridge on the river, or a field of sunflowers with a dilapidated barn. While she worked, her devoted friend Esme was quite content to sit and read her book.

One water colour of a crowded garden café was executed at dawn. But what were all those people doing, up so early? That was Esme. Every ten minutes or so, Phyllis asked her to move tables and sit differently, to make up for the fact that the place was deserted.

From 1992 onwards, every November, Phyllis and Esme would fly to Hong Kong for a three-week visit to Government House, as guests of Chris and Lavender Patten. During the Blitz, Phyllis had lived in Golders Green with Lavender's mother, Joan Walker-Smith. Sadly, Joan's husband was killed a month before she was due to give birth, so it was Phyllis who had helped ease her distress, by organising a gynaecologist and a taxi to the hospital. At sixteen years old, Lavender found the affectionate bond between herself and Phyllis grow a little stronger, when her mother died.

In contrast to her own quiet Church of England family, Lavender found herself amazed at the spiritual zeal that guided Phyllis's life, and how happily she would talk about God.

To the Patten family, Phyllis was known as Auntie Pig – the

perfect, self-sufficient guest who would keep family and dinner-party guests alike entertained with the most extraordinary stories.

'We used to give Phyllis one of the bedrooms with an outside terrace,' says Lavender, 'and she used to hold court; all the stewards, cleaners and aides would go to see her, apparently to look at her painting, but they just loved having chats with her. Phyllis was one of those people who could talk to anyone easily, no matter their nationality or background.

'We admired her for breaking free of her previous existence and for having done so well on her own. Growing up, there had been periods when I didn't see her for years and years, and then she would appear and bowl us over with her personality. She was my brother Malcolm's Godmother but we didn't see her a great deal. Phyllis would dive into your life briefly, fill it with excitement and then leave; she was like a shooting star.'

Phyllis adored her surrogate family, describing the Governor General as the most huggable of men, with a tremendously affectionate nature. No matter which dignitary the Governor was with, if he caught sight of a hat above an easel among the eucalyptus trees, he would shout out, 'Hello there, Auntie Pig!'

In the late afternoons, Phyllis would set aside time to write letters on official crested notepaper to her friends the broadcaster and journalist Derek Jameson and his wife Ellen. As usual, Phyllis could hardly contain her excitement at painting in such a beautiful location: *Marvellously spoilt are Esme and I . . . Water colours from the terrace of our suite, from dawn till dusk.*

Yet her moments caught on camera are not serene. And it was in Hong Kong that she showed Esme a mole on her upper arm that had been bothering her. That mole would later prove to be the first symptom of malignant melanoma cancer.

Phyllis always grumbled about wearing what must have been a badly-fitting set of false teeth. Dreadful! So as not to detract from the enjoyment of painting, when she was out alone with her easel, she refused to put them in. Her appearance, Lavender Patten remembers as a hoot: 'She really did look like a tramp, with a painting hat – one of those wide, floppy cloche hats and old painting clothes. And once, when we had the Duchess of Kent staying, Phyllis had gone downstairs in her painting kit, without her teeth, and they met in the front hall.'

'Well, I thought I'd better curtsey,' Phyllis later told her hostess, 'but then I apologised for not having my teeth in.'

As a result of her yet-to-be-discovered illness – and a lack of teeth – most of the photographs in Hong Kong capture her with sunken cheeks, while her eyes have the startled darkness of a bush-baby.

The directors of the Geographers' Map Company planned a surprise eightieth birthday party for Phyllis at the Berkeley Hotel, in London, on 6 September 1986. At a champagne reception, their founder was presented with a red rose from eighty of her employees. In the corner of the room was the surprise present, which Esme had succeeded in keeping a secret from Phyllis. Underneath layers of wrapping paper and bows was an oil painting – a portrait of Bella done by Alfred in 1933 – two years before her death. It had later been sold to a private collector in the Cotswolds.

No one in the company had ever heard Phyllis speak about her late mother. The indignity of Bella's final days had stained her image for ever, as far as Phyllis was concerned. Whereas she had known and loved her mother, others, she believed, could not understand the distortion of insanity. Rather than allow the slightest word to taint her further, Phyllis chose not to speak of her at all. But Bella was never far from her thoughts.

'We knew there was a portrait of her which we managed to

track down,' Nigel Syrett recalled. 'We didn't know what Mrs P would think, so we just went for it.'

As everyone gathered around to watch Phyllis receive her gift, to Esme's horror, as she tore the paper from the four-foot frame, her face stretched with shock. 'Mama, Mama,' she cried. The tears that ran down her face were, the guests believed, of sheer happiness at being reunited with her darling Mama.

For some six months afterwards, the dark painting dominated the Shoreham flat and Esme would catch Phyllis paralysed by its gaze; lost in the past and lost in the face of her mother. In the portrait, her once-happy cheeks are now firmly set, unable to smile. Dark wavy hair sits rigidly on her head and echoes her dark, open-necked blouse and eyes, that reveal she is beaten. Beaten by disappointment and beaten by her husbands.

'I had no idea what Phyllis was thinking,' Esme said, 'for she would never talk about it.'

After lunch one day with Phyllis at her Shoreham flat, Ellen Jameson remembers her saying, 'I'll show you something very special,' as she led Ellen to Bella's portrait.

Silence. For just one connection with her mother's face still overwhelmed Phyllis in quite an extraordinary way.

'Who do you think this is?' she asked quietly.

'Your mother?'

'Yes. You must look at this and forget all the other things you may have heard about her.'

On life's journey, the past can be a heavy load. It can follow you into your future or it can drag you back.

One morning, the weight of Bella's unhappiness suddenly became too much to carry. 'Get rid of it, Esme,' Phyllis cried. 'I detest that painting!'

Today, Bella's portrait belongs to Mary West, daughter of

Tony and Daisy Gross, and it hangs at her home in King George Street, Greenwich. Here is the house where Tony and Daisy lived for many years. Upstairs is the whitewashed bedroom converted into Tony's studio, and in the courtyard garden is the printing workshop. The walls are adorned by Tony's works and Daisy's fashion sketches.

Mary's father has been gone for over sixteen years, her mother fourteen. Propped up on one of his long wooden tables is a black and white framed photograph of Tony and Daisy. In a floral print dress, she squints at the camera, her head on one side while Tony, in a white shirt, with a neat moustache and his hair combed back like his father's, lets the hand with his cigarette relax. Between them is a little boy – their son, Jean-Pierre, and on Daisy's knee, Mary is perched in a gingham frock.

Shortly before the photograph was taken, the family had experienced a major domestic upheaval. In 1939, France was no place to be for a half-Jewish Englishman.

'My parents left France,' says Mary, 'with one suitcase, that is all. And they never went back to live there again.' They settled for a while in Flamstead, Hertfordshire, where Phyllis would chatter in French to her sister-in-law, whom Bella had dubbed 'the fashionable semi-demi'. Mary remembers their aunt taking her and her brother for walks in the woods and playing games with them.

In her father's studio, Mary leafs through his childhood albums; a sepia world of memories bound for ever in leather. There are no wedding photographs of any of the family, but there, in matching sailor suits, Tony and Phyllis pose for a portrait, their three- and four-year-old heads together, their dark hair and eyes glistening. They pop up again and again, laughing, digging sand-castles on the beach at Ostend, Phyllis swamped by ringlets and in a tiny fur coat, holding a birdcage, Tony, watching, captivated by the canaries inside. In a white party frock, with white socks and white shoes, Phyllis stands by Elijah, her baby elephant, her face pulled into a smile of fear and excitement. There's a snapshot of Bella, her head in profile so her pearl earrings catch the light, as does her glossy hair, exquisitely swept up on her head. An assortment of Surrey gentry are seated outside the conservatory during one of the celebrated garden parties at The Firs.

Laughter in another shot, as General Livingstone, in his uniform, squeezes the waist of Bella and his wife, Wuffy, who would later become one of Sandor's conquests. A portrait of Sandor, at thirty, looking defiantly past the camera. Smartly poised with the tight posture of a small man, his mouth hints at a sneer. Fifty years later, there is Sandor again, taken the night before he died, seated at a table in a restaurant of the *Queen Mary*. He is dining alone. His suit is immaculate, the remnants of his hair shining black on his walnut head. His hard skin has shrunken, his arrogance replaced by bitterness; his mouth is unrepentant.

CHAPTER THIRTY-TWO

On We Go

Isn't it lovely to have behaved in life the same as in work. Whether starving or smoked salmoning, we ride on irrespective, should ups and downs bring us there again.

Letter from Phyllis to Ellen Jameson

'We always wanted to die in a plane crash,' Esme insists. 'We travelled a lot by plane and before take-off, we would shake hands and say, "Thank you – it's been a nice life." You see, we had no worries, everything was straight. I certainly never thought I could live by myself.'

It would be nothing so easy. It would take Phyllis over seven months to succumb to melanoma cancer. The results from a biopsy on the mole on her upper arm had not been good. Further exploratory operations discovered the cancer had spread to her stomach and the rest of her body.

'She always encouraged us in a deep faith,' her friend Ellen Jameson says. 'Phyllis embraced death as her next journey, and she believed totally in this glorious place called heaven which would be a better place than this. The disease quickly robbed her body of strength and she hated becoming confined to a wheelchair.'

Phyllis went on a final outing on 14 May 1996, to Euro Disney in Paris, where she celebrated sixty years of the company, thirty years of the Trust, and her ninetieth year. There, before 250

317

members of staff, gathered in a suite festooned with red, white and blue *A-Z* balloons, she gave a last speech. Clutching the microphone that Nigel Syrett held to her mouth, her frail voice sounded thinner than ever. It was, according to Esme, Nigel and the staff, one of the most beautiful, unrehearsed speeches they had ever heard.

'You see, Phyllis was so proud of them,' says Ellen. 'She groomed each one of them, to fulfil a potential that no one else had seen. It was a great talent of hers, to be able to nurture.'

Her world, her company, was a tight little community. Outsiders were rarely employed; when they were, Phyllis preferred to take on new young people who could be trained in a supportive atmosphere. No one, she felt, should suffer or endure as much as she had done, simply to make a living. And despite being a single woman, she encouraged a family-friendly policy.

Of course, Phyllis must have known that this would be her only opportunity to speak to them all together before her death. She had meant her words to inspire and she had meant them to truly understand how dear every individual had been to her. She was saying goodbye to her family.

Afterwards, naturally, everyone wanted to hug her, to kiss their beloved Mrs P. Esme did her utmost to dissuade them, as even the slightest pressure on her skin left Phyllis in the most terrible pain. 'None of the staff,' she explained, 'had realised the agony Phyllis had kept to herself, until a giant Mickey Mouse tried to give her a squeeze after her speech and she recoiled in pain. "Don't touch me. Please don't touch me," she whimpered.'

The occasion had sapped the energy she had managed to muster up, and Esme remembers Phyllis whispering: 'Get me out of here.'

In her final two months, Phyllis found the boundaries of her life tightened again. This time it was to her small bed, which gave a panoramic view of Shoreham seafront. 'To stop was a terrible shock. Everything,' according to Esme, 'had been work, work, work, in her life.' The voracious letter-writer, the voracious reader, the voracious conversationalist was too weak to stir, and Esme remembers her as too far gone to care.

The July and August heat weakened her further. For nearly the whole day, Esme would sit on a chair by her side and talk to her. On the pale pink walls of the bedroom hung over ten of her own tiny paintings – sunrises, sunsets, landscapes, seascapes. For hours, she would stare into their memory and then the following day ask Esme to swap them around.

On Thursday, 28 August 1996, nearly a month before her ninetieth birthday, Phyllis died with Esme at her bedside. Those who could be spared from work at the *A-Z* offices attended her funeral service the following week at The Downs Cemetery, where friends and family paid their last respects to the little coffin covered in white lilies. In the following weeks and months, Nigel Syrett would miss her matter-of-fact phone calls, which had come at any time and sometimes as early as 6 a.m. on a Sunday morning.

'Hello, darling, what's happening, Nigel? How about Manchester?'

He would miss his friend, rather than his boss, a woman who had treated him more like a son than an employee, and who respected his diligence.

At the age of seventeen, Nigel had been working for two years on a wobbly old table; to make matters worse, it was on casters and used to slide about on the wooden floors.

'You need a desk,' Phyllis had said to him out of the blue. 'If you can make £2,000 commission this month, I will buy you a new desk.'

Nigel had his eye on one, in a shop along the Edgware Road. He met his target and Phyllis kept her word.

319

The first Christmas without Phyllis must have been incredibly difficult for Esme. One of the cards she received was an official one, from the Governor of Hong Kong, Chris Patten and his wife, Lavender, and their three daughters. On the front of the card was one of Phyllis's last paintings of Government House. The words written inside would be of great comfort to Esme and echoed all the feelings of those who had loved Phyllis:

Esme dearest,

We think of you and pray for you often. It is very hard for you, I know you were such wonderful friends, but you know she would want you to carry on with all your busy life. 'On we go' indeed.

One of the first articles I read about Phyllis Pearsall in the *Daily Mail* described how she had always wanted to be taken seriously as an artist. Map-making, she explained, saved her from using her painting as a means of paying the rent. Her art, she believed, ought to be cherished and not crudely exploited to make money. The irony was that no matter how many paintings she sold or art exhibitions she organised, the business would always float at the top of her thoughts. In the article, she had posed expertly for the photographer behind her large easel on the Shoreham promenade, her tiny face crinkled by an enormous smile and haloed by a straw coolie hat. In her left hand, she balanced a wooden paint palette and a fistful of sable paint-brushes.

They say that by a certain age, you get the face you deserve. I stare for I don't know how long at the photograph, trying to see if any marks have been left on her face from what life had thrown at her, in handfuls. Her flinty eyes, hint at an elderly lady who defies doctors, traffic wardens and Foreign Office officials. The sparrow tilt of her head, like her posture, is defiant. There are no frown lines. Staring out is the undiluted gaze of a woman who has not been distracted by bringing up a family. If she had ever taken time out to grieve over the children she never had, there was no trace of sorrow.

One thing is for certain. Phyllis did *not* like interrupting a canvas to have a photograph taken. Portraits of her that hang in The Geographers' A-Z Map Company offices are all promoting the *A-Z*, and the few framed snaps at home were mostly taken from behind as she, unawares, gazed at the canvas on her easel.

In the *Daily Mail* photo, she appears quite chic, with a crisp white shirt beneath a cocky-angled collar. Staff at her company remember that Mrs P, as they would call her, often turned up at the offices looking as if she had just stepped out of Harrods – in later years, Yves Saint Laurent took up much of her wardrobe – and at other times she would pitch up in tatty mustard-coloured cords, held up by string, her short, snow-bobbed hair in disarray.

Ellen Jameson was always fascinated by the bright and fashionable clothes Phyllis wore, even in her eighties: 'For one party Derek and I held, she arrived looking gorgeous in trousers tucked into brown leather cowboy boots, and I remember thinking, I wish I'd thought of wearing that.'

On the canvas she has interrupted, a few flickers of shoreline are visible; whether water colours or line drawings, there is a quirky, free-hand wobble to her work, like the twitch of a lie-detector needle. Her impatience to capture a scene before the light flitted gave rise to her characteristic quick, light strokes, in brilliant colour, usually in Caribbean shades of creamy pinks, yellows and blue. Whereas some might see a thunderous grey shadow hanging over the sea, Phyllis would pick up on the slightest shaft of light and let it illuminate her entire painting.

Her final exhibition, entitled *Alive with Joy*, was held at The Little Gallery in Arundel, where it ran from 21 May until the last week of June 1995. There, 136 paintings were on show, from *Bonfire on Henfield Common* (1960) to *House and Chickens of the*

Goure Sons, Brehement (1992) and *Victoria Harbour, Kowloon, Hong Kong* (1993).

It nearly didn't happen. The gallery owner had committed suicide before the exhibition opened on 21 May, but left instructions in a note, found with his body, that Phyllis was to go ahead with the show. *Alive with Joy* then seemed a horribly ironic name and an evangelical-sounding title to those who had not met Phyllis. But here was a woman whose enthusiasm for every day's new adventure could not be thwarted. Even in her late eighties, she used exclamation marks as if they were going out of fashion and gave media interviews full of remarks like, 'I fall in love with everything I lay my eyes on!'

By coincidence, I arrive at The Geographers' A-Z Map Company two years to the day that Phyllis Pearsall died. The forty-minute train journey out of Victoria to Borough Green in Kent slides from the confusion of urban knottiness to parachute-soft fields. The company is a two-minute walk from the station, housed on a small business estate. It is a modern, square, biscuit-coloured building. Inside, the air is static and the silence is airtight. The boardroom carpet, a sage colour, is trimmed with an *A-Z* logo. Huge, antique oak desks are kept in pride of place from the old office.

In the corridors, the walls are decorated by dozens of drawings and sketches by Phyllis Pearsall. The suffocating concentration of draughtsmen is everywhere, their eyes fixed on their computer screens, their work seeming every bit as painstaking as the old methods. Phyllis, they say, could be heard in the drawing office as she scuttled into the building, her powerful high voice drifting up the stairs and heralding an inspection. Here, forty draughtsmen and one hundred and ten employees work on over two hundred and fifty publications. People do not come and go here. Most of the old-timers, as they are known, have been with Phyllis for over forty years, inching their way up from apprentices to directors of the company.

Surprisingly, Phyllis did not request that her ashes be scattered in the strong wind that pulls along the Shoreham seafront, although this would have set her free to dance in the air for ever. In the end, she chose her adopted family before her freedom. Mrs P's journey was to end beneath a rowan tree, planted in her memory, outside the *A-Z* offices. It is a quiet spot, which her former employees pass every day on their way into work.

Programme notes for the Memorial Exhibition and Open Day at The Geographers' A-Z Map Company Limited.

'Mrs P', as she liked to be known, saw no barriers between one aspect of her talent and another. She would paint, write, read accounts, plan new cartographic projects wherever she happened to be – and it was not unknown for her to try several activities at the same time!

Whilst we all did our best to keep up with her seemingly boundless energy and sharp probing mind, she embraced us all equally, as friends and colleagues – part of her larger family.

Mrs P has given us the opportunity to develop our individual talents and work in an environment based on trust, respect for the individual and with a level of security only made possible by her selfless consideration in creating The Geographers' Map Trust. She also gave us a motto – *On We Go* – and as a team we can, and will, do just that.

Index

**SIMON &
SCHUSTER**

LA DIVA NICOTINA
The Story of How Tobacco Seduced the World
Iain Gately

A fascinating and witty dissection of tobacco tracing
its development from ritual refreshment to universal
habit. Alluring and glamourous, deceitful and deadly,
La Diva Nicotina relates the story of this most
addictive of plants, from its beginnings amongst the
ancient civilisations of South America to the present
day. From Mayan gods to Marlboro Man, from
Casanova to President Clinton, *La Diva Nicotina*
examines the roles tobacco has played in its long
association with men and women, including its
functions as spiritual messenger, as sexual
ambassador, as a cure for cancer, global currency and
ultimately as an assassin.

ISBN 0 7432 0812 9
PRICE £14.99

**SIMON &
SCHUSTER**

VANILLA BEANS & BRODO
Real Life in the Hills of Tuscany
Isabella Dusi

Five years ago, Isabella Dusi and her husband left
their native Australia and settled in the close-knit
community of Montalcino, a beautiful mountain eyrie
and home to an eclectic tribe of Italians. In *Vanilla
Beans & Brodo*, Isabella writes an affectionate and
humourous acount of a year in the Tuscan hills.
Following the Montalcinese through the seasons, she
captures the spirit of the place: the fierce rivalry
between the village neighbourhoods, the football
fever, the prestigious archery tournament, and the
delicious cuisine and much prized wine.

Described by *The Times* as 'enticing' and 'vivid' by the
Daily Express, *Vanilla Beans & Brodo* is an evocative
portrait of Montalcino, a village with a passionate and
bloody history, that will surely challenge the long
held image that Tuscany moves at a leisurely and
docile pace.

ISBN 0 7432 0934 6
PRICE £13.99

Scribner

THE GIRL IN THE PICTURE
The Remarkable Story of
Vietnam's Most Famous Casualty
Denise Chong

'Masterly . . . reads like the best kind of novel – both moving and startling' *The Times*

On 8 June 1972, nine-year-old Kim Phuc, severely burned by napalm, ran from her burning village and into the eye of history. Her photograph, seen around the world, helped turn public opinion against the Vietnam War and is one of a handful of images that remain branded in the public consciousness. Denise Chong has written a detailed, humanistic account of everyday life in the wake of the Vietnam War, as well as a meditation on the aftermath of celebrity, and the power of an image.

'A fascinating account of the life of an extraordinary human being' *Time Out*

ISBN 0 7432 0703 3
PRICE £7.99

POCKET
BOOKS

TO SEE YOU AGAIN
The Betty Schimmel Story
Betty Schimmel & Joyce Gabriel

The Nazi occupation of Europe destroyed families,
broke up lovers and disrupted all semblance of
normal life for many people. In Budapest in 1944 it
shattered the dreams of a young Jewish couple, Betty
Schimmel and Richie Kovacs. Betty survived being
sent to the concentration camp at Mauthausen but it
seemed that Richie was lost. However, Betty was
determined to build a new life for herself and she
married Otto, a fellow death camp survivor, who
adored her.

But in an extraordinary twist of fate, nearly three
decades later Betty encounters Richie again who tells
her he has never stopped loving her. Clearly she has
the most terrible and important choice to make –
should she run away with the love of her life or stay
with the man who has been her devoted husband and
the father of her children?

ISBN 0 671 02213 X
PRICE £5.99

POCKET
B O O K S

HILLARY'S CHOICE
Gail Sheehy

'Very good, sensational reading, with plenty of sharp,
plausible insights'
Spectator

Hillary's Choice is a love story – but one whose rocky
moments, rather than remaining private, have been
publicised beyond any imagining. What is the real
story of this marriage? In *Hillary's Choice*, Sheehy
takes the Clintons from the moment their eyes met in
school to reveal the power shifts, the genuine passion,
and the ultimate price Hillary has paid for her love
and her ambition.

'Gail Sheehy's expertise lies in the charting
of rites of passage'
Times Literary Supplement

'Insightful . . . Sheehy's analysis of Hillary's psyche
is highly persuasive'
New York Observer

ISBN 0-671-03278-X
PRICE £8.99

**SIMON &
SCHUSTER**

This book and other **Simon & Schuster** titles are available from your book shop or can be ordered direct from the publisher.

Please send cheque or postal order for the value of the book, and add packing within the UK inc. BFPO 75p per book; OVERSEAS inc. EIRE £1 per book.

OR: Please debit this amount from my:

VISA/ACCESS/MASTERCARD ....

CARD NO ....

EXPIRY DATE ....

AMOUNT £ ....

NAME ....

ADDRESS ....

....

SIGNATURE ....

Send orders to:
SIMON & SCHUSTER CASH SALES
PO Box 29, Douglas, Isle of Man, IM99 1BQ
Tel: 01624 675137, Fax 01624 670923
www.bookpost.co.uk
email: bookshop@enterprise.net for details
Please allow 28 days for delivery.
Prices and availability subject to change without notice.